Moses and Abraham Maimonides: Encountering the Divine

Moses and Abraham Maimonides: Encountering the Divine

DIANA LOBEL

BOSTON
2021

Library of Congress Cataloging-in-Publication Data

Names: Lobel, Diana, author.
Title: Moses and Abraham Maimonides : encountering the Divine / Diana Lobel.
Description: Boston : Academic Studies Press, 2021. | Series: Emunot: Jewish Philosophy and Kabbalah | Includes bibliographical references and index.
Identifiers: LCCN 2021000541 (print) | LCCN 2021000542 (ebook) | ISBN 9781644695845 (hardback) | ISBN 9781644695852 (adobe pdf) | ISBN 9781644695869 (epub)
Subjects: LCSH: Maimonides, Moses, 1135-1204. | Abraham ben Moses ben Maimon, 1186-1237. | God (Judaism) | God (Judaism)--Name. | Presence of God. | Revelation--Judaism.
Classification: LCC BM755.A23 L63 2021 (print) | LCC BM755.A23 (ebook) | DDC 296.3/112--dc23
LC record available at https://lccn.loc.gov/2021000541
LC ebook record available at https://lccn.loc.gov/2021000542

ISBN 9781644695371
ISBN 9781644695852 (adobe pdf)
ISBN 9781644695869 (epub)
Book design by Lapiz Digital Services
Cover design by Ivan Grave

Published by Academic Studies Press
1577 Beacon Street
Brookline, MA 02446, USA
press@academicstudiespress.com
www.academicstudiespress.com

For Penelope and Adeline,
two bright sparks of divine light and love.

Contents

Acknowledgements ix
Introduction xi

Part One: Moses and Abraham Maimonides on Created Light, Created Word, and the Event at Mount Sinai 1

1. Abraham Maimonides on Created Light in the Cleft of the Rock: Exodus 33:22 5
2. Maimonides on Created Light: An Esoteric Interpretation 26
3. Abraham and Moses Maimonides on Cloud and Glory: Exodus 16:9–10/Guide III:9 34
4. Abraham Maimonides on Created Light in the Preparation for the Sinai Event 41
5. Maimonides on the Theophany at Mount Sinai 54
6. Abraham Maimonides on the Created Word at Mount Sinai: Between Maimonides and R. Abraham he-Ḥasid 67
7. Abraham and Moses Maimonides on Created Light in the Vision of the Nobles 78

Part Two: *Ehyeh asher Ehyeh* and the Tetragrammaton: Between Eternity and Necessary Existence 87

8. Introduction: *Ehyeh asher Ehyeh* and the Tetragrammaton 91
9. Rabbinic Interpretations of *Ehyeh asher Ehyeh* 96
10. The Interpretation of Saadya Gaon 100
11. Saadya's Long Commentary to Exodus 3:13–15 104
12. Abraham Maimonides on Saadya Gaon 107
13. The Interpretation of Maimonides 111
14. Abraham on Eternity and Relationship 121

Conclusion 126
Notes 133
Bibliography 187
Index 202

Acknowledgements

My interest in the Torah commentary of Abraham Maimonides grew out of my study of the dissertation of Rabbi Ezra Labaton, z"l, *A Comprehensive Analysis of Rabenu Abraham Maimuni's Biblical Commentary*, Brandeis University, 2012, for which I served as a reader; this book pays tribute to his life and work. I am indebted to Professor Bernard Septimus for tracking down additional sources and for our study of the texts together in August 2016. I hope I have done justice in some small way to the results of our rich conversation, as well as invaluable exchanges with Warren Zev Harvey, Josef Stern, Esti Eisenmann, Nahem Ilan, Rabbi David Roth, Hillel Ben-Sasson, Marc Bregman, Yonatan Negev, Miriam Bronstein, Miriam Goldstein, Eli Shaubi, Scott Girdner, and Stan Dorn. I would like to express appreciation to the dedicated and skilled assistants who made the material production of this book possible, including Julia Carroll and Ayla Goktan, who prepared the bibliography, and Johnathan Kelly, who assisted with the index. In addition, I thank my colleagues and chairs in the Department of Religion at Boston University, including Kecia Ali, David Frankfurter, and Stephen Prothero, and Michael Zank, director of the Elie Wiesel Center for Judaic Studies; our Department and Center administrators Wendy Czik, Theresa Cooney, Ryan Sullivan, and Anna Stroinski; Brian Anderson and Sean Faeth from the office of CAS-IT; and Rhoda Bilansky from the ILL division of Mugar Library. I thank the Boston University Center for the Humanities, which provided subvention for the book's publication, and Dov Schwartz, Alessandra Anzani, Kira Nemirovsky, Ilya Nikolaev, and Ekaterina Yanduganova of Academic Studies Press for their support of the project.

An earlier version of Part II appeared as "*Ehyeh asher Ehyeh* and the Tetragrammaton: Between Eternity and Necessary Existence in Saadya,

Maimonides, and Abraham Maimonides," *Review of Rabbinic Judaism* 23 (2020): 89–126. I thank Alan Avery-Peck and Brill's *Review of Rabbinic Judaism* for permission to publish a revised version of the article.

I offer special appreciation to Professor Zev Harvey for sharing his genuine love for philosophical investigation, for embodying the Socratic ideal of philosophical dialogue and discovery. The book also unfolded through illuminating study with Miriam Bronstein and Stan Dorn. I thank Eli Shaubi, Scott Girdner, and the anonymous readers for Academic Studies Press for their insightful comments on the manuscript, and Eli Shaubi for his expert assistance with transliteration.

I am grateful for the communities of prayer and study that so enrich my life, and for moments of sacred Presence, both in music and in the silence. I honor with deep gratitude the beautiful loving kindness of Janet Lobel, Albert (Avraham Yehiel) Lobel, z"l, Francine Lobel, z"l, my grandmothers, Shirley Goodman, z"l, and Bertha Lobel, z"l, and Reb Moshe Holcer, z"l, whose gentle spirit will always be a guiding light.

I am appreciative of the gifts to this world of Tina Mulhern, Gina Bova, Rosa and Mark Drapkin, Debi Adams, Walter Ness, Barbara Brandt, Beth O'Sullivan, Tony Rivera, Ted and Betsy Kaptchuk, Tom Alden, Rabbi Yonah, Rabbi Liza Stern, Rabbi David Roth, John Paul, Katrina, Steel, Faith and Abigail, Irene, Aunt Fran Cohen, Penelope, and Adeline.

I am deeply appreciative of family, friends, and friends in spirit, who have walked together every step of the way, from the beginning to the present moment.

Introduction

Moses Maimonides (1138–1204) was born in Cordoba, Spain, and considered himself an heir to the Andalusian philosophical tradition, developed by his generational contemporaries Ibn Bājja (d. 1138), and Averroes (Ibn Rushd, 1126–1198). In a letter to his translator Samuel Ibn Tibbon evaluating readings in philosophy, he recommends no Jewish philosophical sources.[1] Likewise, in the *Guide of the Perplexed*, he cites no Jewish sources. He cites Aristotle, Alexander of Aphrodisias, Plato, al-Fārābī, and Ibn Bājja; he is also clearly indebted to Avicenna (Ibn Sīnā, d. 1037) and al-Ghazālī (d. 1111). While it is evident that he has read Saadya Gaon (882–942), Judah Halevi (c. 1075–1141), Abraham Ibn Ezra (1089–1164), and Abraham Ibn Daud (1110–1180), he never openly acknowledges them by name.[2]

In contrast, his son Abraham Maimonides (1186–1237) writes a commentary to the Torah in which he grapples explicitly with the commentaries of earlier Jewish exegetes, including Saadya Gaon, Samuel ben Ḥofni (d. 1034), and Abraham Ibn Ezra, commentators who represent the Gaonic-Andalusian rationalist tradition of Biblical exegesis. Yet Abraham Maimonides grew up in Egypt, and while he defends Maimonides' philosophical positions, he shows little interest in the Andalusian tradition of Arabic Aristotelians, and even makes critical remarks about the dangers of the philosophical path.[3]

Maimonides was clearly proud of his Andalusian origin; throughout his life, he signed his name in Hebrew as "Moshe ben Maimon *ha-Sefaradi*" ("the Spaniard," *al-Andalusī*).[4] Maimonides regarded himself, along with Averroes, as a final heir of this Andalusian school, which was actually quite small. The Spanish Aristotelian tradition traced its roots in the East to the tenth-century Islamic philosopher al-Fārābī (d. 951), rather than to Avicenna (Ibn Sīnā), whose works came to prevail in the East.[5] The figure who sparked the Aristotelian revival in Spain was Ibn Bājja, who was followed by Ibn Ṭufayl (d. 1185) and Averroes.[6] As Joel Kraemer points out, this was not a school in a formal, institutional sense, but rather a group of thinkers who shared a framework of ideas, arguments, source material, and terminology, pursuing common questions through a shared methodology.[7] Sarah Stroumsa adds that Maimonides' identification with this school was not typical for medieval Jewish thinkers. Whereas modern scholars group Jewish thinkers into schools such as "*kalām*," "Neoplatonism," and "Aristotelianism," medieval Jewish thinkers did not generally identify explicitly with one school, and were not identified as members of a school by others.[8] It is thus especially noteworthy that Maimonides, commenting to his translator Samuel Ibn Tibbon on a philosophical curriculum, demonstrates identification with an Aristotelian tradition; he recommends Aristotle over Plato, and gives stern instructions to read Aristotle with authoritative commentators Alexander of Aphrodisias, Themistius, and the contemporary Andalusian Averroes.[9] In the *Guide*, he again indicates his Andalusian intellectual affiliation, noting that he himself has studied under a student of the contemporary Andalusian philosopher Ibn Bājja, and that he has met a son of the Andalusian astronomer Jābir Ibn Aflaḥ (d. ca. 1150).[10]

Because of religious persecution, Maimonides was forced to flee al-Andalus with his family and eventually settled in Egypt. Abraham Maimonides thus grew up in an entirely different intellectual milieu than did his father. There is no evidence that philosophical and scientific works had reached Egypt; scholars in Egypt might have known them only through Maimonides' citations and summary of their ideas.[11] His father, an Aristotelian who had actually studied primary source texts from the Andalusian philosophical tradition, was a rare exception in this intellectual environment.[12]

In addition to his father, among Abraham Maimonides' close associates were R. Abraham ibn Abī'l-Rabī' he-Ḥasid (d. ca. 1223), who seems to have held an official post, and his father-in-law, R. Ḥananel ben Samuel, who served in Abraham Maimonides' rabbinic court (*bet din*), perhaps as its head.[13] Both R. Ḥananel and R. Abraham he-Ḥasid were members of a circle of Egyptian pietists; Abraham Maimonides refers to R. Abraham ibn Abī'l-Rabī' he-Ḥasid as "our master in the path of the Lord."[14] Abraham Maimonides is thus the heir of two traditions—the Aristotelian Andalusian philosophical tradition, exemplified by al-Fārābī, Ibn Bājja, and Averroes, of which his father was a proud exemplar, and the Sufi-influenced pietism of his Egyptian milieu.[15]

Abraham Maimonides is well-versed in this complex of intellectual trends, and selectively integrates these trends according to his own distinctive sensibility.[16] It is clear that he has read and come into contact with a wide variety of Jewish and Islamic texts and traditions, and creates his own unique synthesis. He understands his father's interpretations well and tries to harmonize them with other streams of thought. But in the end he is his own person and disagrees with his father. For example, while Moses Maimonides asserts that a thinker who upholds the theory of God's glory as created light is one of insufficient intellectual capacity, Abraham Maimonides does not hide that he himself finds this view plausible. Moreover, he omits explicit language of the Active Intellect, prominent in the thought of his father. Abraham Maimonides is well aware of his father's abstract metaphysical concept of Necessary Existence, but draws less precise philosophical boundaries between metaphysical necessity and temporal eternity than does his father. Abraham Maimonides accepts Saadya's conception of the created light and the created word of God, which are dismissed by his father as secondary interpretations. Nevertheless, he is well aware of the great intellectual stature of his father, and seeks to defend his father's interpretations and harmonize them with his own.

In his Commentary to the Torah, Abraham Maimonides makes two significant programmatic statements outlining his exegetical agenda.[17] In his comment to Exodus 33:22, R. Abraham states that he seeks to harmonize the interpretation of his father with that of thinkers who interpret God's glory as a sensory created light, the most prominent being Onqelos and Saadya Gaon. In this statement, he writes that "it is not impossible in this and [matters] like it to connect what my father intended with what the scholars who preceded him intended [by noting] that there is some sensory or sensory-like viewing of the created light." Thus Abraham Maimonides indicates his larger exegetical purpose: to harmonize the approach of his father, a strict Aristotelian-Andalusian philosopher, with other exegetical approaches he has inherited, such as those of Saadya. In a second programmatic statement, in his comment to Exodus 3:14, he makes a conceptual identification between Saadya's interpretation of the divine name *Ehyeh asher Ehyeh* as eternity, and the assertion of his father that the name signifies Necessary Existence. He writes, "And there is no difference [between this] and what my father mentioned in his explication of this exalted name (*hādhā al-shem ha-nikhbad*), that it points to Necessary Existence." Thus Abraham Maimonides seeks to harmonize Saadya's conception of eternity with his father's conception of metaphysical necessity.

Moses Maimonides is an abstract scientific thinker. Through his study of Avicenna, he is aware of Sufi vocabulary, but gives it a philosophical inflection. In contrast, Abraham Maimonides, while accepting certain metaphysical concepts such as that of Necessary Existence, has a Sufi-influenced pietist sensibility. Elisha Russ-Fishbane has described the writings of Abraham Maimonides and his circle as a form of "intellectual illuminationism" or "philosophical mysticism," and notes the extraordinary impact of the Sufi-influenced language of *Guide* III:51.[18] Our investigation will to some extent confirm this appraisal. Abraham Maimonides does accord the intellect an important role in spiritual ascent. However, we must also recognize a significant distinction between the philosophical sensibilities of Maimonides and his son, as Russ-Fishbane himself acknowledges.[19] While III:51 is the climax of the *Guide*, it is only one strand of discourse in the work.[20] Maimonides grapples with philosophical and scientific questions that perplexed the Andalusians of his time, most significantly the conflict between Aristotelian natural science and Ptolemaic astronomy. Maimonides terms this "the true perplexity."[21] Maimonides is a dialectical thinker, carefully examining and sifting through conflicting philosophical perspectives, searching for philosophical and scientific understanding through relentless dialectical investigation.[22] While Abraham Maimonides may accept some of the outlines, vocabulary, and concepts exemplified in his father's writings on scientific and metaphysical matters, his real interests lie elsewhere—in ethical and spiritual purification as a path to arrival at the divine. He understands his father well, but chooses to pursue the questions and approach that most interest him. Abraham is simply not fascinated in the way his father is with questions of scientific cosmology. While he is as interested as his father in attaining an audience in the inner court of the divine ruler, he is less interested in the study of mathematics, physics, and biology that

Maimonides argues is the path to that inner court.[23] In his desired audience with the divine, Abraham Maimonides would likely pose different questions before his maker than would Maimonides.[24] In one striking difference, Abraham Maimonides omits a key concept central to the thought of his father—that of the Active Intellect—and using visual, sensory language, suggests that one can attain a "glimpse" of the divine essence.

While Abraham Maimonides has great respect for his father's abstract philosophical interpretations of Scripture, he is also more sensitive to a plain-sense contextual reading, bringing in citations from commentaries of Saadya Gaon, Samuel ben Ḥofni, and Abraham Ibn Ezra. In this study, we will analyze the way this difference in philosophical and exegetical sensibility expresses itself in the contrasting and intersecting approaches of Maimonides and his son Abraham to the concepts of created light, created word, and the event at Mount Sinai, and to the divine names *Ehyeh asher Ehyeh* and the Tetragrammaton. Our study will reveal the ways Abraham Maimonides mediates between the approach of his father and his own intellectual and spiritual understanding, and the ways that Abraham's interpretations shed new light on the work of Maimonides.

A brief overview of the book's chapters will orient the reader to our study. Part one explores the themes of created light, created word, and the revelation at Mount Sinai, with a particular focus on the question of experiential illumination. In Chapter 1, we analyze Abraham Maimonides' interpretation of the image of God's glory that Moses perceives in the cleft of the rock. In both his Torah Commentary and his pietist Compendium (the *Kifāya*), Abraham speaks of attaining "a glimpse of God's exalted essence [or existence]." Abraham's language of illumination suggests a background in spiritual practices known from the writings of his Pietist circle.

In contrast, Maimonides suggests that the concept of God's "created light" arises from an inferior interpretation for those who cannot achieve an abstract conception of illumination as purely intellectual. In chapter 2, we see that detailed exegesis reveals that Maimonides also hints at an esoteric interpretation, according to which "created light" signifies the Active Intellect or the separate intellects. Thus the "vision" of the glory at Mount Sinai was not a collective vision of sensory light, but rather signifies openness to inspiration from the Active Intellect.

Chapter 3 explores the Israelites' experience of created light in the desert. Abraham Maimonides emphasizes the inner dimension of spiritual life, even in the group religious experience of the Israelites in the wilderness. Although the nation shared a common experience of witnessing the light of God's glory, each individual experienced this as an event of individual spiritual illumination. Here, as at Mount Sinai, Abraham Maimonides alludes to the Sufi practice of emptying or inner solitude (*khalwa*), even in the historical experience of the nation as a whole.

Chapter 4 turns to the theme of created light in preparation for the revelation at Mount Sinai. Both Maimonides and his son interpret Exodus 19:22 as warning that one must engage in a slow, internal process of preparation to achieve vision of the Lord. However, the two diverge in what such vision means. Maimonides insists in *Guide* I:5 that all language of vision with respect to God is metaphorical; "seeing God" is a metaphor for intellectual understanding. The two will thus also disagree on what preparation for this "seeing" entails. While Maimonides describes an intellectual process including studying the rules of logic and inference, Abraham emphasizes a spiritual, pietistic process of purification of the heart and mind, without the goal of scientific study of creation. For Abraham Maimonides, study of the sciences is at most preparatory; for Maimonides, understanding of the scientific order of the universe is central and intrinsic to contemplation of God.

Chapter 5 turns to the revelation at Mount Sinai itself. We discover that Maimonides borrows the phrase "the great event of witness" (*al-mashhad al-ʿaẓīm*) from Judah Halevi. However, Maimonides divests the phrase of its anti-al-Fārābīan polemic, co-opting it to describe the Sinai event in accord with his own philosophical theory of prophecy. He suggests that the event at Sinai was a *sui generis* vision of prophecy; like the glory, the "voice" heard at Mount Sinai is a metaphor for information received from the Active Intellect. "Created light" and "created voice" are two sensory metaphors for intellectual apprehension. Both signify that we come to understand the truth of the Necessary Existent and the way divine intelligence is expressed in nature.

Chapter 6 turns to the created word experienced at Mount Sinai. We find that Abraham Maimonides draws upon the experiential dimension of the Sinai event expressed by R. Abraham he-Ḥasid. However, whereas Abraham he-Ḥasid insists that the voice that the people heard on

Mount Sinai was an undifferentiated, unintelligible sound, for Abraham Maimonides, the people heard the Ten Words. Like Abraham he-Ḥasid, Abraham Maimonides holds that the event at Mount Sinai made the people of Israel suitable vehicles for reception of the prophetic experience for generations to come.

Chapter 7 turns to the vision of the created light by the nobles of Israel in Exodus 24:9–11. However, Abraham describes the vision as a singular apprehension, likened to clarity, brightness, and purity. By contrast, in *Guide* I:5, Maimonides criticizes the nobles and the material nature of their vision. Whereas Maimonides suggests that the nobles deserved to die because of their rushing forward, Abraham suggests that no harm befell the elders because they prepared themselves spiritually.

Part One demonstrates that Abraham Maimonides sought to harmonize the approach of his father with that of Saadya on the topics of created light, created word, and the event at Mount Sinai. In Part Two, we see this harmonizing impulse again with respect to the divine names. In chapter 8, we find that there are two approaches to the divine name *Ehyeh asher Ehyeh* in rabbinic and medieval Jewish philosophical literature. One is historical, experiential, and existential; "I will be" means "I will be with you; I will be present." A second is metaphysical, and connects the name *Ehyeh asher Ehyeh* to the Tetragrammaton.

Chapter 9 explores rabbinic interpretations of the name *Ehyeh asher Ehyeh*, both metaphysical and historical. We observe that one manuscript variant of Onqelos translates the term as *ehe ʿal ma de-ehe* ("I will be what I will be" or "I will be according to what I will be"). This could be a metaphysical assertion of God's eternal existence or a historical assertion that God will act according to circumstances. Rabbinic midrashim include both historical and eternal interpretations. In one interpretation included in the *Tanḥuma*, *Ehyeh asher Ehyeh* is not a name in itself but a stand in for the names that God will be called according to the qualities God expresses in different historical circumstances. A purely historical twist found in the medieval midrashic collection *Exodus Rabbah* and in the Babylonian Talmud suggests that *Ehyeh asher Ehyeh* signifies one who will be with the nation in present and future tribulations.

Chapter 10 turns to Saadya Gaon's interpretation of *Ehyeh asher Ehyeh*. Saadya parallels both sides of rabbinic interpretation, the metaphysical and the historical. In his stand-alone Arabic translation of the

Torah (the *Tafsīr*), he translates *Ehyeh asher Ehyeh* as "the eternal (beginningless) that will not cease to be (*al-azalī alladhī lā yazūl*)." Other comments of Saadya reflect a historical reading, in which *Ehyeh asher Ehyeh* is not in itself a name, but a stand-in for names that will be appropriate according to the circumstances, an approach that parallels Midrash *Tanḥuma*.

Chapter 11 demonstrates that the two approaches—the metaphysical and the historical—are integrated and explicated at length in Saadya's long commentary to Exodus 3:13–15. Abraham Maimonides, in his commentary to the Torah, cites Saadya's translation and a very short fragment—or perhaps a quotation from a paraphrase—from Saadya's long commentary. Saadya suggests that *Ehyeh asher Ehyeh* in Exodus 3:14a indicates eternity in the past and the future, as we see in his *Tafsīr*. Thus the one term *Ehyeh* in Exodus 3:14b can be translated by the one term "the eternal" (*al-azalī*), which includes both past and future. Saadya has not yet arrived at Maimonides' notion of metaphysical necessity. His concept of eternity is concerned with the infinitude of God—stretching from the past to the future—in contrast to the finitude of creatures who come to be and pass away.

Chapter 12 investigates Abraham Maimonides' interpretation of Saadya's position. Abraham Maimonides agrees with Saadya that the concept of eternity (*azaliyya*) includes not only eternity in the past but eternity in the future. Abraham shows interest in harmonizing the interpretations of Saadya and his father; he identifies Saadya's conception of eternity with his father's conception of Necessary Existence. Abraham pushes Saadya's conception of eternity in the direction of necessity and non-contingency.

Chapter 13 turns to Maimonides' interpretation of the divine names. Like Halevi and Ibn Ezra, Maimonides associates the name *Ehyeh asher Ehyeh* with the Tetragrammaton. Maimonides suggests that there may be an etymological and semantic derivation of the Tetragrammaton of which we are not aware. The Tetragrammaton does not derive from God's actions, but represents God's essential nature, which is simple, necessary being. Through deliberate use of ambiguous language, Maimonides provokes the reader to ponder the relationship between the Tetragrammaton and the name *Ehyeh asher Ehyeh*. Maimonides suggests, in accordance with the interpretation of his son, that *Ehyeh asher Ehyeh* offers an explanation of the Tetragrammaton.

Chapter 14 explores Abraham Maimonides' explication of conceptions of eternity and relationship in the name *Ehyeh asher Ehyeh.* Abraham asserts that the first pronouncement of *Ehyeh* (*Ehyeh asher Ehyeh*, Exodus 3:14a) relates to God's exalted essence, which it is difficult for language to express, while the second *Ehyeh* ("Thus say to the children of Israel, *Ehyeh* sent me to you," Exodus 3:14b) signifies God's relationship to humanity; "*Ehyeh* has sent me to you" suggests that God sent Moses to Israel as an act of divine providence. Abraham suggests that the name *El Shaddai* also expresses Necessary Existence; this position softens the philosophical precision of his father, who reserves the concept of Necessary Existence for the Tetragrammaton, yet adds an experiential dimension to apprehension of the divine names.

In our conclusion, we investigate the three contexts in which Abraham Maimonides alludes to catching a glimpse of the divine essence, and contrast his approach to the intellectualist mysticism of his father. In investigating the concept of intellectualist mysticism, we note the ways Abraham Maimonides integrates the intellectual approach of his father with his own focus upon illuminative, experiential awareness.

A final introductory word will be of aid to the reader. The following chapters offer an exploration of texts and concepts in the history of Jewish thought that are not immediately transparent. This study is as much a journey through these texts and ideas as it is about the thinkers who investigate them. Medieval Arabic thinkers argue that to accept the authoritative pronouncement of an author—a stance they term *taqlīd*—does not do justice to the spirit of independent inquiry and engagement expressed by these thinkers and the texts they love. Approaches to illumination and the divine Name invite careful reflection, a savoring of ideas with the intuitive as well as the discursive mind, much as we savor poetry. The words of these texts guide the reader to experiential insight that lies behind and beyond the words themselves. Readers are invited to journey deeply into these texts, to ponder the ideas they express, and hence to enter into the intellectual and spiritual worlds of Moses and Abraham Maimonides.

Part One

Moses and Abraham Maimonides on Created Light, Created Word, and the Event at Mount Sinai

In penetrating studies, Nahem Ilan and Elisha Russ-Fishbane point out that for Abraham Maimonides, even in collective religious experiences, such as that of the Israelites at Mount Sinai, each individual's experience is internal.[1] Our study will confirm this view. At the same time, we will demonstrate that Abraham Maimonides takes seriously the visual dimension of God's created light and the material dimension of God's created word in a way that his father Maimonides did not. This will put his positions in many cases closer to those of Saadya and Halevi than to those of his father.

I begin with Abraham Maimonides' interpretation of created light in the scene at the cleft of the rock depicted in Exodus 33–34. I will then bring evidence that in contrast to Abraham, who conceives of created light as quasi-sensory, Maimonides interprets the created light in intellectual terms, both exoteric and esoteric. I will go on to examine other events in which Abraham Maimonides depicts created light—the vision of the glory in the wilderness, the preparation for the Sinai event, the Sinai event itself, and the vision of the nobles. In each case, I will compare the view of Abraham Maimonides with that of his father, showing the ways that Abraham follows and departs from the intellectualist approach of Maimonides, and at times seeks to bridge the approaches of Saadya, Halevi, and his father.

1

Abraham Maimonides on Created Light in the Cleft of the Rock: Exodus 33:22

In Exodus 33:22, we read:

> "And it shall come to pass when my glory passes by, that I will put you in a cleft of the rock and I will cover you with my hand while (until) I pass by. And I will take away my hand, and you shall see my back, but my face shall not be seen."

Abraham comments on this verse:

> An indication/hint of the passing (by) of the created light; or of the occurrence (*khuṭūr)*[1] of a flash (*lamḥ*)[2] of the exalted essence (*al-dhāt al-muʿaẓẓama*). The first is closer (*aqrab*) to the wording (*lafẓ),* while the second is closer to the meaning (*maʿna).*[3]
>
> "My hand"—which is derived from *kaf,* which is the hand—has a borrowed meaning of "cloud," if the glory (*kavod*) that is referred to is the created light; or of "safeguarding" and "protection" if what is indicated by the word *kavod* refers to a mental flash and speculative apprehension.
>
> And everything that my father and teacher (may his name be for a blessing) mentioned about these matters is more fitting to the exalted nature of the matter requested and the

> attainment of the requestor (peace be upon him), while what others mentioned is closer to the wording.[4] And I, too, cannot refrain from adding something about this according to my understanding. "I will also add my opinion" (Job 32:10).
>
> In my view, it is not impossible in this and [matters] like it to connect what my father (may his name be for a blessing) intended with what the scholars who preceded him intended [by noting] that there is some sensory or sensory-like viewing of the created light's illumination (*ru'yat ḥiss aw tashabbuh ḥissiyya li-nūriyyat al-makhlūq*), by means of which [Moses] was guided or helped to [achieve] intellectual apprehension of the greatness of the creator.[5]

Abraham tells us explicitly his exegetical agenda: he seeks to harmonize the interpretation of those who uphold the theory of the created light—the most prominent being Onqelos and Saadya Gaon—with that of his father.[6] Saadya articulates his views on the created light succinctly in the *Book of Doctrines and Beliefs* and at greater length in his commentary to the Biblical book of Daniel.[7] In the *Book of Doctrines and Beliefs*, Saadya writes:

> God has a special light, which he creates and makes manifest to His prophets in order that they may infer therefrom that it is a prophetic communication emanating from God that they hear. . . . However, when they beheld this light, they were unable to look upon it on account of its power and brilliance. . . .
>
> Moses, accordingly, asked his Master to give him the strength to look upon this light. The latter, however, answered him that the first rays of this light were so powerful that he would be unable to view them clearly with his naked eyes, lest he perish. He would rather cover him up with a cloud or the like until the first rays of this light has passed because the greatest strength of every radiant body is contained in its initial approach. All this was implied in the statement of Scripture: "And I will cover you with my hand until I have passed by" (Exodus 33:22). When, then, the first portion of the light had passed, God removed from Moses the thing that had covered him, so that he might be able to look at the back of the light as Scripture says, "And I will take away my hand and you shall see my back" (Exodus 33:23). As for the Creator

himself, however, there is no means whereby anyone might see him. That is indeed in the realm of the impossible.[8]

In reflecting on the passing by of the glory in the cleft of the rock, Abraham suggests that the notion that a created light passed by is closer to the wording (*lafẓ*) than the notion that the text is speaking about intellectual illumination, which is an interpretation based on meaning (*ma'na*). In several other contexts in his commentary in which he makes a distinction between linguistic expression (*lafẓ*) and meaning (*ma'na*), he suggests that both interpretations are legitimate.[9] Here, too, Abraham is sympathetic to both approaches. In a plain sense reading of the text, it sounds as if God places Moses in the cleft of the rock and shows him a visible light. Yet Abraham, like Onqelos, Saadya, and his father, is sensitive to the problem of anthropomorphism. If the glory that passes by is a visible, manifest presence, how do we understand God's assertion "I will take away my hand, and you shall see my back, but my face shall not be seen"? Shall we infer that God has a physical hand, face, and back?

In order to avoid the physical connotation of hand, Abraham interprets the phrase to suggest a cloud that somehow covers the light. As we have seen, this is indeed the approach of Saadya, who in the *Book of Doctrines and Beliefs* suggests that the cloud covers the light to protect Moses from its intensity, giving him time to habituate to the light. On the other hand, Abraham argues that an abstract interpretation is closer to the meaning. The abstract interpretation is that the divine glory refers to a mental, intuitive flash of understanding of God's essence. It befits the nature of what Moses is requesting that when Moses asks "Show me your glory," God bestows upon him a spark of insight into the divine essence, rather than a visible show of light. In this second reading, glory is given a metaphorical interpretation. In accordance with this interpretation, the "hand" with which God shields Moses refers to a mental protection that God grants him in his process of arriving at understanding. What this suggests is an analogy to Saadya's interpretation. If God wanted to shield Moses from the intensity of physical light, perhaps God also wants to shield Moses from the intensity of spiritual and intellectual insight.

Abraham thus tries to harmonize two views: one in which the light of God's glory is physical and sensory, and one in which "God's glory" is a metaphor for intellectual illumination. Abraham suggests that the illumination of the created light, which has a sensible aspect, may also have guided Moses to intellectual apprehension of the greatness of the creator.

a. Abraham's Language of Illumination: "Through your light, we see light"

We should note that Abraham uses a very similar phrase in his Compendium (the *Kifāya*) to discuss the goal of the spiritual path: "a flash/glimpse (*lamḥ*) of [God's] exalted existence (*wujūdihi al-ʿaẓīm*)."[10] He ties this explicitly to his father's discussion in *Guide* III:51, quoting the same verse in I Chronicles, in which David enjoins his son Solomon to know and serve God.[11] Abraham writes:

> This path is very distinguished, and its end is contiguous with arrival/attainment (*wuṣūl*) . . . and [when] the rational part of the soul is engaged in the attainment of the necessary religious/legal (*sharʿiyya*) and philosophical (*ḥikmiyya*) studies that are useful for the fulfillment of the aims of the Law, as well as the acquisition of what would lead one to the special worship of the Creator of [all] beings, which consists in apprehending him (*idrākuhu*), that is, glimpsing his exalted existence (*lamḥ wujūdihi al-ʿaẓīm*) and sincerity (*ikhlās*) in love of him and passion (*ʿishq*) for him and being present before him, as David intimated in his testament to Solomon: "And you, Solomon, my son, know the God of your father, and serve him with a whole heart and a willing mind." And my father and teacher, the memory of the righteous be blessed, has already interpreted this at the end of the *Guide*. And when one's thoughts are dedicated to him, exalted be he, and are [so] preoccupied [with him as to forget] about anything else, that constitutes arrival/attainment (*wuṣūl*), as we shall note in the chapters on *wuṣūl*.[12]

Abraham echoes his father's language, his prooftext, and some of his intellectualist conceptions. He notes the importance of legal and philosophical study and, like his father, identifies the special service of the creator with understanding God, just as Maimonides (influenced by

Avicenna) does in his outline of the special service of intellectual prayer in *Guide* III:51:

> After love comes this worship to which attention has also been drawn by [the Sages], may their memory be blessed, who said: "this is worship in the heart." In my opinion, it consists in setting thought to work on the first intelligible and in devoting oneself exclusively to this as far as this is within one's capacity. Therefore you will find that David exhorted Solomon and fortified him in these two things, I mean his endeavor to apprehend (*idrākihi*) him and his endeavor to worship him after apprehension has been achieved. He said: "and you, Solomon my son, know the God of your father and serve him, and so on. If you seek him, he will be found by you, and so on." The exhortation always refers to intellectual apprehensions, not to imagination; for thought concerning imaginings is not called knowledge, but that which comes into your mind. Thus it is clear that after apprehension, the aim is total devotion (*al-inqiṭāʿ*) to him and the employment of intellectual thought in constantly loving him. Mostly this is achieved in solitude (*khalwa*) and isolation (*infirād*).[13]

However, we should notice significant differences in the two discussions. Abraham omits Maimonides' language of setting thought to work on the first intelligible. Throughout the firmly attested writings of Abraham Maimonides, we find almost no reference to the Active Intellect, a concept prominent in Maimonides' thought.[14] While both speak of a special worship that includes passionate love for God, Maimonides specifically emphasizes "the employment of intellectual thought" in passionately loving [God]. We can note, too, that elsewhere, when Maimonides does speak of the apprehension of God's being (*wujūd*) in the world to come, he uses the verb "to apprehend [with the intellect]" (*taʿqil*), rather than any verb having to do with glimpsing or seeing. In his Commentary to the Mishnah, *Pereq Ḥeleq*, Maimonides writes:

> The statement [of the Rabbinic text] "they delight in the radiance of the divine Presence" means that these souls delight in what they apprehend (*taʿqil*) of the creator, just as the holy

> angels (*ḥayyot ha-qodesh*) and the other ranks of angels delight in what they apprehend of his existence (*ʿaqalū min-wujūdihi*).[15]

Maimonides goes out of his way to translate the visual language of radiance (*ziv*) into a non-visual intellectual idiom. By contrast, Abraham Maimonides defines apprehending God (*idrākuhu*) in illuminative, visual terms as attaining a "glimpse [of] [God's] exalted essence/being (*lamḥ wujūdihi al-ʿaẓīm*)."

We find another striking use of the term *lamḥ* in the Compendium in a discussion of the parts of the soul. Abraham writes that the rational part of the soul (*al-nāṭiq*) is its noblest part, "the image of God and his likeness;" it is that by which is apprehended (*yudrak*) whatever can be apprehended of God's existence, majesty, greatness, and splendor, concerning which his prophets said, "so have I looked for you in the sanctuary, to see your power and your glory" (Psalm 63:3).[16] He then adds:

> The rational part [of the soul] is employed in glimpsing the majesty of his holiness (*lamḥ jalāl qudsihi*) and [of] his spiritual creatures—I mean, the angels—which are separated forms, apprehended by the intellect (*ʿaql*), not perceived with the senses, or [else] imagined under [some] likeness in "a prophetic vision."[17]

Abraham asserts that the angels, intellectual forms, can be known by the intellect (*ʿaql*). However, the majesty of God's holiness cannot be known by intellect; it can only be apprehended (*yudrak*) by a glimpse (*lamḥ*). Thus for Abraham, while pure intellect is one faculty of soul necessary for spiritual ascent, it is not the essence of the soul, even of the rational part (*al-nāṭiq*). The rational part of the soul includes a capacity beyond that of the strict scientific intellect, and it is this extended capacity that is able to glimpse the greatness of the Creator.

It is true that in several additional passages in the Compendium, Abraham includes a central role for the speculative intellect in the process of spiritual ascent. In one passage, Abraham speaks about rising to the upper world through contemplating the intelligibles and the speculative sciences (*tafakkur fī'l-maʿārif wa'l-ʿulūm al-naẓarī*ya).[18] However, the context suggests that for Abraham, engaging in speculative science is not necessarily intrinsically valuable; the value of speculative reason is that it enables the soul to disengage from the material world and ascend to the upper world. Thus the role of reason is primarily an instrumental one for the soul's spiritual purification.

Another passage seems to accord intrinsic value to the intellect. In this passage, Abraham describes the intellect in Maimonidean terms as the form (*ṣūra*) of the soul, the image of God, and the bond between a human being and the divine.[19] Abraham writes:

> Also the bond (*ṣila*) between the human being and his master [exists] through his form (*ṣūra*), by means of which he understands and grasps (*yudrik*) what he does of his Creator, and thinks about him and is preoccupied with Him. And as that form ascends to its source, which is God, its attachment to [God], exalted be He, is strengthened, and as it descends to [the level of] its substratum, which is matter, its attachment to its source is weakened, and there are precluded from it His lights (*anwār*), exalted be He, and His splendor, concerning which the prophets said, "Through your light, we see light" (Psalm 36:10).[20]

Abraham's language here is reminiscent of Maimonides' description of intellectual ascent to prophecy in *Hilkhot Yesodei ha-Torah* 7:1, and the Biblical phrase "in your light, we see light" is cited by Maimonides in his descriptions of intellectual illumination in *Guide* II:12 and III:52.[21] However, we notice some subtle shifts in Abraham's language. When Maimonides quotes the Biblical phrase "through your light, we see light," he is speaking of the overflow (*fayḍ*) of the Active Intellect. In contrast, Abraham's language of illumination omits the phrase "Active Intellect." Abraham speaks of God's "lights" in the plural without mention of the Active Intellect or the separate intellects; his plural reference to "lights" suggests spiritual vision. While for Maimonides, all illumination takes place through the intellect, Abraham's model of illuminative perception is more expansive, including perceptive capacities beyond the discursive intellect, and vision of a reality that transcends the intellect alone.

The imagery of light is of course complex and nuanced; intellectual and spiritual meanings easily shade into one another. We find this blending illustrated richly in the works of al-Ghazālī, a thinker widely known in Abraham Maimonides' Egyptian milieu. Elisha Russ-Fishbane has noted the presence of Sufi illuminationist imagery characteristic of the writings of Suhrawardī, and anticipated by Avicenna and Ibn Ṭufayl, in the writings of Abraham Maimonides and the Jewish pietist movement in Egypt.[22] For example, the illuminationist Suhrawardī offers a detailed description of experiences of various kinds of light that can occur to seekers along the path.[23] Suhrawardī was also clearly indebted to al-Ghazālī, who speaks of God as the true light, the Light of lights.[24]

It is crucial to note that for Sufi-influenced thinkers such as al-Ghazālī, light is not a mere metaphor. It is worth reflecting carefully upon the astute explication of one contemporary scholar, Kristin Zahra Sands:

> When the mystic experiences spiritual light, he is not experiencing something similar to light, but rather sees a light far more powerful and "real" than physical light. The mystic does not choose a metaphor to describe his visionary experience: the metaphor or symbol does not point to something other than itself but rather is an indicator of its own self and the mystic has merely perceived this reality. Seen from the outside, the mystic's description of this reality appears to be a metaphor, but this is only because the observer has not grasped the true nature of things.[25]

It is clear that Abraham Maimonides knew the work of al-Ghazālī; his chapters on trust, humility, abstinence, governance of the faculties, and solitude in the Compendium show close parallels to these discussions in al-Ghazālī's *Iḥyā' 'ulūm al-dīn*.[26] Al-Ghazālī devoted an entire treatise, *Mishkāt al-anwār* (*The Niche of Lights*), to explication of the ontological status of light and illumination. For example, he writes in the *Mishkāt*:

> There are in the world of dominion noble and high luminous substances called angels. Light overflows (*tufīḍ*) toward human spirits, and because of these lights these angels may be called "lords"—that is why God is "Lord of the lords." These angels have the first level in the luminosity.[27]

Moreover, imagery of light is present throughout al-Ghazālī's writings. In a remarkable passage in the *Ihyā'*, al-Ghazālī distinguishes two forms of acquiring knowledge: the way of inference and the process of learning (*ta'allum*), and the way of inspiration (*ilhām*).[28] He goes on to explain that Sufis prefer the way of inspiration. When a Sufi engages in spiritual practices:

> It is God who takes care and charge of his servant's heart by enlightening with the light of knowledge. And when God takes charge of the heart's affairs, his mercy floods it and his light shines in it and man's heart is dilated and there is disclosed to him the mystery of the Kingdom, and there is lifted from the face of his heart by the favor of the [divine] mercy the veil [of delusion or inattention], and there gleams in it the realities of the divine things. The only requirement for man is to dispose himself by simple purification and to furnish ardor along with a sincere will and total yearning and continual lying in wait for the mercy which God most high will open to him.
>
> To the prophets and the friends of God the matter was disclosed and light poured forth (*fāḍa*) into their hearts, not by study and the writing of books, but by abstinence in worldly things and freeing themselves from attachments to them and emptying their hearts from preoccupations and devoting themselves most ardently to God most high. . . .
>
> At this point, if his will is sincere and his intention [ardor] pure and his perseverance proper [good], and he is not pulled by his passions or distracted by inner concerns with worldly attachments, the gleams of the Truth will shine in his heart. In its beginnings it will be like the rapid lightning and will not remain. Then it will return and it may tarry. And if it returns it may remain, and it may be snatched away. And if it remains, it may, or may not be, prolonged.[29]

Abraham Maimonides uses imagery of light shining upon prophets and friends of God in a way quite similar to that of al-Ghazālī, often using the prooftext "through your light, we see light" (Psalm 36:10), sometimes using the term overflow (*fayḍ*)[30]. For both thinkers, the *fayḍ* is light, but not necessarily intellectual light; it is a spiritual light that may include, but also transcends the intellect. For example, in his discourse on the government of the faculties, Abraham Maimonides writes:

> Your aim in regard to the welfare of your soul should be that it be free from dullness and bright, in order that it may contemplate (*iṭṭilā'*) what it is able to of the light that shines upon it from the overflow (*fayḍ*) of [God's] light—of which it is said, "through Your light, we see light"—and of which it is said regarding the request to be enlightened by it, "for You light my lamp; the Lord my God lightens my darkness" (Psalm 18:29).[31]

Note that in this context, Abraham Maimonides is not speaking of an ancient Biblical exemplar; he is offering direct guidance to his reader about ideal spiritual practice to receive infusion of divine light.

A similar conception arises in the Compendium in the context of a discussion of the Sabbath. Abraham Maimonides describes three kinds of Sabbath observers. The first simply rests; the second thinks of the purpose of the Sabbath, reflects on the creation of the world, and categorizes the parts of the universe and what is created on each day of creation.[32] He adds to this a third level of observance:

> [One who reflects on these matters] becomes absorbed in this scientific reflection (*al-fikra al-'ilmiyya*) until he is transported to the true sanctity and rejoices in the Maker for what He has illuminated within his inward being (*ashraqa 'alā bāṭinihi*) of the lights of his majesty (*anwār jalālihi*), through his reflection upon him, and adduces proofs for his greatness from the greatness of what he has made. And he apprehends (*adraka*) the nobility of the intellectual and religious-legal bond that (exists) between [God] and him as was intended by the Sabbath in his declaration, exalted be he, in his legislation, "between me and the children of Israel it is a sign forever."[33]

Abraham Maimonides' approach here certainly accords with the contemplation of creation (*i'tibār*) and religious rationalism we find in thinkers such as Baḥya Ibn Paqūda and Maimonides.[34] The language of light shining on one's inward being is close to that of Baḥya, who also describes the yearning of the soul to achieve union with the divine light.[35] But the plural phrase "lights of His majesty" should give us pause. This is experiential language for witnessing spiritual light, such as we find in the writings of al-Ghazālī and illuminationist Sufi teachers.

Indeed, as Eli Shaubi has pointed out, in Abraham's view, there seems to be an internal light that the spiritual practitioner receives and cultivates. Abraham notes a Sufi meditative practice of sitting in darkness:

> The Sufis of Islam practice solitude in dark places and isolate themselves in them to the point that the sensitive part of the soul is suspended even from seeing light (*ḍaw'*). This requires a strong inner light (*nūr bāṭin qawī*) with which the soul is preoccupied so as not to experience loneliness or distress (*tastawḥish*) because of external darkness.[36]

The passage goes on to describe finding intimacy in solitude, as in a greeting that sages extend to one another, "May God make you one who finds companionship in solitude and feels lonesome (*yastawḥish*) in the crowd." Abraham Maimonides continues:

> David also said, in reference to his intimacy with [God], exalted be He, during his solitude in the darkness of night and in the desert and the waterless wastes, "Yea, though I walk through the valley of the shadow of death, I will fear no evil, for Thou art with me; Thy rod and Thy staff, they comfort me" (Psalm 23:4).[37]

The strong inner light developed by the meditator provides a comforting, intimate presence that illuminates any darkness.

Shaubi notes further that the preparation for the theophany at Sinai, described by Abraham Maimonides in his comment to Exodus 19:10, includes preparation to receive God's light, as described in Abraham Maimonides' comment on Exodus 19:11 ("God will come down [in the sight of all the people on Mt. Sinai]") : "This is an allusion to the revelation of light that is called the glory of God."[38] Shaubi writes perceptively:

> It is worth pointing out that in R. Abraham's example of the Sabbath observers, as well as in the case of the Children of Israel ahead of the theophany at Sinai, the light is a product of "God's splendor". In the case of the Sufi practice of seclusion in dark rooms, the light is described as an "internal light". It is unclear whether R. Abraham sees this light as an external act of God

> shining His light or as a pure mental state reached by a pious individual, or even if both of these lights are identical.[39]

The important question Shaubi poses is whether the inner light one develops in meditation represents illumination of one's own inner being or is a reflection of the light of God's glory. Perhaps the distinction between external and internal is artificial; Abraham Maimonides speaks of what "[God] has illuminated within his inner being of the lights of His majesty." God's light sparks the inner light of the spiritual practitioner, which in turn strengthens the meditator's ability to perceive spiritual light. God's light illumines and strengthens one's inner flame.[40]

A further contrast between the illuminative language of Maimonides and Abraham Maimonides can be discerned in the two thinkers' discussions of providence. In *Guide* III:17–18, Maimonides explains that divine providence accords with one's intellectual attainment. In *Guide* III:51 he explains that great sages who suffer do so when they have turned their minds from God, and thus the intellect—the bond between humans and God—is severed. In this context, Maimonides cites Psalm 91: "when you pass through the waters, I will be with you, and through the rivers, they shall not overflow you," and adds that "everyone who has rendered themselves so worthy that the intellect in question overflows toward him, has providence attached to him, while all evils are prevented from befalling him."[41]

While he cites the same prooftext, Abraham Maimonides offers a much less intellectual conception of personal providence than his father. Abraham Maimonides writes:

> When [his] piety (*salāḥ*) is strong and [his] performances are good and [his] reliance upon him, in all matters is in order, and the servant is preoccupied with the love of him, and turns away from everything except him, and "the spirit of the Lord and the love of him" are firmly established in him so that his lights shine upon him, and he receives intimation of his nearness to him and of his great solicitude for him, then detrimental causes have no effect upon him, but [it is] as it has been said, "when you pass through the waters, I will be with you, and through the rivers they shall not overflow you. . . ."[42]

As Russ-Fishbane observes, for Abraham Maimonides, providence is not a matter of attachment to the Active Intellect, but of piety and reliance on God (*ittikāl, tawakkul*). Russ-Fishbane calls attention to Sufi language of intimacy and proximity (*qurb*) added by Abraham Maimonides in his discussion of providence.[43] For Maimonides, it is intellect that creates the providential bond between God and humans, while for Abraham Maimonides, God's "lights" provide an additional sense of personal caring and comfort, such as we find in Baḥya Ibn Paqūda.[44] We can also note again the experiential language of spiritual lights shining upon one. In *Guide* III:52, citing Psalm 36:10, "through your light, we see light," Maimonides states explicitly that the light that is always providentially observing one is the light of the [Active] Intellect. In Abraham Maimonides, the language of intellectual illumination is certainly present. However, the Active Intellect is absent, and his use of the term "lights" in the plural suggests spiritual vision, perceived by faculties of soul more expansive than the intellect alone. We should note, too, that in contrast to his son, Maimonides never uses the term "lights" in the plural. Maimonides' chief concern is to preserve the absolute unity of God. Intellect or Active Intellect is Maimonides' sole concession to plurality in the divine realm.[45]

It is true that, like al-Ghazālī and Maimonides, Abraham Maimonides does accord the intellect a role in spiritual ascent.[46] However, it is important to add that Abraham Maimonides does not view philosophy as the primary method of this ascent.[47] The role of intellect for Abraham Maimonides is contemplative, but not philosophical in the sense of Aristotelian demonstrative philosophy. For Abraham Maimonides, while intellect is key in the ascent to God, philosophical and scientific demonstration lack the centrality and passion they find in the thought of Maimonides. For Maimonides, the essence of a human being is the speculative intellect (*ʿaql*); it is the intellect that achieves immortality, and it is through intellect that we achieve whatever conjunction is possible with the divine.[48] While both thinkers emphasize passionate love for God, for Maimonides, passionate love arises from the dazzlement of intellectual wonder and awe, a heightened state of intellect such as described by Aristotle in *Metaphysics* XII:7 and Spinoza in *Ethics* V:21–42. By contrast, Abraham Maimonides describes ascent to and infusion of light without the theme of intellectual perplexity and dazzlement. For Abraham Maimonides, the scientific and philosophical intellect is just one aspect of one's being that plays a role in spiritual ascent, along with the sensory-experiential and affective dimensions.[49]

The relationship between these two modes of cognition is a subject of debate among medieval Jewish and Islamic thinkers. Judah Halevi argues that the most accurate knowledge of God is more akin to sense perception than to intellectual knowledge. Halevi suggests that the God of Abraham, which he identifies with the Tetragrammaton, is known experientially, by taste (*dhawq*) and witness (*mushāhada*), while the God of Aristotle, which he identifies with the generic divine name *Elohim* (God), is known by logic and inference (*qiyās*):

> Now it has become clear to me the difference between God and Lord, and I understand what [the difference is] between the God of Abraham and the God of Aristotle. The LORD, may He be blessed, one longs for with a longing of taste (*dhawq*) and witness (*mushāhada*), while we [only] incline logically (*qiyāsan*) to God.[50]

Halevi thus draws a sharp distinction between knowledge through syllogism (*qiyās*), and knowledge through taste (*dhawq*) and witness (*mushāhada*).

We have seen that in the *Iḥyā'*, al-Ghazālī draws a distinction between knowledge acquired through the process of learning (*ta'allum*) and knowledge acquired spontaneously through inspiration (*ilhām*).[51] In his spiritual autobiography *Deliverer from Error* (*al-Munqidh min al-ḍalāl*), he draws a similar distinction between what can be known by study or learning (*ta'allum)* and what is known by immediate experience (*dhawq*).[52] Likewise, in the *Mishkāt al-anwār*, al-Ghazālī indicates a stage of knowing beyond that of the ordinary rational faculty, attained by the prophets and friends of God through what he terms "the holy prophetic spirit" and "the specific prophetic taste (*dhawq*)," which he compares to taste (*dhawq*) in poetry and music.[53]

Scholars debate the significance of *dhawq* and *mushāhada* for al-Ghazālī.[54] Alexander Treiger argues that for both al-Ghazālī and Avicenna, witnessing and tasting take place through the faculty of intellect; *mushāhada* designates an intellectual vision of intelligibles, while *dhawq* signifies the intellectual pleasure of knowledge that "has become so internalized as to be an integral part of one's being," a direct and incommunicable experience that has no analogy and must be experienced for oneself.[55] However, while Treiger suggests that *dhawq* takes place through the intellect, the analogy of poetry and music suggests something beyond the scientific intellect. Poetry and music must be experienced for oneself precisely because such appreciation has an aesthetic quality that distinguishes it from syllogistic knowledge. We can recall the insight of William James:

> . . . mystical states are more like states of feeling than like states of intellect. No one can make clear to another who has never had a certain feeling, in what the quality or work of it consists. One must have musical ears to know the value of a symphony; one must have been in love one's self to understand a lover's state of mind. Lacking the heart or ear, we cannot interpret the musician or the lover justly, and are even likely to consider him weak-minded or absurd. The mystic finds that most of us accord to his experiences an equally incompetent treatment.[56]

Music is thus a prime example of direct experience that cannot be captured in language. Likewise, al-Ghazālī states explicitly that there are "flashes" (*lawā'iḥ*) of the unseen available to the prophetic spirit that cannot be grasped by speculative reason alone.[57]

As Treiger notes, al-Ghazālī omits Avicenna's stipulation that all knowledge, including witnessing, is syllogistic in nature.[58] This caveat is helpful for distinguishing the approach of Maimonides from that of Abraham Maimonides. For Maimonides, as for Avicenna, all knowing, including prophetic knowing, has a syllogistic structure, which mirrors the syllogistic structure of reality. In this philosophical theory of prophecy, prophets simply arrive at syllogistic knowledge more rapidly than others, perhaps instantaneously.[59] Maimonides uses the Avicennian term *ḥads* to describe this faculty of quickened, intuitive intellect, the effect of divine overflow (*fayḍ*) upon the rational faculty. Maimonides never uses the Sufi term *dhawq* for intuitive understanding, just as he never uses the term *mushāhada* for witness of the divine.

Abraham Maimonides is closer to al-Ghazālī; he does not insist upon the syllogistic nature of all knowledge, and he does not emphasize the necessity for philosophical demonstration. In contrast to his father, Abraham Maimonides does use the term *mushāhada* for witness of the divine, and uses the term *dhawq* for intuitive understanding of Scripture, and for the direct spiritual experience engendered through prostration in prayer. Abraham Maimonides also speaks of other non-discursive ways of knowing: "the meditations of the heart," "a vision of the heart," and "the paths of the heart and the destinations of the mind." For Abraham Maimonides, discursive and non-discursive, intellectual and sensory-affective modes of knowing are complementary and mutually reinforcing.[60]

Abraham Maimonides and his circle of Pietists certainly saw themselves as heirs to Maimonides. They drew upon Maimonides' intellectualist language of illumination and heightened its experiential dimension, drawing upon what Abraham Maimonides termed "sensory or sensory-like vision."[61] For example, we find the following remarkable passage in the compiled document published by Paul Fenton as "A Mystical Treatise on Prayer and the Spiritual Quest:"

> Then [one should engage in] reflection (*fikr*) on his exaltedness and invocation (*dhikr*) of his Name, until love is impressed in his heart, through which he turns to Him on high, until he arrives at a state of unity (*waṣala ilā maqām al-tawḥīd*), which is the annihilation of humanity (*fanā' al-bashariyya*) and the manifestation of divinity (*ithbāt al-rubūbiyya*). This is the true unification (*al-tawḥīd ʿalā al-ḥaqīqa*) which is the intended goal of the verse "Hear O Israel, the Lord our God, the Lord is one (Deuteronomy 6:4)," and the verse "you shall love the Lord your God with all your heart, with all your soul, and with all your might (Deuteronomy 6:5)." Whereupon the heart will be filled with His lights (*anwārihi*) through continuing recollection of Him and occupying oneself in reflection upon His exaltedness, His awesomeness, being in the divine Presence in His state of holiness, and the bliss of contemplating his Beauty and Majesty.[62]

The author of this passage—perhaps R. Abraham he-Ḥasid—draws upon evocative illuminationist imagery, depicting God's light, beauty, and majesty. The author uses Sufi experiential language of annihilation of the human ego (*fanā'*) to describe the true meaning of unification (*tawḥīd*), as expressed in the declaration of the *Shemaʿ* that God is one.

We see another striking example in a letter found in the Cairo Genizah, which may be also written by Abraham he-Ḥasid. In this passage we hear about an intellectual contemplation of the Cause of causes:

> Through his revelation, he shall receive spiritual intuition and ascensions in the visions of those possessed of mystical knowledge. Then he shall ascend and drink plentifully from the source of life, after which he shall thirst no more for eternity. In him shall be granted the request of the prophets, "that glory may praise you without end." By "glory" is meant the intellect..., through which we pray and commune with [God], perceiving what may be perceived of the radiant divine light, as David said, "through your light we see light."[63]

The Pietist author of this letter describes the mystical ascension of the intellect only suggested in *Guide* III:51–54. He builds on the notion we will see in Maimonides that the intellect is the glory of God. However, the sensory language of "drinking" and "thirsting" suggests that the radiant divine light perceived is not purely metaphorical, but also has an experiential, sensory-affective dimension.[64]

The experiential dimension is also suggested in documents we have concerning Abraham Maimonides' father-in-law, R. Ḥananel. A letter apparently addressed to R. Ḥananel's son Ḥayyim offers a prayer for R. Ḥananel's forty-day spiritual retreat. This letter is the only direct evidence we have thus far that the Jewish Pietists of Egypt engaged in forty-day spiritual retreats—known as *arbaʿīn*—practiced by Sufis in their contemporary milieu.[65] In this letter, the author wishes R. Ḥananel the spiritual fruits of his journey, as were granted to the prophets and friends of God:

> May God be a protector and friend during his journey, a guardian and preserver, a companion and guide, just as he was for his prophets and friends during their journeys and solitary retreats (*khalwātihim*), in their vision/beholding (*mulāḥaẓa*) of the Majesty and Beauty, Splendor, and Perfection of the divine Presence, and in their immense longing that He might infuse them (*li-yufīḍ ʿalayhim*) with an unmediated perception of the divine (*ʿilman laduniyyan*),[66] unveil for them (*li-yukāshif*)

> the mysteries of His holy books, and assist them both in the knowledge and practice contained in them.[67]

In another fragment, R. Ḥananel himself writes:

> Any person who has experienced an unveiling (*inkashafa*) of his inner vision, strives and trains with [spiritual] discipline, guarding his soul from desires and pleasures, restraining his bodily members when in motion and when still, that perhaps He may bring his goal to fruition and nourish him during solitary meditation with serenity and sweetness. If this is granted but once a month, once a year, even once in one's entire lifetime, it would bring him supreme happiness and exceeding repose.[68]

Abraham Maimonides' language of illumination must be read in the context of these striking first-person accounts of spiritual practice and experience offered by his close associates. Inspired by *Guide* III:51, the Egyptian Pietist circle developed a concrete spiritual practice; their light imagery reflects the fruit of such practice. Whereas for Maimonides, communion with the divine light consists in intellectual union with the Active Intellect, for the Pietist circle intellectual union includes experiential viewing of spiritual light, a glimpse of the divine beyond that of the speculative intellect—a viewing which, in the words of Abraham Maimonides, "may guide [one] to intellectual apprehension of the greatness of the creator."[69]

Maimonides and Abraham Maimonides thus differ with respect to the language of glimpsing a flash (*lamḥ*) of the divine. In the introduction to the *Guide*, Maimonides uses the image of lightning flashes, but does not use the specific term *lamḥ*; he writes that "sometimes truth flashes out (*yalūḥu*) to us so that we think it is day," and suggests that Moses is one for whom "the lightning flashes (*yabruqu ʿalayhi al-baraq*) time and time again, so that he is always, as it were, in unceasing light."[70] As we will see in chapter 7 below, in the *Commentary to the Mishnah*, Eight Chapters, chapter 7, Maimonides suggests that Moses knew more after his request to see God's glory than before, and in the *Mishneh Torah, Hilkhot Yesodei ha-Torah* I:10, suggests that Moses apprehended "something of God's being." However, in the *Guide*, he nowhere states that Moses achieves a glimpse of God's exalted essence or existence. To the contrary, in *Guide* I:54, he interprets the passage in the cleft of the rock to insist that even Moses cannot perceive the essence of God, only God's attributes of action.[71] Thus while Abraham Maimonides is eager to identify his path to knowledge of God with that of his father's teachings in the *Guide*, there are distinct differences in their conceptions. While the notion that Moses is able to achieve a glimpse of God's essence or existence may draw upon suggestions in Maimonides' pre-*Guide* writings, the language itself is Abraham Maimonides' innovation.

Abraham Maimonides' position in his commentary to Exodus 33:22 is thus closer to the visual and experiential models of Saadya, Halevi, al-Ghazālī, and Ibn Ṭufayl than to his father's distinctly intellectual approach.[72] It is, however, reminiscent of two passages in *Guide* I:21. In the first passage, Maimonides offers an interpretation of the phrase "and I will cover you with my hand until I have passed by" that compares with Saadya's in interesting ways. Maimonides suggests that if one longs for an apprehension beyond that which one's intellect is capable of, the faculty of apprehension may be deceived or destroyed, unless divine help attends him. Saadya offered a similar interpretation of the phrase "and I will cover you with my hand." However, for Saadya, God shielded Moses from the intensity of the created light with a cloud, while for Maimonides, God protects Moses with a mental shield so that he is not harmed by seeking to understand what his intellect cannot bear. What is similar in the interpretations is the notion that God is trying to protect Moses from something that will be too powerful for him to withstand.

Abraham echoes and expands on this point in the *Kifāya*, in his chapter on the two forms of solitude (*khalwa*). He writes there:

> It has already been said to the master of prophets in reference to (this divine) protection, "and I will cover you with my hand until I have passed by" (Exodus 33:22). Then he said "the Lord gives grace and glory (*ḥen ve-khavod*); no good thing will he withhold from them that walk uprightly" (Psalm 84:12), as an allusion to what He, exalted be he, overflows (*yufīḍ*) on those who walk with uprightness in the paths that lead (*al-masālik al-muwaṣṣila*) to him if they walk uprightly, until they arrive (*yaṣilū*).[73]

God's glory is here an emanation afforded to those who walk uprightly. If one prepares oneself morally and spiritually, God will protect one so that one will not be burnt by the overwhelming power of God's light.[74] While for Maimonides, preparation is moral and intellectual, for Abraham Maimonides, preparation entails walking in the paths of piety, the spiritual practices he offers in the *Kifāya*. We are reminded as well of al-Ghazālī's description of the moral and spiritual preparation necessary for receiving God's light.

In a second passage, at the end of *Guide* I:21, Maimonides goes on to acknowledge that the profound subject of prophetic revelation is subject to many different interpretations, and that one is free to choose whichever one wishes.[75] Maimonides here offers several interpretive options. First, one might think that in the cleft of the rock, Moses asked to understand God's essence, and was given instead an understanding of God's attributes of action. This is the interpretation Maimonides offers as his own, both in *Guide* I:21 and I:54. Second, he notes that one might believe that in addition to this intellectual apprehension, there was an apprehension due to the sense of sight, which had for its object a created thing, through seeing which intellectual apprehension achieves perfection. He ascribes this interpretation to Onqelos. This is the harmonizing view that Abraham appears to adopt. Seeing a created light might enable one to understand intellectual truths.

However, Maimonides offers a third possibility, which may hold the key to an esoteric position. If visual apprehension occurs in a vision of prophecy, then the created light may be said to be an emanation from the Active Intellect. Basing himself upon al-Fārābī, Maimonides' theory of prophecy asserts that what we call prophecy is a light emanated from the divine Active Intellect, first upon the human intellect, and then upon the imaginative faculty, which produces images.[76] Thus, the glory that Moses is said to encounter in the cleft of the rock may represent an inner illumination of either the intellect or the imaginative faculty. Likewise, the voice that, Maimonides asserts, passes before Moses may represent a reception from the divine intellect.

There is no getting around the fact that Maimonides offers as one interpretative option that Moses' apprehension in the cleft of the rock is due to the sense of sight or the sense of hearing, in addition to intellectual apprehension. In his second interpretation, Maimonides ascribes to Onqelos the view that what is seen or heard is something physical; Maimonides appears to hold that this is a less harmful interpretive option than ascribing physical characteristics to God.[77] But need the sense of sight or hearing necessarily be physical sight or hearing? In his third option, the vision of prophecy is visual, but not physical; it is an internal vision. What the interpretation we will explore here adds is that the created light or the created word is not necessarily physical, but may be the light of understanding of the Active Intellect.

In summary, Abraham Maimonides states that he seeks to harmonize two views: one in which the light of God's glory is physical and sensory, and one in which "God's glory" is a metaphor for intellectual illumination. Abraham suggests that the sensory illumination of the created light may have guided Moses to intellectual understanding; in both his Torah Commentary and *Kifāya*, he speaks of attaining a glimpse of God's exalted essence or existence. While for Maimonides, light signifies conjunction with the Active Intellect, for Abraham and his Pietist associates—as for Sufi-influenced thinkers like al-Ghazālī—light is visual and experiential, suggesting a more expansive and integrated model of human perception of the divine; what is perceived of the divine transcends that which can be grasped by the intellect alone. Abraham Maimonides omits the central Maimonidean concept of the Active Intellect, and speaks in experiential terms of overflow of the lights of God's majesty. This language suggests a background in the spiritual practices attested to in the writings of his Pietist associates.

In the next chapter, we turn to the esoteric interpretation of Maimonides suggested by *Guide* I:21, that God's "glory" or "created light" represents the light of the Active Intellect.

2

Maimonides on Created Light: An Esoteric Interpretation

In two fascinating studies, Esti Eisenmann argues through detailed exegesis that Maimonides does not simply reject the interpretation of the glory as created light, but rather reinterprets it to suggest either the prophetic emanation that the prophet receives or the Active Intellect itself.[1] Thus what occurred at Mount Sinai was a historical event, just as the revelation at the burning bush was a historical event. But neither was a visible light show. Rather in both cases what took place was an event of inner illumination and understanding—one, in the understanding of Moses and the other, in the understanding of Moses and the nation.

Let us look at some of the evidence that Eisenmann adduces for the thesis that the created light signifies the Active Intellect.[2] In several places, Maimonides identifies the created light with the glory. We thus may base ourselves on clear statements he makes about the glory. In his commentary to Mishnah *Ḥagigah* II:1, he states that "the intellect is the glory of the Lord."[3] In *Guide* III:52, he identifies the Active Intellect with the glory of God and *Shekhinah*, citing the verse "Through your light, we see light" (Psalm 36:10). Likewise, at the end of *Guide* III:51, he tells us that prophets and excellent people are beneath the degree of Moses, Aaron, and Miriam, but that the apprehension of their intellects becomes stronger when separated from the body, quoting Isaiah 58:8: "And your righteousness shall go before you; the glory of the Lord shall be at your rear."[4] He adds that, having reached this condition of enduring permanence, that intellect remains in one and the same state. He thus clearly identifies the intellect as the glory of the Lord.

Following classical commentators, several modern scholars, including Howard Kreisel, Jacob Levinger and Esti Eisenmann, have put forth the view that for Maimonides, the voice of God symbolizes the Active Intellect. Eisenmann extends this argument to the created light. The crux of her argument is that when Maimonides claims that the use of the created light is an inferior interpretation this is meant to signal to advanced readers that the true interpretation is allegorical, that is, intellectual. When he offers the two interpretations side by side, the common reader can interpret the created light as a miraculous light outside the soul, while the advanced reader knows that it actually signifies the Active Intellect.

Perhaps the clearest textual argument for this esoteric approach is the fact that Exodus 24:16, "and the glory of the Lord dwelt/rested upon Mount Sinai," is interpreted twice— in I:25 and I:64— and both times it is interpreted exclusively as created light. In this way, Maimonides does not deny the historical event at Mount Sinai (as he does not deny a historical occurrence at the burning bush). But given that elsewhere (end of I:5) he tells the reader that the interpretation depicting a visible created light is an inferior interpretation, there must be a hidden superior interpretation that he has not stated explicitly. This could be either 1) that Mount Sinai took place in a collective vision of prophecy (hinted at in *Guide* II:32–33 and I:46); and/or 2) that what occurred at Mount Sinai was a collective or individual reception of the Active Intellect.[5]

The notion that Maimonides is hinting that the created light is in fact intellectual light, the light of the Active Intellect, is of course not a plain or surface reading, but requires one to weave together various statements from various chapters, as, Maimonides suggests in his introduction, one must do.[6]

In *Guide* I:4, Maimonides asserts that every mention of seeing referring to God has the figurative meaning of intellectual apprehension. Since God does not have a body, God cannot be seen by the physical eye. Among the many verses he cites is Genesis 15:1: "The word of the Lord came to Abram in a vision."[7] What is important here is that Maimonides is asserting that the event of the covenant between the pieces takes place in a vision of prophecy. Thus the smoking oven and flaming torch, as well as all of the animal sacrifices, are products of Abram's prophetic imagination, rather than physical objects seen in the external world.[8] In Maimonides' al-Fārābīan theory of prophecy, they are products of the light of the Active Intellect, which overflows to the prophet's vision.

In I:5, Maimonides argues that in the quest for knowledge, one should feel awe, refrain, and hold back until one gradually elevates oneself intellectually. Maimonides asserts that this is the genuine meaning of the verse "and Moses hid his face because he was afraid to look upon God" (Exodus 3:6). This, he asserts, is "an additional meaning of the verse over and above the external meaning, which indicates that he hid his face because of his being afraid to look upon the light manifesting itself—and not that the deity, who is greatly exalted above every deficiency, can be apprehended by the eyes." As Eisenmann points out, Maimonides holds that the plain sense of the verse is that Moses was afraid to look upon a light manifesting itself; Maimonides will not allow that any sense of the verse indicates that God was visible to the physical eyes.[9]

At the end of *Guide* I:5, Maimonides reiterates that "whenever the words seeing, vision, and looking occur in this sense, intellectual apprehension is meant and not the eye's sight, as God, may he be exalted, is not an existent that can be apprehended with the eyes."[10] He then adds an important caveat: "If, however, an individual of insufficient capacity should not wish to reach the rank to which we desire him to ascend and should he consider that all the words [figuring in the Bible] concerning this subject are indicative of sensual perception of created lights—be they angels or something else—why, there is no harm in his thinking this."[11]

The plain sense of Maimonides' own words is that there is no harm in believing that a human being can see created beings or lights, for these physical manifestations do not endanger the absolute incorporeality of God. Eisenmann, however, suggests that Maimonides' true view is that the created light or glory is either the Active Intellect or an intellectual emanation from the Active Intellect that appears internally in the prophet's mind in visions of prophecy, such as he spells out with respect to Abram's covenant between the pieces.[12] This suggestion would appear to collapse the two meanings, external and internal, of the statement in Exodus 3:6 that "Moses hid his face, because he was afraid to look upon

God." Moses was cautious and paced himself in his receiving of intellectual understanding. Thus, he paced himself in receiving illumination from the light of the Active Intellect.

But according to this interpretation, what do we make of Maimonides' statement at the end of I:5 to the effect that there is no harm in believing that that there is "sensory perception of created lights?" Eisenmann suggests that this is a contradiction of the seventh type. That is, Maimonides deliberately creates an apparent contradiction between a metaphorical interpretation, whereby light refers to intellectual illumination and a physical interpretation, whereby light is external and visible to the senses. The discerning reader will weave together Maimonides' varied statements to recognize that the created light is in fact intellectual light, that is, the light of the Active Intellect.[13] Thus "sensory perception of created light" need not be literally sensory and external, but may refer to internal prophetic vision.[14]

Whether or not we attribute Maimonides' ambiguity here specifically to the seventh contradiction, we can note that the notion of light as intellectual is familiar to us from *Guide* III:52:

> This king, who cleaves to him and accompanies him, is the intellect that overflows toward us and is the bond between us and him, may he be exalted. Just as we apprehend him by means of that light (*ḍaw'*), which he caused to overflow toward us—as it says, "through your light, do we see light" (Psalm 36:10)—so does he by means of this same light examine us; and because of it, he, may he be exalted, is constantly with us, examining from on high: "can any hide himself in secret places that I shall not see him?" (Jeremiah 23:24).[15]

Maimonides thus uses images of light as well as water to depict the overflow (*fayḍ*) that brings intellects from potentiality to actuality and causes prophetic visions.[16] The term he uses here for light (*ḍaw'*) is precisely the term used by al-Fārābī when comparing the Active Intellect to intelligible light.[17] Likewise, in *Guide* II:12, he writes:

> As for our remark that the books of the prophets likewise apply figuratively the notion of overflow to the action of the deity, a case in point is the dictum, "they have forsaken me, the fountain

> of living waters" (Jeremiah 2:13)—which refers to the overflow of life, that is, of being, which is life without doubt. Similarly, the dictum, "for with you is the fountain of life" (Psalm 36:10), signifies the overflow of being. In the same way the remaining portion of this verse, "through your light, we see light" has the same meaning—namely, that through the overflow of the intellect that overflowed from you, we intellectually cognize, and consequently, we receive correct guidance, we draw inferences, and we apprehend the intellect.[18]

God's light is thus an overflow of intellect and an overflow of being.[19] Maimonides asserts that the separate intellects are created beings. Thus, Eisenmann's hypothesis is that for Maimonides, the created light, God's glory, and the *Shekhinah* are all Maimonidean expressions for the separate intellects or the Active Intellect. We can add that this is corroborated by the prooftext Maimonides cites in *Guide* III:9, where he writes: "For near Him, may He be exalted, there is no darkness, but rather, perpetual, dazzling light (*al-ḍaw' al-bāhir al-dā'im*), whose overflow (*fayḍ*) illuminates all that is dark, as it is said in the prophetic parables, 'and the earth shined with His glory" (Ezekiel 43:2). God's glory is the overflow or emanation (*fayḍ*) of the light of intellect, which is also bestowed by God upon humans, on account of which we are said to be made in God's image.[20]

In *Guide* I:10, in his discussion of ascending and descending, Maimonides adds that "[Moses] ascended to the top of the mountain upon which the created light had descended."[21] By the parallelism we see in *Guide* III:52, Moses' intellectual light is ascending to meet the intellectual light descending from the Active Intellect—or more precisely, intellectual connection is taking place. At Mount Sinai the created light of the Active Intellect descends upon those prepared to receive it.[22]

Maimonides returns to the event at Mount Sinai in I:64, writing that "the glory of the Lord is sometimes intended to signify the created light that God causes to descend in a particular place in order to confer honor upon it in a miraculous way: 'and the glory of the Lord abode upon Mount Sinai, and then [the cloud] covered it, and so on' (Exodus 24:16)."[23] In the interpretation we have been pursuing here, the descent of the created light represents the revelation and reception of the Active Intellect. What is new here is the language of conferring honor in a miraculous way. On a plain reading of Maimonides' text, one might think that he is here following the conception of Onqelos and Saadya that the created light is a miraculous, external manifestation. However, Maimonides may want to indicate that openness to the revelation of the Active Intellect can also be seen as a kind of miracle.

Maimonides goes on to explain that the greatest honor we can accord to God is apprehension, that is, understanding. We honor God by words indicating our understanding; we communicate to others that which we have apprehended by our intellect. Maimonides makes this point in II:5, interpreting the verse from Psalms: "The heavens tell of the glory of God" (Psalm 19:2). The plain sense of the Biblical verse is actually Maimonidean; the magnificence of the heavens is a silent witness to their creator. Here, however, Maimonides builds on the Aristotelian notion that the heavens are living beings who praise God through their understanding. As he writes, "for he who praises through speech only makes known what he has represented to himself. Now this very representation is the true praise, whereas the words concerning it are meant to instruct someone else or to make it clear concerning oneself that one has had the apprehension in question."[24] Thus, understanding, mental representation, is the true praise. In II:5, the glory of God is the wisdom manifest in creation, and in both II:5 and I:64, we honor or give glory to God by understanding and communicating that wisdom.

In I:64, Maimonides adds that beings that have no apprehension, such as the minerals, "also as it were honor God through the fact that by their very nature they are indicative of the power and wisdom of him who brought them into existence. For this induces him who considers them to honor God, either by means of articulate utterance or without it if speech is not permitted him."[25] Thus, the magnificent complexity of nature is part of God's glory and causes those who discern it to honor God through praise and understanding.[26]

An esoteric interpretation of created light may also be confirmed in a passage in Maimonides' *Epistle to Yemen*. Maimonides is here countering the interpretation of Deuteronomy 33:2, "He appeared from Mount Paran." A Jewish convert to Islam claimed that this verse alludes to the appearance of Muhammad. By contrast, Maimonides argues that this verse refers to the heavenly "light" that descended on Mount Sinai:

> When the Deity was about to reveal himself on Mount Sinai, the heavenly light did not descend suddenly like a thunderbolt, but came down gently, manifesting itself gradually first from the top of one mountain, then from another, until he reached his abode on Sinai… [Scripture] speaks of the light that glimmered from Mount Paran, which is further removed from Sinai, but of the light that radiated from Mount Seir, which is mirrored to it, and finally of the revelation of the full splendor of God on Sinai which was the goal of the theophany as is related in the verse, "and the glory of God abode on Mount Sinai" (Exodus 24:16), "and the Lord came from Sinai" (Deuteronomy 33:2).[27]

Here, as in the *Guide*, Maimonides interprets the glory of God in Exodus 24:16 as a created light. He then goes on to cite a well-known midrash on Deuteronomy 33:2 which suggests that God first sent the Torah to other nations, including the children of Esau and Ishmael, who symbolize in rabbinic thought Christianity and Islam. Howard Kreisel points out astutely that "by citing a midrash in which God's 'appearance' is interpreted as the revelation of the Law, Maimonides may be signaling that the appearance of the 'light' should be construed figuratively. The light is not a visible light at all. It refers to the content of the Torah that was accepted by the Jews and rejected by the adherents of the other religions."[28]

This figurative interpretation of light is not necessarily identical to the light of the Active Intellect, but it does provide another context in which Maimonides interprets the created light that descended on Mount Sinai in a figurative sense. We should not assume that he believes that the "created light" is a visible light.

In summary: we have supported here Eisenmann's intriguing reading of Maimonides' theory of created light and glory, according to which the created light is the light of the Active Intellect that illumines the mind of the prophet. In several passages, Maimonides identifies created light with the terms glory and *Shekhinah*. At Mount Sinai, the created light of the Active Intellect descends upon those prepared to receive it. Maimonides also indicates that the glory represents the wisdom of God manifested in nature. This, too, is an expression of the Active Intellect, and the prophet/philosopher who perceives the magnificent complexity of God's nature and God's glory honors God through his or her understanding and appreciation.[29]

Against this Maimonidean background, Abraham Maimonides presents a view of the glory and created light that is closer to that of Onqelos, Saadya, and Halevi.

3

Abraham and Moses Maimonides on Cloud and Glory: Exodus 16:9–10/*Guide* III:9

Our investigation began with a passage in which Abraham Maimonides suggests that in the cleft of the rock, Moses perceived a quasi-physical light that also illuminated his understanding. Whereas for Maimonides, only those with insufficient capacity for understanding need to conceive of a physical created light, Abraham embraces this harmonizing interpretation as his own.

We see another example of Abraham's connecting the vision of created light and intellectual understanding in his comment to Exodus 16:9–10.[1] Depicting the vision of glory in the wilderness, Abraham finds in the Biblical text the theme of spiritual preparation. We read in the text that Aaron says to the Israelites, "Draw near before the Lord" (Exodus 16:9); in the next verse, they look towards the wilderness, "and behold, the glory of the Lord appeared in a cloud." Abraham interprets "draw near" as referring to spiritual and intellectual, rather than physical, preparation and drawing near; he suggests that they draw near in their inner being (*bāṭin/bawāṭin),* a term which is prominent in Sufi thought and in the Sufi-influenced *Duties of the Heart* of Baḥya Ibn Paqūda. Abraham comments to Exodus 16:9:

> There was not a tabernacle (*mishkan*) at that time, and no place to which one could suggest that they would be commanded to draw near. Thus it seems according to my understanding from this that Moses commanded Aaron to say first to all the community of Israel that they should prepare themselves in an inner preparation (*yatahayyu' tahayyu' bāṭin*), and ready themselves (*yast'idūn*) to draw near before Him (*bi-l-qurb bayna yadayhi*) in their thoughts and their inner beings (*bi-afkārihim wa-bawāṭinihim*) to witness what they would witness of Him (*li-yushāhidūn ma yushāhidūnahu*).[2]

Abraham thus emphasizes the inner dimension of spiritual life even in the group religious experience of the Israelites in the wilderness. Although the nation shared a common experience of witnessing the light of God's glory, each individual experienced this as an event of individual spiritual illumination.[3] We should also note that the term *qurb*, signifying drawing near or proximity, has a special Sufi and Pietistic resonance. It is used by classical Sufi thinkers such as al-Qushayrī as a term for spiritual intimacy and proximity, a usage echoed by the Egyptian Pietist R. Abraham he-Ḥasid, who argues that the Israelites were privileged with proximity (*qurb*), one of the spiritual levels or stations (*maqāmāt, marātib*).[4]

In his comment to Exodus 16:10, Abraham suggests that drawing near in these passages is not, as in later passages in the Torah, an allusion to drawing near to an altar or a sanctuary, but drawing near to the holy:

> Their inner beings and thoughts (*bawāṭinuhum wa-afkāruhum*) drew near, and they emptied (*akhlū*) their inner beings of everything other than God and they turned completely from their tents and dwellings (*maḥālātihim wa-manāzilihim*) [to look toward] the dwelling/descent of the holy (*maḥall al-qedushah*), and immediately the created light descended (*ḥalla*). And in witnessing it (*mushāhadatihi*) there was undoubtedly guidance to perceive His oneness and greatness. No one who did not behold and see it [with their own eyes] can understand this condition/state (*ḥāl*).[5]

In suggesting that the people empty their beings of everything other than God, Abraham alludes to the Sufi practice of emptying/inner solitude (*khalwa*), even in the historical experience of the nation as a whole.[6] The passage also plays on the Arabic verbal root *ḥ-l-l* (to dwell), suggesting a move from physical dwelling or presence to spiritual presencing or alighting. We will thus explore the use of this root in Saadya, Halevi, and al-Fārābī, which will shed light on Abraham's use of the root in this passage.

a. The Root *ḥ-l-l* in Arabic and Judeo-Arabic Literature; Light Imagery in the *Kuzari*

The Arabic root *ḥ-l-l* signifies alighting, descending and stopping, or abiding in a place; medieval thinkers use the root *ḥ-l-l* to describe the sense in which a human being may become an abode or resting place for the divine.[7] For example, Saadya Gaon, in the *Book of Doctrines and Beliefs*, describes a certain group of Christians who work out the doctrine of the Trinity using as an analogy "the descent (*ḥulūl*) of the light of God on Mount Sinai and its appearance in the burning bush and the tent of meeting."[8]

In the *Kuzari*, Halevi's Jewish Sage uses the verbal root *ḥ-l-l* repeatedly to describe God's Presence among the Jewish people. For example, the Sage explains that "this community had at last become sufficiently pure for the [divine] light to rest upon it (*ḥulūl al-nur 'alayhā*)."[9] In fact, God is ever awaiting a community that will accept the divine light:

> Whenever a few or a group [from among humanity] purifies [itself], the divine light rests upon them (*ḥallahu*), and guides them through subtle acts of grace, and wonders which break the natural order.[10]

God promises that there will always be prophets to teach the divine laws, a promise God kept during the period of his favor and the dwelling (*ḥulūl*) of the *Shekhinah* among the Israelites, i.e. during the period when the Temple stood.[11] Every day in the silent Amidah prayer, Jews pray that Jerusalem will once more be a dwelling place (*maḥall*) for the divine Presence.[12]

The tenth-century philosopher al-Fārābī uses the verb *ḥ-l-l* in the context of a theory of prophecy, to denote the Active Intellect's "entering" or "descending" upon or "inhering" in the human subject who has attained the acquired intellect.[13] We see here the ambiguity of the verb *ḥalla*, which is reflected in the variety of ways the verb can be translated. It is not clear whether al-Fārābī conceives of the Active Intellect as a transcendent principle that "descends" upon the individual human intellect, or as an immanent principle that "inheres" in the human mind which has been fully developed. The ambiguity of the verb serves al-Fārābī well in his project of reinterpreting traditional religious concepts in a philosophical key. The verb allows him to subtly shift from the traditional conception of prophecy as a divinely initiated gift from without, to the philosophical notion of prophecy as a natural process of intellectual development from within. We will see that this ambiguity will figure in Maimonides' theory of prophecy as well.

b. Abraham's Conception of Dwelling (*ḥ-l-l*)

Returning to Abraham Maimonides' passage, let us focus on his multivalent use of the root *ḥ-l-l*. He writes that after the inner spiritual and intellectual purification of their inward beings and thought, they turned from their physical dwellings or tents (*maḥālāt*) to look toward the dwelling/descent of the holy (*maḥall al-qedushah*), and immediately the created light descended (*ḥalla*). Abraham's articulation here calls to mind Halevi's theme of divine light resting on the community. It also recalls a formulation by Maimonides in his description of prophecy in the *Mishneh Torah* (*Hilkhot Yesodei ha-Torah* 7), reflecting the view of al-Fārābī. Maimonides writes:

> One of the foundations of religion is the knowledge that God engenders prophecy in humans. But prophecy only rests (*ḥalah*) upon a sage possessed of great wisdom, powerful in [governing] his ethical dispositions—never mastered by his irrational part, but always mastering it through his reason—[and] possessed of a most ample and sound intellect. When someone abounding in all these qualities and sound of body . . . progressively sanctifies himself, forsaking the ways of the commonality who walk in

> temporal darkness, and continually spurs himself on, training his psyche to give no thought whatever to vanities or temporal inanities and designs, his mind rather directed ever upward, bound fast below the Throne in contemplation of the holy and pure Forms, reflecting upon the Holy One's wisdom (blessed be He) [manifest] in everything from the First Form to the earth's center, through which he comprehends [God's] greatness—then straightaway the Holy Spirit comes to rest upon him (*miyad ruaḥ ha-qodesh shorah 'alav*). When the Spirit rests (*tanuaḥ*) upon him, his soul partakes of the angelic rank called *Ishim* [i.e. the Active Intellect].[14]

Maimonides opens the passage with a Hebrew echo (from the Hebrew root *ḥ-w-l*) of the Arabic root *ḥ-l-l*—prophecy "rests" (*ḥalah*) upon a sage. In Mishnaic Hebrew, the verb *ḥalah* means "to take effect," and the root *ḥ-l-l* can bear that connotation in Arabic as well.[15] However, the continuation of the passage suggests that Maimonides deliberately chose the Hebrew word to echo the Arabic sense of "resting upon," as he draws parallels with rabbinic and Biblical Hebrew by closing the passage with the phrases "the Holy Spirit rests (*shorah*) on him,"[16] and "when the Spirit rests (*tanuaḥ*) upon him."[17]

Abraham clearly echoes Maimonides' conceptualization of preparation for prophecy, both conceptually and terminologically. In both texts, people prepare themselves, emptying their minds of everything other than God, and then immediately the holy descends (*ḥalla*; *shorah*). Moreover, Abraham's suggestion that the people move from physical presence or dwelling in space to spiritual dwelling parallels his father's emphasis on mastering one's irrational impulses and directing the mind upward to the angelic Forms. The difference between the two passages is that whereas Maimonides is discussing prophecy as an individual inner attunement, Abraham suggests that the people together witnessed a visible light, a collective vision of prophecy, in a formulation close to the visual language of Halevi. He also strikingly uses the Sufi language of "witness" for witnessing God (*yushāhidūnahu*), a formulation prominent in Halevi but absent in the writings of his father.[18] Moreover, the philosophical and scientific dimension of preparation for witness of the divine is absent in Abraham's account.

Abraham's statement that the people "turned completely" from their physical dwellings/tents to witness the descent of the holy is somewhat problematic. It is clear that the people do not leave the embodied state for a purely intellectual realm, as they see a visible light. However, this light may be conceptualized as an interface between the spiritual and physical realm—precisely the harmonizing approach his father rejects as inferior, for those of insufficient understanding.

Abraham suggests that in seeing or witnessing it, there was guidance to perceive God's oneness and greatness, and that no one who did not behold and see it with their own eyes can understand this condition or state. This statement recalls the approaches of Saadya and Halevi to the glory. Saadya claims that the created glory is meant to verify through the prophet that the words they hear in prophecy are actually from God.[19] Halevi goes further than Saadya, insisting that the prophets learn something from beholding the spiritual forms that constitute the glory.[20] As noted above, Halevi repeatedly uses imagery of vision and light to depict the experience and descent of the divine.[21]

Abraham Maimonides, too, ascribes a didactic function to the light.[22] In the wilderness, vision of the glory brings guidance to perceive God's oneness and greatness. Similarly, in the cleft of the rock, Moses perceived sensibly the illumination of the created light, by means of which he was guided to intellectual apprehension of the greatness of the Creator. Thus like Halevi, Abraham brings together themes of seeing and understanding. As Halevi notes explicitly in *Kuzari* IV:5–6, visual witness is a powerful tool to attaining spiritual and intellectual apprehension.[23]

While he does not quote his father in this context, Abraham follows the approach of Maimonides in the lexical chapters of the *Guide*, which interpret verbal roots for closeness (*q-r-b*) and dwelling (Maimonides: *sh-kh-n*; Abraham: *ḥ-l-l*) to point to spiritual or intellectual proximity. However, whereas his father dismisses the necessity for physical vision, Abraham suggests otherwise. For Abraham, the sensory act of seeing serves an important, perhaps preparatory dimension to the achievement of intellectual apprehension. By seeing the actual glory or created light of God, one draws near in understanding to the holy.

Abraham seeks to make clear that the glory is a diaphonous cloud, one that protects the eyes by concealing the brilliance of the light, while also allowing one to see the radiance shining through.[24] The eyes would not be able to look at the glory if it were not somewhat concealed by the cloud; thus the cloud functions like a dimmer on a bright light. He compares the cloud to a light covering, rather than a heavy cloud in a time of winter. Abraham does not dismiss the physical cloud and glory, but suggests that the image also alludes to the way our matter prevents us from apprehending that which is separate from matter as it truly is, and adds that this allusion "contains subtlety and mystery (*diqqa wa-sod*)."[25] Abraham offers a fascinating dialectical view of the role of the cloud: without a cloud, one would not be able to witness the divine glory. However, the cloud also prevents us from witnessing the divine as it really is. Abraham thus alludes to Maimonides' discussion in *Guide* III:9, which is related to Maimonides' interpretation of the event at Mount Sinai.

In *Guide* III:9, Maimonides writes that we are veiled from God and that He is hidden (*masṭūr*) from us by a heavy cloud, or darkness, or similar allusions to our being incapable of our apprehending God on account of matter. Maimonides thus suggests that all mentions of clouds are allegorical. God is not a physical being who can be hidden by clouds. It is the fact that we are material beings that makes us incapable of fully apprehending that which is separate from matter. We see once again a contrast between the approach of Maimonides and that of his son. For Maimonides, all language about clouds surrounding God or God's glory is metaphorical. By contrast, for Abraham, God's created light is a real light that must be covered by a real cloud, even while the light may in addition refer to intellectual illumination and the cloud may in addition refer to the way our matter prevents us from fully apprehending that which is immaterial. We will return to Maimonides' interpretation of the Sinai event; we begin with preparation for the event.

4

Abraham Maimonides on Created Light in the Preparation for the Sinai Event

Maimonides indicates several times that the external, physical interpretation of the glory as created light is an inferior one for those who do not have the intellectual capacity to understand spiritual matters on a purely intellectual plane. Abraham, however, takes a both/and rather than an either/or approach. He depicts the revelation of the glory to Moses at the cleft of the rock in both inner and outer terms, suggesting that the illumination of the created light may guide Moses, aiding him in intellectual apprehension.

He offers a similar approach to the question of vision in the preparation for the Sinai event. In Exodus 19:21–22, we read: "The Lord said to Moses, go down, warn the people, lest they break through to the Lord to gaze, and many of them perish. And let the priests also, who come near to the Lord, sanctify themselves, lest the Lord break forth (*yehersu*) upon them." Abraham comments:

> The expression *yehersu* (break forth) can be understood in two senses, one revealed/external (*ẓāhir*) and one hidden/internal (*bāṭin*). The external/revealed meaning is transgressing/overstepping the boundary in contemplating (*ta'ammul*) the

> created light. The second is an allusion to the inner transgressing of the mind of what it is incapable of, and they [sic] are destroyed, as what happened to Ben Azzai when he entered into Pardes and was destroyed. And my father already spoke of this and explained it completely at the beginning of the *Guide.*[1]

Abraham thus fully accepts the notion that the priests—who, he will explain, are the firstborn, as the official priesthood was not instituted until after Sinai—see a created light. The verb he uses is contemplate (*ta'ammul*), which can have a connotation of looking, but is more strongly associated with inner meditation and reflection. Thus he suggests that the purpose of a visual revelation of light is not, as Saadya would have it, simply to verify that a prophetic vision is authentic and comes from God. Rather, the purpose of the light is to teach something about the divine.

He explicates these two levels by emphasizing that the meaning of "must sanctify themselves" is an allusion to inner sanctification of the mind. He then argues that the expression *yehersu* (break through) is a reference to the prohibition of inner breaking through, transgressing intellectual boundaries. He argues that if the priests were specifically being warned against not breaking through to see light through the visible eye, Exodus 19:22 would have said "And also the priests who draw near to the Lord, do not break through (*al yehersu*)!" Thus the command that the priests "must sanctify themselves (*yitqaddashu*)" assumes they will see the light, and commands the priests to be careful lest they transgress intellectual boundaries.

Abraham goes on to cite the translation of Onqelos for the phrase *pen yifrots* ("lest He break out"). He notes that Onqelos translates the phrase, "Lest the Lord kill (*yiqṭol*) among them." However, he notes that in some versions, he saw *yitqof* ("overpower"). He writes:

> This is a powerful reading (version), subtle in meaning, in accordance with which the meaning is that what they think about in their thoughts should not overpower their minds, as the light of the sun overpowers the seer, and they be destroyed, as the vision is destroyed if one stares with one's eyes at the sun. And it is as if he interpreted the reading in which he translated *yitqof* in accordance with the other reading [in which he translated *yiqṭol* ("kill")]. And understand this.[2]

Like his father, Abraham brings in Onqelos as support for his own understanding of the text. Here he makes a comparison between physical vision and intellectual seeing, and suggests that just as one can destroy the eyesight if one looks directly at the blinding light of the sun, so there is danger of destroying the mind if we overstep its safe limits. In his interpretation of the experience of Moses in the cleft of the rock, Abraham suggested that the "hand" that covered Moses could be a protection that protects the mind. This accords with his interpretation here that the priests are warned to create such a boundary in the mind, lest their minds be destroyed.

He makes this comparison explicit in a long discussion in the *Kifāya* in the chapter on the two forms of solitude (*khalwa*). In his discussion of inner and outer solitude, Abraham draws a comparison between the outer temple (*miqdash*) and the inner temple (*miqdash*), to which the desire and the longing (of Israel) is (directed) because of its complete good (*khayr*). He adds to this an exegesis of Psalm 84:12, "For the Lord God is a sun and a shield; the Lord will give grace and glory (*ḥen ve-khavod*); no good thing will he withhold from them that walk uprightly." Abraham writes:

> By [David's] statement, "for the Lord God is a sun and a shield" (Psalm 84:12), he means that in the overflow of His being (*fayḍ wujūdihi*) that pours forth (*fā'iḍ*) upon those who arrive (*al-wāṣilīn*) [and] is compared to light—as it has been said, "through your light, we see light"—there is (experienced such) complete spiritual delight of what is apprehended as there is (in) the sensory pleasure of the light of the sun. And in it there is also the danger of destruction for one who is blinded by it, as it has been said in the Torah, "and let the priests also who come near to the Lord sanctify themselves, lest the Lord break forth upon them" (Exodus 19:22), and as has been reported in the traditions of the ancients, "Ben Azzai looked and became demented" (b. *Ḥagigah*. 14b and Tosefta *Ḥagigah* 2:3). Now that [danger] is like [that which is due to] the light of the sun proper, which causes the sight of him that looks at it to turn away because it is too weak to bear it, if he has been bold enough to look at the sun itself and not contented himself with the light of

> the rays that proceeds from it; or [it is like] the danger of being burnt by its heat, if one sits in it naked [and] uncovered and one does not have upon oneself anything that would serve as protection from its heat. He said, therefore, that God, exalted be He, causes his light to pour forth (*yufiḍ nūrahu*) upon his servants who arrive [at him], and protects them by means of his shelter. He is, then, the sun, and he is [also] the shield that shades and protects from its heat and its great light.[3]

As the verse from Psalms states, God is both sun and shield; God overflows spiritual-intellectual light, and affords mental protection from that light. In further exegesis of the psalm, Abraham goes on to add the example of Moses, the master of the prophets:

> It has already been said to the master of prophets in reference to (this divine) protection, "and I will cover you with my hand until I have passed by" (Exodus 33:22). Then he said "the Lord gives grace and glory (*ḥen ve-khavod*); no good thing will he withhold from them that walk uprightly" (Psalm 84:12), as an allusion to what He, exalted be He, overflows (*yufiḍ*) on those who walk with uprightness in the paths that lead (*al-masālik al-muwaṣṣila*) to him if they walk uprightly, until they arrive (*yaṣilū*).[4]

In his exegesis of Exodus 33:22 in his Torah Commentary, Abraham Maimonides suggests that the "hand" that covers Moses protects him from God's glory, like the cloud that covers the glory on Mount Sinai. In this passage in the *Kifāya*, if we follow Biblical parallelism—between the terms "sun and shield" and "grace and glory"—the term "grace" (*ḥen*) seems to function as the overflow from God (the "sun"), while "glory" (*kavod*) is the protection (the "shield"). If Abraham seeks to be consistent with this terminology, perhaps we must reverse the terms, and suggest that the sun is the glory, while the shield is God's grace. Regardless of terminology, Abraham's conception is consistent. He draws a fascinating comparison between Moses in the cleft of the rock and the priests; for both, God creates a boundary in the mind lest their minds be destroyed.

Eli Shaubi offers an intriguing interpretation of the passage. As noted previously, Shaubi poses the question of whether the inner light of those who "attain" represents illumination of one's own inner being or is a reflection of the light of God's glory. Reflecting upon this passage, Shaubi writes:

> We may perhaps interpret this last sun-metaphor in such a way so as to shed light on this question [of whether the inner light and the light of God's glory/splendor are identical], considering his use of the verse "Through Your light do we see light", which seems to mention two separate "lights": "Your light" being a reference to the "attainers" who have attained a strong internal light, and the latter light being an apprehension of a light pouring forth from God's splendor. Hence, the internal light, possessed by the "attainers" and compared to a "shield" that protects them from the "sun", precedes the ability to apprehend the external—perhaps prophetic—light that bedazzles its onlookers and is compared to the sun.[5]

Shaubi thus suggests that in the Biblical phrase "through Your light, we see light," "Your light" is the internal light the meditator cultivates, through which he or she can see the light pouring forth from God's glory (which Shaubi terms "splendor").

Shaubi thus suggests that a strong inner light creates a shield that enables one to receive and withstand the intensity of the light of God's glory. Note that in a passage discussed earlier, Abraham has written:

> Your aim in regard to the welfare of your soul should be that it be free from dullness and bright, in order that it may contemplate (*taṭṭali'*) what it is able to of the light that shines upon it from the overflow (*fayḍ*) of [God's] light—of which it is said, "through Your light, we see light"—and of which it is said regarding the request to be enlightened by it, "for You light my lamp; the Lord my God lightens my darkness" (Psalm 18:29).[6]

Abraham's language thus suggests that the strong inner light is itself an overflow of God's light, a light that illuminates one's inner darkness. In his discourse on the sun and the shield, Abraham adds that the light received by the contemplator is the overflow of God's being (*fayḍ wujū-dihi*). God's overflow thus includes both the kindling light of God's glory and the lamp of inner illumination that is kindled; perhaps this is the significance of Abraham's plural reference to God's "lights" that illuminate the soul. One's inner light provides a reflective mirror to God's light, an inner resonance to the radiance of God's splendor.

In summary: Shaubi suggests that "Your light" refers to the inner illumination that gives homeopathic support, strengthening the meditator's ability to behold the splendor of God's glory. Developing an inner light can inoculate one against the intensity of God's glory. Shaubi thus suggests that inner light precedes the ability to see God's glory.[7] However, the reverse may hold true as well: that through the light of God's glory, the meditator is empowered to see inner light in meditation. In either case, the light represents a quasi-sensory illumination which transcends, although it may include, intellectual understanding. What is clear is that there is an infusion of divine light, and a quickening and sparking of the meditator's own inner light, a synergy in which light reflects and intensifies light.

Abraham then turns to a further interpretive problem. In Exodus 19:24, we read, "And the Lord said to him, 'Go down, and you shall come up, you and Aaron with you; but let not the priests and people break through (*al-yehersu*) to come up to the Lord, lest he break forth upon them (*pen-yifrots-bam*).'"

Abraham writes:

> The question remains how to harmonize this with the words, "And let the priests also, who come near to the Lord, sanctify themselves, lest the Lord break forth upon them (*pen yifrots bahem*)" with his word here, "But let not the priests and the people break through," because it seems that they are equal to all the people in the prohibition. And it appears from what my grandfather interpreted in the name of the Sages that the meaning of the saying "Those who draw near," is those distinguished (*al-mukhtaṣṣūn*) in speculative drawing near. And that is indisputable. However, if there is not drawing near in place at all,[8] then *yitqaddashu* (sanctify themselves) is in their inner beings (*bawāṭinihin*) at the time of their speculative advancement (*taqaddumihim al-maʿnawī*). And this corroborates all that I explained. For it says in the first prohibition of the people, "Lest they break through to the Lord

> to see" (Exodus 19:21). And here, in their prohibition [the text reads], "Let not the priests or people break through to come up to the Lord," because the priests are not prohibited from the inner seeing. Rather [the opposite]: they are commanded to prepare themselves (*isti'dād*) for it. But they and the people are prohibited from going up the mountain. But these [ideas] are subtle; only select individuals can get a glimpse of them (*yalmaḥuhā*) and how mighty and awesome is their discovery. And in explaining and speaking of them [there is] boldness and how great is the danger. But God is good and forgiving (Psalm 86:5).[9]

Abraham's citation of his grandfather in this passage is intriguing; the passage also echoes the interpretation of Maimonides. Maimonides cites Exodus 19:22 only once in the *Guide*. In *Guide* I:5, he explains that the verse "And Moses hid his face, for he was afraid to look upon God" (Exodus 3:6) has two interpretations. One is that he hid his face because he was afraid to look upon the light manifesting itself. The second, he explains, is that:

> When one has achieved and acquired knowledge of true and certain premises, and has achieved knowledge of the rules of logic and inference and of the various ways of preserving himself from errors of the mind, he should then engage in the investigation of the subject. When doing this, he should not make categoric affirmations in favor of the first opinion that occurs to him and should not, from the outset, strain and impel his thoughts towards the apprehension of the deity. Rather, one should feel awe and refrain and hold back until he gradually elevates himself. It is in this sense that it is said, "And Moses hid his face, for he was afraid to look upon God;" this being an additional meaning of the verse over and above its external meaning (*al-ẓāhir*) that indicates that he hid his face because of his being afraid to look upon the light manifested itself.[10]

Maimonides goes on to explain that the nobles of the children of Israel were overhasty, strained their thoughts, and achieved apprehension, but only an imperfect one. Likewise, Nadav and Avihu were burnt in the tabernacle of the congregation for the same reason, for being overhasty in intellectual grasping. Maimonides then comments:

> This having happened to these men, it behooves us all the more, as being inferior to them, and it behooves those who are inferior to us, to aim at and engage in perfecting our knowledge of preparatory matters, and in achieving those premises that purify apprehension of its taint, which is error. [One] will then go forward (*yataqaddam*) to look upon (*li-laḥẓ*) the divine holy Presence (*al-ḥaḍra al-qudūsiyya al-ilāhiyya*): "And let the priests also, who come near to the Lord, sanctify themselves, lest the Lord break forth upon them" (Exodus 19:22). And Solomon has been the person who wishes to reach this rank to be most careful. He said warningly in parabolic language, "Guard your foot when you go to the house of God" (Ecclesiastes 4:17).[11]

Thus while Abraham explicitly mentions his grandfather in this context, he also clearly has in mind his father's interpretation. In addition to their common explication of Exodus 19:22 as signaling intellectual preparation, Abraham echoes Maimonides' language of advancement (*taqaddum*). Maimonides writes: "[One] will then go forward (*yataqaddam)* to look upon (*li-laḥẓ)* the divine holy Presence;" while Abraham writes of the phrase "those who draw near:" "However, if there is not drawing near in place, then *yitqaddashu* (sanctify themselves) is in their inner beings (*bawāṭinihim*) at the time of their speculative advancement (*taqaddumihim al-ma'nawī*)."[12]

Abraham argues that both the priests and the people are prohibited from physically ascending the mountain. The priests are enjoined to prepare themselves internally for intellectual and spiritual attainment. According to Abraham's commentary, in Exodus 19:10, all the people, including the priests, are bidden to purify themselves internally ("go to the people and warn them to stay pure"); in Exodus 19:24, both the priests and the people are commanded not to ascend the mountain ("but let not the priests or the people break through to come up to the Lord, lest he break out against them"). In Exodus 19:22 ("the priests also, who come near the Lord, must stay pure, lest the Lord break out against them"), the priests are not being warned against spiritual vision of God. Rather, they are being warned to prepare themselves and use caution in their intellectual ascent, just as Maimonides teaches in *Guide* I:5. In his comment to Exodus 19:10 ("go to the people and warn them to stay pure"), Abraham argues that the priests already had external purity; they and the people are warned to maintain mental purity. The priests are given a further warning in Exodus 19:22, because they will be making a greater intellectual/spiritual ascent, and need to be careful to do this slowly.

Maimonides' exposition in *Guide* I:5 is highly intellectual; he speaks of achieving knowledge of the rules of logic and inference, and the danger of premature cognitive commitment, making categoric affirmations in favor of the first opinion that occurs to one. He lauds Moses for his intellectual caution, and argues that the apprehension of the nobles was tainted with imagined images, because they were overhasty. If one really wants to understand the mysteries of physics and metaphysics, one must undergo a long process of intellectual and spiritual preparation and self-cultivation. One who undergoes that slow, steady, and cautious journey will be rewarded with true understanding, "[One] will then go forward (*yataqaddam*) to look upon (*laḥẓ*) the divine holy Presence (*al-ḥaḍra al-qudūsiyya al-ilāhiyya*)." This is Maimonides' interpretation of Exodus 19:22; the "priests" mentioned in this verse are those individuals who, like Moses, use appropriate intellectual caution, and prepare themselves (*yitqadashu*) for the holy work of understanding the divine.

For Maimonides, "looking upon the divine holy Presence" is an intellectual process; the language of vision is purely metaphorical. To see the divine Presence is to understand. Because Moses exercised appropriate caution in hiding his face before the divine light, "God, may he be exalted, let flow upon him (*afāḍ ʿalayhi*) so much of his bounty and goodness that it became necessary to say of him, 'and the figure of the Lord shall he look upon' (Numbers 12:8)."[13] Maimonides is here following the rabbinic tradition that Moses was rewarded with the vision in the cleft of the rock for hiding his face at the burning bush.[14] Maimonides takes this rabbinic tradition in an intellectual direction: because he exercised appropriate intellectual caution, Moses was rewarded with genuine intellectual understanding.

Abraham, however, does not dismiss the sensory seeing of created lights. He agrees with his father that in Exodus 19:22, the priests are commanded to prepare themselves for vision of the divine, but he does not describe this vision as intellectual. In his commentary to Exodus 19:10

(which he cross-references to Exodus 19:22), Abraham uses Sufi, pietistic language of solitude (*khalwa*) to further develop his conception of this preparation. In commenting on the phrase "and [tell them to] sanctify themselves (*ve-qiddashtam*)," he writes:

> The meaning intended by this "holiness" (*qedushah*) is an internal holiness through the preparation of the heart and an external [holiness] through withdrawing from/avoiding impurity, or through bathing, according to the position of Ibn Ezra, may his memory be for a blessing. And [Scripture's] statement after that about preparation indicates to you inner sanctification[15] to elucidate this spiritual state (*maqām*), "and the priests who draw near to the Lord should also sanctify themselves (Exodus 19:22)." For without doubt, they had already attained external sanctification.
>
> And the meaning of internal holiness is the purification of the heart from the squalor of the mind, about which it is said, "God knows the thoughts of humans, that they are vanity" (Psalm 94:11), as well as occupying themselves with the perfection/wholeness (*kamāl*) that they will receive, as David, peace be upon him, said, "I study [you] by the way of wholeness (*askilekha be-derekh ṭamim*), when will you come to me?" (Psalm 101:2).[16] And this is internal solitude (*al-khalwa al-bāṭina*). Or perhaps there are some prophetic ways whose details are unknown to us. Thus he, may he be praised, commanded that their preparation would take two days, for he knew that in that time they would complete their preparation for the attainment (*al-iʿtidād li'l-wuṣūl*) that they would attain (*yaṣilūn*) on the third day.[17]

The suggestion that in these three days the people may have been prepared for prophecy at Mount Sinai is echoed in a citation Abraham attributes to his teacher, R. Abraham he-Ḥasid. Commenting on Exodus 19:9, "[and Moses told]," Abraham writes:

> R. Abraham he-Ḥasid said that there is a hidden matter (*amr muḍmar*) in this that the Sages alluded to regarding his saying, "Behold, I come to you in a thick cloud." This is that when [God]

addressed Moses with these words, he told them that he would prepare them for prophecy through inner conditions which Scripture does not specify due to their exalted nature.[18]

Abraham's commentary on Exodus 19:10 also echoes his chapter on two forms of solitude (*khalwa*) in the *Kifāya*. There, he describes the same harmony between external and internal solitude:

> [The two forms of] solitude (*al-khalawāt*) are among the most distinguished of the elevated paths. This is the way of the great friends of God (*awliyā'*) and through it, the prophets attain or arrive (*bi-hā wuṣūl al-anbiyā'*).[19] It is divided into external solitude and internal solitude. The aim of external solitude is the attainment of internal solitude, which is the ultimate rung of the ladder of attainment—nay, it constitutes attainment (*wuṣūl).* Let us then say in reference to that internal solitude—which is complete sincerity (*ikhlāṣ*) of the heart, to attain which David prayed, saying: "create for me a pure heart" (Psalm 51:12), and [which] Asaph attained, according to his statement, "my flesh and my heart fail, but the rock of my heart and my portion is God" (Psalm 73:20)—[that it] consists of emptying the heart and the mind of everything except him, may he be exalted, and of their being filled with and inhabited by him.[20]

The motif of emptying the heart and the mind of everything except God is found in al-Ghazālī, both in his spiritual autobiography *Deliverer from Error* (*al-Munqidh min al-ḍalāl*) and in his chapter on solitude in the *Revival of Religious Sciences* (*Ihyā' 'ulūm al-dīn*), a chapter with close echoes in Abraham's work.[21] We are also reminded here of Maimonides' exaltation of the value of solitude in *Guide* III:51, and his suggestion that in the central moments of Jewish individual and communal prayer, the goal is to attain a focused state of meditative concentration, emptying the mind of everything other than God.[22] However, for Maimonides, there is a further dimension to intellectual worship:

> There are those who set their thought to work after having attained perfection in the divine science, turn wholly toward God, may He be cherished and held sublime, renounce what is other than He, and direct all the acts of their intellect toward an

> examination of the beings with a view to drawing from them proof with regard to Him, so as to know His governance of them in whatever way it is possible. . . . This is the rank of the prophets.[23]

For Maimonides, a key component of intellectual worship is contemplation of "the divine science," which includes physics and metaphysics, the natural order through which God governs the universe. In contrast, Abraham's ways of solitude do not emphasize this scientific content. While we have seen that Abraham's Sabbath meditation does reflect upon the cosmos, creation, and the giving of the Sabbath, nowhere do we see Abraham engage in the complexities of physics and metaphysics.

We have noted that Abraham Maimonides does find a role for intellect in his ascent to spiritual attainment. For example, in a comment to Exodus 34:5, in which the Lord descends in the cloud, Scripture writes that "[the Lord] stood with him there [and proclaimed the name of the Lord]." Abraham writes:

> A borrowing [or: allusion] and expression for the notion of attainment and intellectual apprehension (*al-wuṣūl wa'l-idrāk al-ʿaqlī*), similar to "mouth to mouth" (Numbers 12:8) and "face to face" (Exodus 33:11), and similar [expressions].

Abraham Maimonides likewise notes the role of the intellect in spiritual ascent in the *Kifāya*. For example, in one passage he writes that "the truly distinguished (*al-khawāṣṣ ḥaqīqatan*) among the adherents of the Law are the servants of the Lord who keep his Law, walk in his way, and follow his prophets whom he has perfected with both intellectual perfection (*al-kamāl al-ʿaqlī*) and religious-legal perfection (*al-kamāl al-sharʿī*)."[24] Abraham Maimonides even acknowledges philosophy (*al-ṭarīq al-falsafiyya*) as a path to what he terms "this exalted perfection" (*hādhā al-kamāl al-ʿaẓīm*), and affirms that "there is no doubt that this path leads to attainment" (*hiya ṭarīq al-muwaṣṣil bi-lā shakk*). However, he notes that this philosophical path of speculation (*al-naẓar*), proof (*al-istidlāl*), and logical demonstration (*al-burhān al-manṭiqī*) poses dangers such as denying the createdness of the world and God's knowledge of particulars.[25] The path of the prophets and pious is more accessible, less arduous, and secure from danger. At the same time, Abraham Maimonides does note that one's observance of the commandments must be accompanied by intellectual reflection and understanding.[26]

Abraham Maimonides thus to some extent shares his father's rationalist sensibility. However, we do not find in the writings of Abraham Maimonides the passion for rigorous philosophical proof that is central to the elder Maimonides' intellectual and spiritual life. While his father embraced the rigorous path of philosophy, Abraham Maimonides himself seems to have preferred the way of the prophets and pious.

In summary, both Maimonides and his son interpret Exodus 19:22 as warning that one must engage in a slow, internal process of preparation to achieve vision of the Lord. However, the two diverge in what such vision means. Maimonides insists in *Guide* I:5 that all language of vision with respect to God is metaphorical; "seeing God" is a metaphor for intellectual understanding. The two will thus also disagree on what preparation for this "seeing" entails. While Maimonides describes an intellectual process including studying the rules of logic and inference, Abraham emphasizes a spiritual, pietistic process of purification of the heart and mind, without the goal of scientific study of creation. For Abraham, study of the sciences is at most preparatory; for Maimonides, understanding of the scientific order of the universe is central and intrinsic to contemplation of God.

For Maimonides, prophecy itself is a highly intellectual process requiring engagement in mathematics, physics, and biology. This scientific dimension is absent in Abraham in favor of a Sufi pietistic ascent. Abraham suggests that perhaps the people prepared themselves for the state of prophecy at Mount Sinai in three days of inner solitude and purification of mind and heart. Maimonides in no way could suggest that a three-day crash course in logic, mathematics, physics, and metaphysics would prepare one adequately for prophecy.

5

Maimonides on the Theophany at Mount Sinai

We have seen that Abraham Maimonides is always concerned to include both external, objective and internal, spiritual and psychological dimensions of divine revelation, prophecy, and religious experience; the created light is for Abraham a visual experience. In contrast, the text of the *Guide* suggests that Maimonides may be preserving the external dimension on an exoteric level, but is more concerned with the internal event of intellectual illumination. Thus, there is evidence that Maimonides interprets the events at Mount Sinai in an esoteric fashion. Let us examine some of the evidence.

In *Guide* III:9, Maimonides writes:

> His manifestation "in a thick cloud" (Exodus 19:9) and in "darkness, cloud, and thick darkness" (Deuteronomy 4:11) is also in order to infer from it about this notion. For everything that is apprehended in a vision of prophecy (*mareh ha-nevuah*) is only a parable for some notion. And that great witnessed scene (*al-mashhad al-ʿaẓīm*) even though it was greater than any vision of prophecy (*mareh nevuah*) and beyond any analogy, it is not without a notion (*maʿna*), that is, His manifestation in a thick cloud. Rather, it is to draw attention/alert (*tanbīh*) to [the fact] that apprehension of His true reality (*ḥaqīqa*) is impossible for us because of the dark matter that encompasses us and not Him, may He be exalted, for He, may He be exalted, is not a

> body. Moreover, it is well known (*mashhūr*) in the religious community that the day of the encounter at Mount Sinai was on a day of clouds, mist, and a light rain. It says, "Lord when you went forth out of Seir, when you marched out of the field of Edom, the earth trembled, the heavens also dropped, yea the clouds dropped water" (Judges 5:4). This is also what is intended in its saying: "Darkness, cloud, and thick darkness" (Deuteronomy 4:11), that He, may He be exalted, is encompassed by darkness, for near Him, may He be exalted, there is no darkness, but rather perpetual, dazzling light (*al-ḍaw*['] *al-bāhir al-dā'im*), whose overflow (*fayḍ*) illuminates all that is dark, as it is said in the prophetic parables, "And the earth shined with His glory" (Ezekiel 43:2).[1]

What is at stake in this passage is the nature of the event at Mount Sinai. If language about clouds in Psalms is metaphorical, is language about the cloud and glory at Mount Sinai metaphorical as well? Was this central event in the religion of Israel and the history of the Jewish people an actual external physical event? Or was it a prophetic vision, an event of inner spiritual illumination? The notion that the revelation was an event of inner spiritual illumination is precisely the view that Halevi sought to refute. In *Kuzari* I:87–91, Halevi uses the language of witness (*mushāhada*, from the root *sh-h-d*) to argue that the revelation at Mount Sinai was a great *mashhad*, a collective religious experience that enabled the Jewish people to offer valid testimony (*shahāda*).[2]

Both Halevi and Maimonides describe the event at Mount Sinai using the phrase "that great *mashhad*" (*hādhā/dhālika al-mashhad al-aẓīm*). The term *mashhad*, too, derives from the root *sh-h-d*. Its earliest lexical uses relate to a place where people are present or assembled, a place of assembly. For example, the places of religious visitation, where ceremonies of the pilgrimage are performed at Mecca, are referred to as *mashāhid Makkah*.[3] This extended sense may bring together the meanings of witness and assembly; it may be that the meaning of gathering, assembly, and pilgrimage derives from the events witnessed there.

The expression *al-mashhad al-aẓīm* is related in Islamic sources to the Day of Judgement, as in Qur'ān 19:37: "So woe to those who disbelieve on account of (their) witnessing a great Day (*mashhad yawm aẓīm*)."[4]

We also find an eleventh-century source, the *Tafsīr* (Qur'ānic commentary) of al-Sulamī (d. 1021–22) which connects the great *mashhad* to the events at the pilgrimage to Mecca. Qur'ān 22:28 proclaims the duty of performing the pilgrimage to Mecca (the Hajj): "that they may witness (*li-yashhadū*) things of benefit to them."[5] On this al-Sulamī, quoting Ja'far al-Ṣādiq (the sixth Shi'i *Imām*, d. 765), writes: "That is the benevolence of God witnessed at that *mashhad,* because (God) has directed them to witness that great *mashhad* (*dhālika al-mashhad al-aẓīm*) . . ." Here "that great *mashhad*" is that which is witnessed during pilgrimage.[6]

We can see how Halevi might have appropriated the phrase and applied it to the revelation at Mount Sinai, drawing a bridge between the great scenes witnessed on Judgement Day and in the Islamic pilgrimage, and the great scene witnessed at Mount Sinai.[7] There might even be a polemical dimension to his interpretation, implying that the true great *mashhad* takes place not at Mecca, but at Sinai.[8]

The term *mashhad* can thus refer to a spectacle, scene, or theophany, something witnessed that attracts attention.[9] It can also refer to testimony.[10] The Arabic root *sh-h-d* is widely used by Islamic thinkers in the context of religious testimony; for example, one becomes a Muslim by the simple statement of faith known as the *shahāda* (testimony) by declaring that there is no God but Allah, and that Muhammad is his messenger.[11] Halevi bridges the gap between the Sufi sense of *mushāhada* as individual religious experience and the broader Islamic notion of *shahāda* as public testimony. Halevi connects these two senses strikingly by depicting the event at Mount Sinai as collective *mushāhada*, a religious experience to which the Jews offer mutually corroborating witness. His Sage explains:

> The masses did not [receive and] hand down these Ten Commandments from individual persons, nor from a prophet, but from God. However, they did not have the capacity of Moses for witness (*mushāhada*) of that grand thing (*dhālika al-amr al-'aẓīm*).[12]

Halevi thus follows one rabbinic interpretation, according to which the nation heard at least some portion of the Ten Words directly from God and then desisted from hearing; the Sage explains that the people had a lesser capacity for *mushāhada* than did Moses.[13] Even given their lesser capacity for an extended period of *mushāhada*, that great theophany (*mashhad*) refuted the psychological theory of prophecy upheld by the philosophers, in which prophecy takes place through inspiration of the Active Intellect:

> Prophecy is not, as the philosophers claim, from an individual psyche that has purified its thoughts and connected with the Active Intellect, which is called Holy Spirit, or Gabriel, and thus been inspired. . . . These opinions were refuted at that great witnessed spectacle (*hādhā al-mashhad al-aẓīm*), and the divine writing which followed the divine address, when He wrote those Ten Words on tablets from a subtle substance and presented them to Moses, and they saw them to be divine writing as they heard that it was divine address.[14]

Halevi's Sage acknowledges that he cannot offer a scientific theory of the event at Mount Sinai. However, this does not detract from its power as evidential proof:

> I do not assert authoritatively that the thing was like this description, and perhaps it was in a way more difficult to comprehend than I could imagine. Nevertheless, the result of this is that whoever witnessed (*shahāda*) those scenes (*mashāhid*) had conviction that the thing was from the Creator, without an intermediary.[15]

Halevi's view is clearly that the revelation at Mount Sinai was a public event witnessed by the entire community. It is true that Halevi uses the Sufi term *mushāhada* to describe all kinds of prophetic witness, so that the event at Mount Sinai could indeed be a collective public experience of prophetic vision. What he is most concerned to refute is the notion that prophetic revelation is a purely internal, intellectual event and a human achievement. For Halevi, God is the initiator of prophetic revelation; it is not cultivated by human effort. The Sinai event is initiated by God as a collective event of revelation.[16]

As Bernard Septimus has suggested, it is plausible that Maimonides drew the striking phrase "that great *mashhad*" from Halevi,[17] and with it the status of the events witnessed at Mount Sinai as national testimony. However, there is a distinction between the way the two use the Arabic root *sh-h-d*. Halevi contextualizes the term *mashhad* within a larger argument that direct religious experience, which he describes as witnessing of the divine (*mushāhada*), is more powerful than knowledge of God through the intellect. Maimonides does not accept this argument.[18] Moreover, he does not use the term *mushāhada* to describe individual religious experience. For example, while Maimonides draws his conception of intellectual prayer in *Guide* III:51 from Avicenna, he avoids the Sufi term *mushāhada* for contemplation of God in favor of terms such as *idrāk* and *fikra* that have a more rationalistic flavor.[19] What seems to have attracted Maimonides to the phrase "that great *mashhad*" is its force in grounding the binding nature of Mosaic prophecy and hence the authority of the Jewish tradition.[20]

a. Maimonides on Visual and Auditory Manifestations at Mount Sinai

Maimonides' psychological theory of prophecy creates a further divergence between his view and that of Halevi. Inspired by the theories of prophecy of al-Fārābī and Avicenna, in *Guide* II:36, Maimonides states categorically that "the true reality and essence of prophecy consist in its being an overflow overflowing from God, may he be cherished and honored, by means of the Active Intellect, first upon the rational faculty, and thereafter upon the imaginative faculty."[21] This is precisely the philosophical view that Halevi sought to refute in *Kuzari* I:87–91. Thus while Maimonides borrows the phrase *al-mashhad al-ʿaẓīm* from Halevi, he divests the phrase of its anti-al-Fārābīan polemic, co-opting it to describe the Sinai event in accord with his own philosophical theory of prophecy.[22]

Maimonides goes on to explain in *Guide* III:9 that everything that is apprehended in a vision of prophecy is only a parable for some notion (*maʿna*). He hastens to add that "that great theophany (*al-mashhad al-aẓīm*) [at Mount Sinai] was greater than any vision of prophecy, and beyond any analogy; nevertheless, it is not without a notion, that is, God's manifestation (*tajallī*) in a thick cloud. This alerts us to the fact that apprehension of God's true reality is impossible for us because of the dark matter that encompasses us and not God."

Maimonides is here a master of equivocal language. He tells the reader openly that since God is not a body, Biblical phrases about clouds covering God do not actually point to physical clouds. It is not physical clouds but our material nature that prevents our intellect from being able to apprehend God. God, he says, is perpetual dazzling light, whose overflow (*fayḍ*) illuminates all that is dark.

The veil of Maimonides' language is not too thick. By including the encounter at Mount Sinai in his discussion of the parabolic nature of clouds, he suggests that the encounter at Mount Sinai was indeed a vision of prophecy. This is notwithstanding his assertion that the great scene was greater than any vision of prophecy and beyond any analogy, just as he asserts in *Guide* II:35 that the prophecy of Moses is greater than any other prophecy and beyond analogy to other prophetic experiences. His language seems to suggest that just as Moses is not a mere prophet, but a *sui generis* or super-prophet, the event at Mount Sinai is a *sui generis* or super-vision of prophecy.

Maimonides asserts that the day of the encounter was a day of clouds and mist, and then adds that the darkness, cloud, and thick darkness are metaphorical, because there is no darkness near God. Thus Maimonides depicts the encounter at Mount Sinai, like events such as the binding of Isaac and Abraham's covenant between the pieces, as a parabolic event that is meant to teach important ideas.[23] It seems clear that Maimonides is hinting that what happened at Mount Sinai was not (or not simply) an external event at a mountain on a rainy day, but an event of illumination, in which Moses received the greatest emanation of the Active Intellect and transmitted some of his understanding to the people.[24]

This is corroborated by *Guide* I:46. In *Guide* I:46, Maimonides explains that sight and hearing have been figuratively ascribed to God to indicate apprehension in general. Thus the Hebrew language can substitute the apprehension made by one sense such as hearing or smell for another. "In this sense, it is said, 'And all the people saw the sounds' (Exodus 20:15), although this encounter [with the divine] (*maqām*) also was a vision of prophecy (*mareh nevuah*), as is well known [and universally accepted] in the religious community (*ma'alūm mashhūr fi'l-milla*)."

Maimonides here indicates that the visual and auditory manifestations at the Mount Sinai event took place in a vision of prophecy. This is startling, as he indicates in *Guide* II:32–33 that not all the people attained the level of Moses or the level of prophecy. At the end of II:32, he writes, "As for the standing [before God] at Mount Sinai, though through a miracle all the people saw the great fire and heard the frightening and terrifying voices, only those who were fit for it achieved the rank of prophecy, and even those in varying degrees." We thus seem to find an outright contradiction between *Guide* II:32–33 and *Guide* I:46. If these visual and auditory manifestations took place in a vision of prophecy, as suggested in *Guide* I:46, this would imply that all the people achieved prophecy. Perhaps in *Guide* I:46, by writing "Although this encounter also was a vision of prophecy, *as is well known [and universally accepted] in the religious community*," Maimonides is signaling that this is a "generally accepted opinion" and not his own view. But that would be odd, as the plain sense of the Biblical text would seem to indicate objective, external historical phenomena, and not a collective vision of prophecy. It is also not clear whether Maimonides means to indicate that the entire event of Mount Sinai took place in a vision of prophecy, or only the visual and auditory manifestations.[25] Perhaps he is using the term prophecy in a loose sense to indicate sub-prophetic phenomena, as suggested in *Guide* II:45.[26] Maimonides' language is thus rather opaque with respect to the status of these visual and auditory manifestations at the event of Mount Sinai and with respect to the prophetic status of the Sinai event.

Bernard Septimus offers a linguistic approach to *Guide* I:46. The term *maqām* literally means "standing." In Sufi terminology, it came to mean a spiritual state or station one attains through preparation, in contrast to a *ḥāl*, which is a gift of God.[27] Abraham he-Ḥasid and Abraham Maimonides adapt this Sufi term to describe the event of standing before God at Mount Sinai, an adaptation they may have derived from Maimonides in passages such as this one.[28] Septimus suggests the following interpretation of Maimonides' language in *Guide* I:46. "All the people saw the sounds" suggests that they perceived the auditory (and visual) phenomena accompanying the Sinai event, i.e. the thunderings and lightnings. But Maimonides adds that this *maqām*, the event of standing before God at Sinai, was also an event of prophetic witness (*mareh nevuah*), a non-sensory prophetic perception.[29]

How can an event of standing before God also take place in a vision of prophecy? In *Guide* III:24, Maimonides explains that one of the lessons of the binding of Isaac is that prophets consider what takes place in prophetic revelation (*waḥy*) as real and to be acted upon. This blurs the distinction between what we generally regard as real, external history, and the realm of dream and imaginative prophetic vision. Dreams and visions can communicate information from the divine, and thus can constitute genuine encounters with the divine.[30]

This approach is confirmed in a literary cross-reference between *Guide* I:46 and *Guide* I:21. Discussing Moses' experience in the cleft of the rock, Maimonides suggests that "that great encounter [with the divine]" (*al-maqām al-aẓīm*) may have been in its entirety a vision of prophecy (*mareh nevuah*). As Septimus notes, since Maimonides prefers the interpretation that Moses' experience at the cleft of the rock was purely internal and intellectual, it is appropriate that he uses the term *maqām* rather than *mashhad* (spectacle/witnessed scene) to describe it. Nevertheless, it is clearly an experience of encounter with the divine, a great event of standing in the presence of God.[31]

Maimonides describes what was witnessed at the event of standing before God at Sinai as "that great witnessed scene" (*dhālika al-mashhad al-ʿaẓīm*). Maimonides does not make it clear whether the lightning, thunders, and even the divine voice are witnessed "prophetically" or through the physical senses. Perhaps in the realm of prophetic witness, the distinction between "internal" and "external" is blurred. All at the event "miraculously" witnessed these sub-prophetic phenomena. Only those who were adequately prepared achieved the genuine level of prophecy.[32]

b. The Voice at Mount Sinai

Indeed, there has been fruitful scholarly discussion in recent years regarding an esoteric interpretation of the "voice" that was heard at Mount Sinai. This interpretation grounds and corroborates Eisenmann's claims with respect to the created light and glory. Like classical commentators such as Narboni and Abravanel, modern interpreters Howard Kreisel, Jacob Levinger, and Esti Eisenmann each come to the conclusion that Maimonides does not believe that the voice is auditory, but rather represents the Active Intellect or information transmitted by the Active Intellect. In *Guide* II:33, Maimonides argues that at Mount Sinai, the people apprehended, that is, understood, the first two of the ten commandments, which can be understood by human intellectual speculation alone, while Moses received the other commandments through prophecy.

He opens the chapter by citing a rabbinic text in the *Mekhilta* that at Mount Sinai, speech was addressed to Moses alone, while Moses repeated to the people every commandment as he heard it.[33] He writes that Moses was spoken to, and that the people heard the great voice, but not the articulations of speech. Maimonides suggests that this is the "external" (*ẓāhir*) meaning of Scripture and of most of the sayings of the rabbis. This would imply that the people heard only an unintelligible sound and that Moses communicated to them all of the Ten Commandments. However, Maimonides then goes on to draw a distinction between the first two commandments and the remaining eight, basing himself upon an alternative rabbinic tradition that the people only heard the first two commandments directly from God ("from the mouth of the Force," *mi-pi ha-gevurah*).[34] Maimonides explains that the status of the prophet and that of everyone else is equal with respect to everything that can be known through rational demonstration. Thus, the people knew the first two commandments, that is, the articulation of the existence and unity of God, from the divine, that is, from their unaided human intellects.

Maimonides distinguishes between the voices and lightnings, like thunder and the loud voice of the trumpet, and the "voice of the Lord . . . the created voice from which the speech [of God] was understood."[35] As we have seen, Maimonides does not fully clarify the status of the auditory and visual manifestations. They seem to be some kind of sub-prophetic accompaniments of the primary event at Mount Sinai. Perhaps, as Levinger suggests, the events of lightning and thunder at Mount Sinai were simply meant to make an impression, to impress on their hearts and minds the truths that they already knew, the first two commandments.[36] The other eight commandments belong to the class of generally accepted opinions; these are what Moses received in prophecy.

We find an intriguing earlier statement relating to the event at Mount Sinai in a work preceding the *Guide*, *Mishneh Torah*, *Yesodei ha-Torah* 8:1. In this earlier work, Maimonides argues that the Israelites did not believe in Moses because of miracles, but rather because "our eyes saw, and not a stranger's; our ears heard, and not another's. There was fire, thunder and lightning. He entered the thick cloud; the voice spoke to him and we heard, 'Moses, Moses, go tell them the following. . . .'"[37] In contrast to his statement in the *Guide*, Maimonides here suggests that the people "heard" more than the first two words known by human speculation alone. Moreover, Maimonides appears to be arguing here that the phenomena of fire, thunder, and lightning were not miracles. If these were not miraculous, an alternative is that they took place in a vision of prophecy, precisely as Maimonides argues in *Guide* I:46. Apparently, the people as a whole attained to a low degree of prophecy, or at least the level of sub-prophetic visual and auditory phenomena, although they did not attain to the level of Moses who came to a full understanding of God's word, and did not just hear a dim voice.[38]

We find a suggestive echo of Maimonides' formulation in *Yesodei ha-Torah* in *Guide* III:24. Like Halevi, Maimonides here parallels traditional rabbinic interpretation of Exodus 19:9: "And the Lord said to Moses, lo I come to you in a thick cloud, that the people may hear when I speak with you, and have trust in you forever." Maimonides writes:

> [Moses] told [the people] . . . at the standing [in the presence of God] at Mount Sinai (*ma'amad har sinai*): be not afraid. This great witnessed spectacle (*al-mashhad al-aẓīm*) that you have seen has taken place only in order that you acquire certitude (*yaqīn*) through witnessing (*mushāhada*). . . . For if I had come to you as a prophet, as you had thought, and I had said to you what had been said to me without your hearing it for yourselves, it would have been possible for you to fancy that what is told by another is true even if that other had come to you with something contradicting what has been made known to you; this is what could have happened if you had not heard it at this event of witnessing (*mashhad*).[39]

Maimonides' position seems to be that both the meteorological phenomena and the voice were created by God to impress upon the people the authenticity of that which God revealed to Moses at Mount Sinai.

What is most important for our purpose is the status of the created voice. As Levinger points out, if both Moses and the people heard the commandments through the created voice but their rank was not equal to that of Moses, this cannot be because Moses' auditory powers were greater.[40] Rather, Moses understood on a deeper level the basic truths of the existence and unity of God.[41] Thus with Levinger, we might find cogent the suggestion set forth by the classical commentators Moses Narboni (ca. 1300–66) and Isaac Abravanel (1437–1508) as an interpretation of Maimonides' position, that one who has apprehended a truth through speculation is able to apprehend the truth through prophecy.[42]

For example, let us imagine two students entering a lecture on the theory of relativity. One who has been trained in physics will hear the words as distinct, intelligible, and conveying meaning; for others, the words will be unintelligible sounds. Thus, the comprehension of those who were at Sinai depended on their degree of preparation.

Abravanel supports this view with an ingenious interpretation of Maimonides' prooftext from Deuteronomy 4:35. The plain sense of the verse reads, "to you it was shown, that you might know that the Lord is God; there is none else beside him." Abravanel reads this verse to mean, "to you it was shown, *because of your knowledge*, that the Lord is God; there is none else beside him." Abravanel writes:

> This has been shown to you in prophecy because you possessed prior knowledge of these two fundamental principles: "that the Lord, He is God," i.e., He is found in the heavens above and the earth below (God's existence, the second commandment); "and there is none else beside Him," i.e., He is one (God's unity, the first commandment). [Hence this verse means,] "because of your knowledge of these two fundamental principles, you have been shown what you have seen here," whereupon Scripture immediately adds, "Out of heaven He made you to hear his voice, that He might instruct you; and upon earth He made you to see His great fire (Deuteronomy 4:36)," for this is what He showed them by virtue of the fact that they were prepared with the prior knowledge they had attained through speculation.[43]

In *Guide* I:59, Maimonides asserts that with every attribute that one demonstrably negates of God, one comes closer to a genuine understanding of God's true existence. Thus there are degrees of understanding of contingent existence as pointing to Necessary Existence.[44] Perhaps, as Narboni and Abravanel suggest, Moses did not even need to hear an auditory voice, but understood the truth purely intellectually, while the people needed to hear actual words to spark their rational understanding of the existence and unity of God.[45]

Thus Levinger proposes that in Maimonides' view, the people may have indeed imagined a voice of God audible through the sounds of thunder and lightning. In contrast, with respect to Moses, the words "heard" and "voice" are completely metaphorical.[46] At Mount Sinai, intelligence from the light of God, symbolized sometimes by the visual image of light and here by the auditory term "voice," overflowed from the Active Intellect to the intellect of Moses. There is thus a parallel between Maimonides' depiction of the voice at Mount Sinai in *Guide* II:33 and Maimonides' comments on the scene at the cleft of the rock in *Guide* I:21. In *Guide* I:21, interpreting the verse "And the Lord passed before his face and called," Maimonides proposes the interpretation "and the *voice* of the Lord passed before his face and called." In the cleft of the rock, then, there was no actual visual or auditory manifestation that passed before Moses.[47] Rather, his intellect was illuminated and he heard, that is came to understand, all one can know about God—the way God governs creation. As explained in *Guide* I:54, what was "proclaimed" at the cleft of the rock is actually what was apprehended intellectually by Moses, the attributes of action, "merciful and gracious, long suffering and abounding in kindness."[48] "Created light" and "created voice" are two sensory metaphors for intellectual apprehension. One can "see the light of God" or "hear the voice of God." Both signify that one comes to understand the truth of the Necessary Existent and the way divine intelligence is expressed in nature.[49]

Now if the account in *Guide* I:54 of Moses in the cleft of the rock does not describe an actual dialogue of words, what might the passage suggest about Mosaic prophecy? In his chapters on prophecy, Maimonides explains the purely naturalistic process by which prophets receive information from the Active Intellect.[50] In Maimonides' cosmology, the first emanation from the Necessary Existent is the First Intellect. From this ensues a series of emanations culminating in the Active Intellect, the principle that brings our intellects from potentiality to actuality. Maimonides asserts that intellect is the bond between God and human beings; we are also told that the light by which God sees us is the very light by which we see God—that is, the intellect.[51] Thus Maimonides suggests that when Moses is with God in that holy state (*dhālika al-maqām al-muqaddas*), asking questions and receiving answers, this is both a purely natural process and a prophetic state of receptivity to intellectual guidance.[52]

This philosophical explanation is in consonance with the way thinkers in many traditions describe contemplative prayer. The seeker enters into a quiet state of focused awareness, brings a thought or question, and receives some kind of guidance, whether at that moment or another time.[53] This is also the way great scientists describe the process of intuitive scientific discovery.[54] Maimonides is speaking of the power of a quiet, focused mind to receive understanding from the most refined dimension of mind or intelligence. We have seen that in *Guide* III:51 he has described the practices of religious observance as training in focused concentration. By eliminating distractions, a receptive mind becomes capable of illuminative understanding. The process might seem miraculous, because the prophet's mind functions by intuition (*ḥads*); it is quicker, more nimble, making creative leaps not possible for discursive reasoning.[55] All the elements of the intuition have been there all along; in a flash of insight they come together in a gestalt.[56]

In a beautiful exegesis of the verse "Through your light, we see light" (Psalm 36:10), Maimonides explains that "through the overflow of the intellect that overflowed from you, we intellectually cognize, and consequently we receive correct guidance, we draw inferences, and we apprehend the intellect."[57] This process applies to both ordinary knowing and prophetic knowing. Reason and intuition are not radically separate; they are two functions of intellect. Maimonides thus depicts the scene in the cleft of the rock—and perhaps even the revelation at Mount Sinai—as a process of receptivity to illumination by the Active Intellect.

6

Abraham Maimonides on the Created Word at Mount Sinai: Between Maimonides and R. Abraham he-Ḥasid

Abraham Maimonides' interpretation of the Mount Sinai event seems to have been shaped by the interpretations of both his father Moses Maimonides and his teacher, the Egyptian Pietist Rabbi Abraham ibn Abī'l-Rabīʿ he-Ḥasid (d. 1223), whom Abraham Maimonides refers to as "our master in the path of the Lord."[1] It seems that in contrast to his father, Abraham Maimonides believes that the people of Israel did achieve the level of prophecy and heard all of the Ten Words at Mount Sinai. We have seen that Maimonides, basing himself upon certain rabbinic statements, argues that the people "heard" the first two of the Ten Words, and at some point asked Moses to intervene and transmit God's word to them, lest they die. He asserts that "the Sages permit considering as admissible that all Israel heard at that encounter one voice one single time—the voice from which Moses and all Israel apprehended "'I' and 'Thou shalt not have', which commandments Moses made them hear again as spoken in his own speech with an articulation of the letters/words that were heard (*tafṣīl aḥruf masmūʿa*)." Then Maimonides goes on to assert that after the people were afraid of hearing the voice, Moses "went forward a second time, received the rest of the commandments one after the other, descended to the foot of the mountain, and made them hear these commandments in the midst of that great *mashhad*." During this time, they were seeing the fires, and hearing the voices [sounds], like thunder and the loud voice of the trumpet.

There is some ambiguity about when the people intervened, both in the Bible and in rabbinic literature. It seems that according to Maimonides, basing himself upon certain rabbinic traditions, the people and Moses "heard" the first two words, and Moses then heard the other eight words, which he went on to repeat to the people.[2]

In contrast, Abraham Maimonides does not make an explicit distinction between the first two and the remainder of the Ten Words. Commenting on Exodus 20:16, "They said to Moses, 'You speak with us and we will hear; but let not God speak with us lest we die,'" Abraham Maimonides explains:

> Since they knew that the law-giving (*tashrī'*) had not been completed, and they did not know that the last word of the Ten Words was the end of what the divine wisdom had decreed to speak to them as a general address. Scripture's saying, "lest we die" was because their powers were too small to bear the continuation of that voice and to hear another word, as was explained to you in Deuteronomy (5:22): "If we hear the voice of the Lord our God anymore, then we will die."[3]

From these comments, it is clear that the people indeed heard all of the Ten Words. Upon hearing the Ten Words, they did not know that God would not transmit to them more of the Torah, and they felt that they could not "hear another word," i.e. that they could not bear to hear any more of the divine voice. It is clear that the people heard all Ten Words, but how much did they understand? Abraham Maimonides does not make his own position clear in his own words; rather than speaking in his own voice or transmitting the opinion of his father, he brings the interpretation of his grandfather R. Maimon that Israel heard somewhat indirectly the word addressed to Moses, as well as the interpretation of his teacher Abraham he-Ḥasid that Israel apprehended only a voice, rather than distinct words. In his commentary to Exodus 20:1, "And God spoke all these words saying." Abraham Maimonides writes:

> From my grandfather [R. Maimon, father of Maimonides]: ". . . And God spoke." The meaning is that the word was to Moses, and Israel heard. And [this is] as we explained [in our comment to Exodus 6:13], that the word that [Moses and] Aaron shared in did not reach Moses and Aaron in the same way. Rather [it came to] Moses mouth-to-mouth (*peh el peh*) and to Aaron through an intermediary. Thus even though this word came at one instant, the apprehensions of the collective (*al-jumla*) who heard [it] varied. From Abraham he-Ḥasid [we read] that Moses was distinct from the rest of Israel in this religious event/spiritual state (*maqām*). For he apprehended the word and he understood its details and teachings/meanings (*madlūlāt*),[4] while Israel only apprehended a voice. They did not achieve understanding of its division into words. The proof of this is [Scripture's] saying, "I stood between the Lord and you to tell you the word of the Lord" (Deuteronomy 5:5). And it says, "The voice of the words you heard [but you saw no image; only [you heard] a voice]" (Deuteronomy 4:12), and its saying, "[These words the Lord spoke to all your assembly in the mountain out of the midst of the fire, the cloud, and the thick darkness] a great voice, and nothing more" (Deuteronomy 5:19). They did not apprehend other than a voice, but this measure of apprehension illuminated their souls and verified for them that what Moses brought them was true and certain. This was Scripture's intention in its saying, "And they will also believe in you forever" (Exodus 19:9). And [R. Abraham he-Ḥasid also] brought a proof that they apprehended [nothing] other than a voice, in Scripture's saying, "And all the people saw the sounds" (Exodus 20:15); Scripture does not mention that they heard voices, all the more so words. And their interpretation [that of the rabbis] on this "sight without hearing" is hyperbole and metaphor.[5]

Abraham he-Ḥasid brings several Scriptural citations to prove that the people of Israel apprehended only a voice, an unintelligible sound, which verified for them the authenticity of Moses' prophecy. This is close to the position of Maimonides. However, Abraham he-Ḥasid differs from Maimonides on two points: 1) Maimonides holds that the people did understand the first two commandments, which are known by rational speculation alone, a point not mentioned by Abraham he-Ḥasid; 2) Maimonides interprets the verse "and all the people saw the sounds" (Exodus 20:18) as referring to the lightning and thunder, whereas Abraham he-Ḥasid interprets it as additional evidence that the people perceived sounds as opposed to hearing distinct words. Abraham Maimonides adds that the rabbinic interpretation of this phrase as referring to "sight without hearing" is metaphorical.

Abraham Maimonides also differs from his father on several points. Maimonides distinguishes between two groups—Moses, Aaron, Nadav, and Avihu, who achieved the level of prophecy, according to their ability and preparation; and the people, who did not necessarily achieve the level of prophecy, but did understand the first two Words, which are apprehensible by the unaided intellect alone. By contrast, like Abraham he-Ḥasid, Abraham Maimonides does not draw a distinction between the first two words and the other eight; he writes the more general statement: "Thus even though this word came in one instant, the apprehensions of the collective who heard [it] varied."

Ezra Labaton, exploring the ambiguity of Abraham Maimonides' position, asks "does 'the perceptions of those who heard' mean that some of the people directly apprehended all of the words of God (contrary to Maimonides and R. Abraham he-Ḥasid)? Or, as Maimonides implies, that the differing levels of understanding correspond to Moses, Aaron, and the seventy elders, who apprehended the divine words, while the people themselves only heard the divine voice, but no words?" Labaton notes that if Abraham believed that the Israelites heard only the first two commandments, as Maimonides teaches, he would have made this point explicit. Labaton also observes that Abraham does not explicitly state that the people heard the word through Moses. Labaton, Wiesenberg, and Fenton all note that it is odd that Abraham brings the position that the people heard only an unintelligible sound in the name of R. Abraham he-Ḥasid, but does not mention his father in this context.[6]

We can only speculate as to Abraham Maimonides' intentions. Does Abraham here hesitate to dissent openly from his father? In other contexts in his commentary, he does disagree openly with certain positions held by Maimonides. Perhaps the status of the event at Mount Sinai is particularly sensitive. In general, Abraham seems to be more concerned with the experiential dimension of the event than is his father. Like Halevi and R. Abraham he-Ḥasid, Abraham describes the event in holistic, experiential terms. The reception is not simply metaphorical. On the other hand, he elsewhere addresses a question that his father does not touch—that of why these ten commandments were included and no others.[7] Perhaps it is because of this interest that he rejects his father's distinction between the first two commandments known by pure speculation and the remaining eight known by prophecy.

Moreover, in contrast to Maimonides and Abraham he-Ḥasid, Abraham Maimonides affirms several times that all the people at Mount Sinai actually achieved the level of prophecy. For example, in his commentary to Exodus 7:1: "And the Lord said to Moses: 'See, I have made you a god to Pharaoh, and Aaron your brother shall be your prophet.' Abraham writes:

> It is impossible that the meaning of "I have made you a god" is God [Allah], as might perhaps come to one's mind. No one has interpreted it thus. Its meaning is a leader, and this is what Onqelos said. And that its meaning is angel/messenger, this is what those who followed him said, and this is more accurate than the others. Accordingly, those who heard the address of Moses, and his messengership to them of the rest of the Law, [were] at the level of prophets, that is, in so far as they heard the word from Moses. Saadya and others also noted this. And it was said of them also that they were prophets from another point of view, that is, that they heard the words of the Lord at the standing [before God] at Mount Sinai (*ma'amad har sinai*). But one should not think that the level of all of Israel was at the level of Aaron [in receiving] prophecy from Moses. For you should know that all the [other] prophets prophesied through the intermediary of an angel, and nevertheless their levels of prophecy differed greatly in accordance with their preparation (*isti'dād*) for reception. The situation is the same with respect to the learning of knowledge from a teacher. The teacher says one statement, which all hear. And they benefit from it in

> accordance with the differences in their understanding and preparation. And this point reveals secrets.[8]

Here Abraham Maimonides says explicitly that the nation were prophets in that they heard the words of the Lord at the encounter at Mount Sinai. However, he may be suggesting that they were prophets in that they heard the word transmitted through Moses, just as other prophets heard through the intermediary of an angel. He cites Saadya, who makes this point in a commentary to Exodus 7:1: "See, I have made you a god to Pharaoh, and Aaron your brother shall be your prophet." Saadya writes:

> God, may He be aggrandized and exalted, when He wishes to speak to a prophet speaks to him through an angel, except for Moses; for [God] himself speaks with him. God said to him, "You will be a god to Pharaoh and Aaron your brother will be your prophet." Thus Moses comes to be in the position of one who speaks between him and God, may He be aggrandized and exalted. Therefore, Moses is called God like the angel, and Aaron is called prophet. And everyone who hears the word from the mouth of Moses is called a prophet.[9]

Abraham may be following Saadya in his view that the people were prophets in that they heard the word transmitted through Moses.[10] Thus while Abraham clearly asserts that the people achieved the level of prophecy at Mount Sinai, he makes ambiguous assertions about what precisely that means. In several places in his commentary, he suggests that just as Aaron received the word indirectly through Moses, so did the people.

On the other hand, in several additional contexts, Abraham makes striking assertions that the people themselves achieved prophecy. In Exodus 20:21, we read, "And Moses said to the people, 'Fear not; for God has come in order to test you, and in order that the fear of Him may be before your faces, so you will not sin/go astray.' And the people stood far off, and Moses drew near to the thick darkness/cloud where God was (*asher sham ha-Elohim*)."

Abraham comments to this verse[11]:

> And the expression "where God was" is lacking [the first term of] the construct state. Its meaning is "where the glory

> of God was." The allusion to the inner meaning (*bāṭin*) is that they separated from that prophetic attainment (*al-wuṣūl al-nabawī*) that they had attained and distanced themselves from it by returning to the physical states, while Moses drew near in thought (or: in the matter).[12] Scripture already explained this inner meaning in the most explicit way in Deutoronomy (literally: *be-Mishneh Torah*), in what God said to him [Moses] at that event of standing [before God]/spiritual state (*maqām*), "Go say to them, 'Return to your tents,' but you, stand here by me" (Deuteronomy 5:26–27).[13]

While Abraham does not here discuss how much of the Ten Words the people understood, he states explicitly that the people when hearing the Ten Words were in a state of prophecy, which they then left.[14] Immediately before this, in his commentary to Exodus 20:20 [20:17], "fear not; for God is come to test you," Abraham writes:

> Perhaps the meaning of the test and what is intended by it is what has been interpreted by my father and teacher (may his name be for blessing) in the *Guide* in the chapter on the test (*Guide* III:24). Or perhaps [its meaning and intention] is from the meaning of habituation. And the meaning of this is to habituate you in the ways of prophecy and its form so that your descendants who will achieve the necessary perfection for prophecy will achieve by this something of what you achieved.[15]

Abraham Maimonides here alludes to an important teaching in his Egyptian Pietist community. Abraham and his community apparently believe that the Biblical phenomenon of prophecy was being revived in their own times.[16] He thus interprets the notion of the "test" in Exodus 20:20 as referring to tempering people in the fire of prophecy, making them suitable vehicles for reception of the prophetic experience for generations to come.[17] Therefore in contrast to his father and Abraham he-Ḥasid, Abraham suggests that *all the people* at Mount Sinai achieved the level of prophecy (and not just, as Maimonides suggests, the sub-prophetic level of perceiving fire, thunder, and lightning).

In his interpretation of Deuteronomy 5:26–27, Abraham does concur with his father's approach. Both Maimonides and his son interpret

Deuteronomy 5:26-27: "Go say to them, 'return to your tents,' but you, stand here by me" to suggest that Moses was transformed intellectually in a permanent way. In *Yesodei ha-Torah* 7:6, Maimonides interprets the verses in Deuteronomy to mean that when prophecy left other prophets, they returned to their tents, the needs of the body, while Moses separated from his wife, that is, his physical needs: "his mind was tied to the eternal Rock[18] and the [divine] splendor never left him; the skin of his face was radiant and he was sanctified like the angels."[19] Abraham expresses this by saying that the people separated from prophetic attainment (*al-wuṣūl al-nabawī*) and returned to their physical state, while Moses drew near; this implies that Moses remained in the state of prophetic attainment.[20] Since Abraham makes no explicit distinction between the first two Words and the other eight, it seems that Abraham holds that the people remained in the state of prophetic attainment throughout the hearing of the Ten Words, and then returned to their physical state, while Moses remained in the state of prophecy to receive the remainder of the Torah.

Abraham Maimonides thus integrates aspects of the approaches of both his father and Abraham he-Ḥasid to the event at Mount Sinai. Like Abraham he-Ḥasid, he insists that the people achieved the prophetic state at Mount Sinai. The potential of this state was transmitted through the generations; the Egyptian Pietists apparently believed that they themselves were now capable of experiencing such prophecy. Thus in his commentary to Exodus 20:17, "[fear not; for God has come to prove/test you], and that his fear may be upon your faces," Abraham comments: "To habituate you to the ways and form of prophecy, so that the perfect ones among your descendants may attain thereby what you have attained." And to this statement 'And his fear be upon you,' he adds, "by recalling always the awesomeness of this spiritual state (*maqām*) that you have witnessed/experienced."[21]

A similar point is elaborated at length by Abraham he-Ḥasid in a fragment of a chapter on the "Fear of God" discovered in the Cairo Genizah and published by Paul Fenton. In that fragment, Abraham he-Ḥasid writes:

> Recall the "preparation and sanctification" (*hakhanah ve-qedushah*), which I have indicated to you, which is the path that leads to Him, and the details of which I have informed you, as

> well as the purifications which I have imparted on you, so that you may be elevated to this spiritual state (*maqām*). Bequeath and teach them to your descendants so that they will be transmitted in your midst without interruption and thus your forebears will hand down the way of [this] path (*tarīq al-sulūk)* to your descendants. If each generation attains to the state of unveiling (*maqām al-kashf),* then they will receive unveiling and become witness (*mukāshaf wa-mushāhid)* to the soundness of the Torah that they possess, how the revelation (*tajallī*) to their ancestors and their acceptance of the law-giving (*tashrīʿ*) [took place]. Thus each generation shall inherit this Torah from Mount Sinai and that spiritual state (*maqām*), as it is said (Deuteronomy 4:9), "Only take heed to yourself and keep your soul diligently lest you forget the things which your eyes have seen lest they depart from your heart all the days of your life, but teach them to your children and your children's children."[22]

Abraham Maimonides thus draws upon the experiential dimension of the Sinai event expressed by Abraham he-Ḥasid. However, whereas Abraham he-Ḥasid insists that the voice that the people heard on Mount Sinai was an undifferentiated, unintelligible sound, for Abraham Maimonides, the people heard the Ten Words. For Maimonides, the "voice" of God is metaphorical, suggesting knowledge of God known by the unaided human intellect, as well as knowledge communicated through prophecy to Moses. It appears that for Abraham, the voice imparted the actual Ten Words.

a. Excursus: Abraham Maimonides on the Created Voice

Abraham adds a complex discussion of the created voice in the context of his comment on Exodus 19:19 ("And God answered him in a voice"). Space does not permit us to fully engage the details of this passage; however, there are a few points of interest for our discussion.

Abraham brings an objection from "some of the sages who are not of our community." The objectors note that the distinction between the prophecy of Moses and that of other prophets is that God spoke to Moses without an intermediary, and this is the meaning of "mouth to mouth" and "face to face." The objectors argue that if the word and speech were created, they would depend on a material substratum; thus the word would be carried by a material substratum, "whether air or something else." Moses' prophecy would thus not be unmediated ("face to face"); rather, it would be mediated by a created word.

Abraham responds to the objection by first noting that in the case of all prophets other than Moses, God communicates through an angel who interprets the word to the prophet. Abraham asserts that the angel—"an imaginative intellectual substance"—acts as an intermediary between God and the prophet. By contrast, in the case of Moses, God communicates through a created word. Abraham asserts that since the created word is not a conscious interpreter—as the angel is in the case of other prophets—the prophecy of Moses is unmediated.[23] That is, Moses' prophecy is unmediated by a conscious, interpreting intermediary.[24]

Alexander Altmann, in a study of Saadya's theory of revelation, notes that in certain *kalām* discussions, the "substratum" of the Word of God is identical with the person in and out of whom the Word of God speaks, not any external substratum such as air.[25] However, Abraham here specifically mentions "air or something else." The mention of air carrying the word is reminiscent of Saadya's theory of the second air, which he articulates in the commentary on *Sefer Yetsirah*. In *Sefer Yetsirah* 4:1, we hear of the *ruaḥ Elohim ḥayyim* (spirit of the living God), from which all things emanate. Saadya interprets this as a subtle air, which he calls "second air" (*avir sheni*). In the subtle air the created Word is produced, from which it moves to the visible air and then to the ear of the prophet. The second air is also the medium of the created glory; Saadya identifies the second air with the Biblical glory (*kavod*), the throne of God, *Shekhinah*, and the Holy Spirit (*ruaḥ ha-qodesh*). In the second air are created the visual and auditory manifestations of divine revelation.[26] Indeed, in the *Book of Doctrines and Beliefs*, Saadya states that the function of the glory is to indicate that the words heard in revelation are from God. Thus for Saadya, revelation is not purely internal and subjective, but has an external, objective basis.[27]

Abraham is clearly aware of *kalām* conceptions, and seems here to show specific awareness of Saadya's commentary to *Sefer Yetsirah*; there is evidence that Maimonides is aware of Saadya's commentary as well.[28] Abraham seems to accept the argument that the created Word exists in a material substance that carries it, and that this substance that carries the word is what speaks, just as the angel—a conscious interpreting being—is a medium between God and the other prophets.

What is especially of note is that whereas Maimonides reinterprets the concepts of glory, throne of God, *Shekhinah*, and *ruaḥ ha-qodesh* metaphorically—as Menachem Kellner has brilliantly demonstrated—Abraham re-populates the spiritual world with ontologically real spiritual entities such as a substantive created word, a visible created light, and angels who are conscious interpreting beings.[29] We can also note that while Abraham suggests that the angels are intellectual beings, he omits the language of his father identifying the angels of classical Jewish thought with the separate intellects of the Arabic Aristotelians. Perhaps he is aware of his contemporary audience, for whom the abstract Aristotelian language of separate intellects would have little significance or appeal.

What then was heard through the voice at Mount Sinai? Whereas Maimonides suggests that Moses alone heard the articulated Ten Words, Abraham Maimonides seems to hold that all the people achieved prophecy and heard all Ten Words. For Maimonides, prophecy is necessary only for revelation of the Words that are not pure intelligibles, known by the intellect alone. Abraham Maimonides does not draw this fine philosophical distinction.

7

Abraham and Maimonides on Created Light in the Vision of the Nobles

We have seen that for Abraham, spiritual light can draw one to intellectual understanding. Abraham reiterates this notion in his commentary on the vision of the nobles (*atsilim*) at the end of the Sinai event.[1] In Exodus 24:9–11, we read: "Then Moses and Aaron, Nadav and Avihu, and seventy of the nobles of Israel went up. And they saw (*va-yir'u*) the God of Israel; and under his feet there was, as it were, a paved work of sapphire, like the very heaven for clearness.[2] Yet he did not raise his hand against the nobles (*atsilei*) of the Israelites; they beheld (*va-yeḥezu*) God, and they ate and drank."

Abraham comments:

> [Scripture's] saying here "And they saw" perhaps [refers] to the seeing of the eye, and in the state of a prophetic vision (*ḥāl mar'eh nabawī*) the created light appeared to them as a man. [The phrase] "Under his feet" is [given] in description of "sapphire stone." And this is the essence of the translation [of Onqelos]. Undoubtedly, these imaginative apprehensions in the vision of prophecy are an indication of apprehensions grasped by the intellect.
>
> Or perhaps [the phrase "And they saw" may refer to] intellectual apprehension alone, which is described in terms of

> vision in order to make it clearer to the understanding.[3] And its meaning (*ma'na*) is that they apprehended what they had not previously apprehended of God's existence. This is like what the text says about the understanding of Moses when he asked to achieve apprehension of the truth: "And you will see my back." This is an indication (*ishāra*) of the greatness of that of which he had achieved apprehension. [And it speaks also of that of which he had not achieved apprehension.][4] "But my face shall not be seen," is an indication that he had not achieved apprehension of the true reality of God's essence (*ḥaqīqat dhātihi*), which is impossible to apprehend, as it says, "For no person shall see me and live."[5]

Once again, Abraham takes a both/and rather than an either/or approach. He does not decide whether the vision of the nobles is an actual visual perception of a created form or metaphorical language for intellectual apprehension. He notes that if this is an imaginative perception in the vision of prophecy, the image in the form of a man is meant to impart intellectual understanding.

At the same time, he suggests that if the seeing is purely intellectual, the language of vision is used to make it clearer to human understanding; that is, Scripture is using metaphorical language. The phrase "And they saw" means that they apprehended what they had not previously apprehended of God's existence; Abraham compares this to what Moses achieved in the vision at the cleft of the rock. Abraham here follows his father who suggests that the phrase "And you will see my back, but my face shall not be seen" indicates that Moses apprehended more after his request than before it, but less than "the true reality of His existence (*ḥaqīqat wujūdihi*)," which it is impossible to apprehend.[6]

However, Abraham differs from his father significantly in the interpretation of the content of the vision.[7] Most importantly, Abraham offers a positive conception of the imaginative vision. He does acknowledge that the nobles' understanding is lower than that of Moses; Moses saw the "back of God," while they only saw "under His feet" However, he suggests that the phrase "like the work of sapphire stone" points to the quality of the vision—a great and singular apprehension, which is likened to clarity, brightness, and purity.[8]

Maimonides comments on this vision in two passages in the *Guide*. In *Guide* I:28, in the lexical chapter on the term "foot," Maimonides focuses on stripping the vision of its anthropomorphism; he follows Onqelos in interpreting "His feet" as referring to God's throne, and translates "under His feet" as "under the throne of His glory." Maimonides approves of this translation and interprets "His glory" as "the *Shekhinah*, which is a created light."[9] He goes on to express the philosophical significance of the parable: the nobles had a vision of the relationship of God to "first matter." Prime matter lacks all form and is therefore capable of assuming any form; it is thus the first corruptible thing created by God. Scripture describes prime matter using the metaphor of "the whiteness of sapphire stone."[10] This is something that is transparent and can take on any color, just as matter can take on any form.[11]

While in *Guide* I:28 Maimonides seems to describe the content of the vision—the relation of the deity to prime matter—in neutral terms, in *Guide* I:5 he explicitly criticizes the nobles and the material component of their vision; he asserts that they were "overhasty, strained in their thoughts and achieved apparehension, but only an imperfect one." This criticism is contrasted to Moses' action at the burning bush: Moses hid his face, for he was afraid to look upon God; he exercised appropriate caution and did not rush forward until he had prepared himself intellectually. By contrast, the nobles rushed forward before they had achieved intellectual perfection, and thus their vision included a corporeal element; they conceived God in bodily form.[12] Moreover, Maimonides suggests that because of the corruption of their apprehension—that is, its physical and anthropomorphic element—they inclined towards things of the body; they ate and drank after the vision. For Abraham, the meaning of their eating and drinking is simply that they did not have to separate from the body after their prophetic experience, as Moses did.[13]

Whereas Maimonides suggests that the nobles deserved to die because of their impetuous rushing forward and were saved from this fate by divine intervention, Abraham suggests that no harm befell the nobles because they were properly qualified through spiritual preparation. He notes this in his commentary to Exodus 24:9–11. On the words "he did not stretch forth his hand," Abraham comments:

> No harm occurred to them, as Onqelos explained, "*la-havvah nizqa*." The reason is their preparation (*isti'dāduhum*) and qualification/fitness. And this was alluded to in the text's saying (Exodus 19:22), "And also let the priests who draw near to the Lord sanctify themselves, lest the Lord break out upon them," at the beginning of the encounter (*maqām*), before the speaking (*dibbur*) [of the Ten Words]. . . .[14]

Abraham thus suggests that the events recounted in Exodus 19–20 and Exodus 24 are part of one *maqām*, or spiritual encounter. Because the priests prepared themselves spiritually for encounter with the divine, the Lord indeed did not "break out upon them"; they were able to achieve a clear and pure understanding: "And the phrase 'Like the work of sapphire stone' according to this interpretation (*ta'wīl*) is an indication of their wide and singular apprehension which is likened to clarity, brightness, and purity." By contrast, Maimonides argues that the nobles did not heed the admonition of Exodus 19:22 to properly prepare themselves, and hence the Lord would have broken forth upon them immediately, if they had not been granted a reprieve.[15]

a. The "Face" and "Back" of the Divine

While father and son differ in their evaluation of the vision, Abraham does reflect Maimonides' approach in his interpretation of the face and back of God. Maimonides addresses the language of face and back in several contexts in his works. In his early work, the *Commentary to the Mishnah,* Eight Chapters, Chapter 7, Moses makes one request, to apprehend the "true reality" of God's existence (*ḥaqīqat wujūdihi*), and is informed by God that this goal is not possible for him as long as he is embodied. As an intellect existing in matter, Moses cannot see the "face" of God, the true reality of God's existence; however, he is granted a lesser apprehension, something "a little below it," a view of the "back."[16] Maimonides does not specify what he means by the apprehension of the "back" in the Eight Chapters. He tells us that God favored Moses with more apprehension after his request than he had before it; he had some recognition of the unique existence of God, but not one firmly and irrevocably established in his soul. Nevertheless, one might infer that this apprehension is an apprehension of God's being.[17]

Likewise in the *Mishneh Torah*, Moses makes one request: "[To] know the true nature of the Holy One's being (blessed be He), so that He would be known to his mind the way one knows an individual whose face he saw, whose form was impressed on his memory, and who is thus distinct in his mind from others."[18] Here, too, Moses is informed that as an intellect embodied in matter, he is incapable of apprehending "His true existence as it is (*amittat himmatse'o*)." Nevertheless, he is granted "something of the true nature of His being (*me'amittat himmatse'o davar*)." Once again, Maimonides suggests that something of God's true nature is revealed to Moses. He hints at what he means by "back" by analogy to someone who sees an individual from the rear, apprehending that person's full body and attire. The context of this passage is precisely an explication of the fact that God does not have a body, and that God's face and back are metaphors. However, Maimonides mysteriously does not explicate in this passage what he means by the analogy of a person's "full body and attire."

What Maimonides does make clear in the Eight Chapters and the *Mishneh Torah* is the epistemological aim of vision of the divine: that God's existence be distinct in one's mind from that of other existents. However, we should note a difference between the two passages. In the Eight Chapters, Maimonides suggests that to see the distinctness of God's existence is a seeing of the face, a level that Moses was not able to attain; he apprehended a little below it. In the *Mishneh Torah*, Maimonides suggests that in his seeing of the back, Moses did achieve some apprehension of the true nature of God's being and God's distinctness from other existents.[19]

We have seen that in both the Eight Chapters and the *Mishneh Torah*, Maimonides seems to suggest that Moses was granted some apprehension of God's being. When we come to the *Guide*, Maimonides explicates the "face" and "back" of God in a new way. In *Guide* I:38, Maimonides tells us that "you shall see my back" means that "you shall apprehend what follows me, has come to be like me, and follows necessarily from my will—that is, all the things created by me."[20]

In *Guide* I:21, Maimonides tells us that that he has already given a hint to the meaning of the seeing of the back in the *Mishneh Torah*, and describes it as "the knowledge of the acts ascribed to Him, may He be exalted, which as we shall explain, are deemed to be multiple attributes."[21] He thus explicates the allusive analogy of seeing God's "full body and attire" as signifying God's attributes of action. Hence in the *Guide*, the apprehension achieved by Moses is no longer apprehension of God's being, but of the things created by God. In *Guide* I:37, a view is also ascribed to Onqelos, in which the back, all things following from God, represents all things beneath the degree of the separate intellects—those things endowed with matter and form. This would imply that the separate intellects themselves are unknowable. Scholars debate whether this is Maimonides' own position, or whether his true position is the view articulated in *Guide* I:38, that Moses is able to apprehend all the things created by God, including the separate intellects.[22]

In *Guide* I:54, Maimonides details the distinction between God and God's creation further, using Aristotelian language of essence and attributes. Moses now makes two requests: to know God's essence (God's "glory") and to know God's attributes of action (God's "ways"). Moses asks for knowledge of God's essence and attributes, and is granted only knowledge of God's attributes of action, God in relation to creation.[23]

Abraham's language is not identical to any of the literary expressions of his father. However, in meaning, he seems to be closest to the Eight Chapters and the *Mishneh Torah*. Abraham mentions that the nobles apprehended what they had not previously apprehended of God's existence, and he compares this explicitly to the understanding that Moses achieved when he asked for apprehension of the truth at the cleft of the rock. According to Abraham, the phrase "And you will see my back" indicates that Moses did achieve a great apprehension of the truth, despite the fact that "he had not achieved apprehension of the true reality of God's essence (*ḥaqīqat dhātihi*) which it is impossible to apprehend, as Scripture says, 'For no person shall see me and live.'" In Abraham's view, Moses achieved the most elevated perception of the divine possible for a human being. Abraham does make a distinction between apprehending God's "face" and apprehending what he calls God's "back," and suggests that Moses was not able to apprehend the true reality of God's essence (*ḥaqīqat dhātihi)* which it is impossible for a human to apprehend. However, Abraham does not draw the contrast his father does in *Guide* I:21 and I:38 between God and the things created by God, nor the distinction he makes in *Guide* I:54 between God's essence and God's attributes of action. Likewise, the question of knowledge of the separate intellects introduced by Maimonides in the name of Onqelos in *Guide* I:37 does not enter into Abraham's discussion. We recall that in his comment to Exodus 33:22, Abraham suggests that Moses may have achieved a glimpse of God's exalted essence. While Maimonides' statements in the Eight Chapters and the *Mishneh Torah* could give the impression that such a glimpse is possible, *Guide* I:54 specifies that it is not possible.

Abraham argues that Moses saw the "back of God"—the greatest degree of apprehension available to a human being—while the nobles only saw "under His feet." But even this vision under God's feet "points to a great and singular apprehension, which is likened to clarity, brightness, and purity." Abraham nowhere criticizes the nobles' vision, and emphasizes the positive achievement of Moses' apprehension, even while acknowledging its limitations. By contrast, in certain passages—those in the *Guide,* written in his later years—Maimonides indicates hesitancy about the ability of humans, including Moses, to achieve direct apprehension of the divine. What Moses knows is not God's being, but God's creation.

Thus we may characterize the distinction between the two thinkers as follows. Maimonides embeds his evaluation of the vision of the nobles within a complex world of Aristotelian physics and metaphysics, including a celestial hierarchy of separate Intellects and spheres and a distinction between heavenly and celestial matter. Abraham shows little interest in the details of the physical and metaphysical structure of the universe—whether the Aristotelian depiction of his father, or the angelic description of Abraham he-Ḥasid.[24] While Abraham acknowledges that Moses may not achieve a complete knowledge of God's essence, his hesitations are not rooted in a complex metaphysical structure. As we see in his *Kifāya*, his interests are those of a mystical pietist—the development of theological virtues such as sincerity, trust, and contentedness, with the aim of arrival at the divine (*wuṣūl*).

Abraham acknowledges that interpretation of the vision of the nobles is not straightforward. He thus adds to his comment on the vision:

> These are allusions (*ishārāt*) which not all minds can glimpse (*talmaḥuhā*); their hints (*talwīḥā*) are not visible to all

> understandings.[25] And [God] is the one who is asked for inspiration (*ilhām*) and understanding, "For the Lord gives wisdom; out of His mouth comes knowledge and understanding" (Proverbs 2:6).[26]

We recall that at the end of his comment to Exodus 19:24, he writes similarly: "These [ideas] are subtle; only select individuals can get a glimpse/flash of them (*yalmaḥahā*), and how mighty and awesome is their discovery! And in speaking of them [there is] boldness, and how great is the danger. But God is good and forgiving" (Psalm 86:5).[27]

The language of illumination and the verbal root *l-m-ḥ* bring to mind the very first comment we cited on Exodus 33:22.[28] Abraham suggests that the glory may indicate an intuitive flash (*lamḥ*) of God's exalted essence. We saw that he uses a very similar phrase in the Compendium to describe the goal of the spiritual path as "a flash/glimpse (*lamḥ*) of His exalted existence (*wujūdihi al-ʿaẓīm*)."[29] In his comments to Exodus 19:24 and 24:11, he suggests that only select individuals can have a glimpse (*yalmaḥuhā*) of the exalted ideas suggested in his commentary. Since he is the author of this commentary, Abraham seems to be suggesting that he himself has had glimpses or intuitive flashes of these intellectual and spiritual secrets.[30]

Part Two

Ehyeh asher Ehyeh and the Tetragrammaton: Between Eternity and Necessary Existence

In Part One, we saw that Abraham Maimonides sought to harmonize the approach of his father to the issue of created light, created word, and the event at Mount Sinai, with the approach of Saadya. We see this harmonizing impulse again in his approach to the divine names. There are two approaches to the divine name *Ehyeh asher Ehyeh* and the Tetragrammaton, both in rabbinic and Jewish philosophical literature: a historical approach and a metaphysical approach. Saadya Gaon articulates these two approaches in his long commentary to Exodus, a fragment of which Abraham Maimonides quotes in his commentary to Exodus. Abraham then seeks to harmonize the metaphysical approach of Saadya with the metaphysical approach of his father.

To contextualize Abraham's exegetical project, we begin with a history of historical and metaphysical approaches in rabbinic literature and Saadya. We then turn to Abraham's harmonizing project.

8

Introduction: *Ehyeh asher Ehyeh* and the Tetragrammaton

Among the mysterious names of God in the Bible, we find the ineffable four-letter name, the Tetragrammaton, Y-H-V-H, described in rabbinic literature as the explicit or articulated name (*shem ha-meforash*), or the distinctive, particular name (*shem ha-meyuḥad*). We find many statements in rabbinic literature regarding prohibitions on pronouncing, writing, and erasing the Tetragrammaton.[1] In daily Jewish prayer, all blessings address God by this mysterious name, although in place of pronouncing it, Jews from very ancient times substituted the name "My Lord" (*Adonai*).[2]

A second mysterious name of God is *Ehyeh asher Ehyeh*. This name is paradoxical precisely because it can suggest two opposing connotations, one fixed and the other fluid. The name might suggest that "I am who I am" or "I will be who I will be" in the fixed sense of an eternal, unchanging essence, or it might suggest that "I will be changing and open according to historical circumstances." A third possibility is that the verse suggests that the infinite, mysterious God cannot be confined to any particular name.

The first two approaches suggest two connotations of the concept of divine Presence. One is that the divine is an eternal Being, whose Presence is constant and unchanging. Another is that this Presence is always aware of changing circumstances, and thus implicitly contains a dynamic element. One approach suggests, "I will always be as I am" and the other "I will be with you as you are." The name is both theocentric and anthropocentric.

The name *Ehyeh asher Ehyeh* is explicitly connected in Exodus 3:13–15 to the Tetragrammaton:

> Moses said to God, "When I come to the Israelites and say to them, 'The God of your fathers has sent me to you,' and they asked me, 'What is His name? what shall I say to them?" And God said to Moses, "*Ehyeh asher Ehyeh.*" He continued, "Thus shall you say to the Israelites: *Ehyeh* sent me to you." And God said further to Moses, "Thus shall you say to the Israelites: the Lord [Y-H-V-H], the God of your fathers, the God of Abraham, The God of Isaac, and the God of Jacob, has sent me to you. This shall be my name forever. And this [is] my memorial for all generations."

However, rabbinic sources are hesitant to give an etymological explanation of the Tetragrammaton as related to the root *hayah* or *havah* and to explicate its connection with the name *Ehyeh*. Their reluctance to lay this out explicitly suggests that the mystery and holiness of the name is meant to mirror and protect the sanctity and transcendence of God.[3]

Warren Zev Harvey, in his article "Judah Halevi's Interpretation of the Tetragrammaton," traces the history of two interpretations of the Tetragrammaton.[4] One, found in rabbinic sources and Judah Halevi (c. 1075–1141), identifies the Tetragrammaton and the name *Ehyeh asher ehyeh* (I will be who I will be), and is historical, experiential, and existential. "I will be" means "I will be with you, I will be present." As Halevi writes, "Let them ask for no greater proof than my presence among them, and name me accordingly."[5] This interpretation is also found in the twentieth century thinker Martin Buber who, like Halevi, notes that it is suggested by the earlier verse Exodus 3:12. After Moses expresses his inadequacy to fulfill his mission, God assures him, "I will be with you" (*Ehyeh 'imakh).* Buber keenly observes that we find an echo of this verse in the prophet Hosea, when God declares that Israel is no longer my people, "and I am no longer *Ehyeh* for them"

(Hoshea 1:9). Buber interprets: "for you I am no longer *ehyeh*, that is, 'I am present.'"[6]

A second strand of interpretation understands both the Tetragrammaton and the name *Ehyeh* metaphysically. This is a strand we find in Abraham Ibn Ezra (1089–1164), a second interpretation by Halevi, and Maimonides (1138–1204). Halevi suggests that *Ehyeh* seems to be derived from the Tetragrammaton, which in turn seems to be derived from the root *hayah*, to be. Its purpose is to prevent the mind from contemplating an existence that cannot be understood.[7] Halevi includes the historical and metaphysical interpretations side by side.

Whereas Halevi asserts that the name *Ehyeh* seems to be derived from the Tetragrammaton, his intellectual interlocutor Abraham Ibn Ezra suggests that both names are derived from the same root *hayah*. But whereas *Ehyeh* is in the first person, the Tetragrammaton is in the third.[8] Ibn Ezra goes further than Halevi in the metaphysical explication of the divine Name. Influenced by the Islamic philosopher Avicenna (980-1037), Ibn Ezra suggests that God is the Necessary Being that sustains all contingent being.[9] In the Franco-German sphere, Rashbam (Rashi's grandson, R. Samuel b. Meir, 1083–1174)—who may have met Ibn Ezra and derived his interpretation from him—makes Ibn Ezra's point explicit: God calls himself "I will be" (*Ehyeh*), whereas we call God, "He will be" (Y-H-V-H). He believes this explicit derivation of the divine Name to be so radical that he has to hide it in coded language (*Atbash*).[10]

A striking example of the integration of metaphysical and historical explanations is found in the modern Enlightenment thinker Moses Mendelssohn, who translates the Tetragrammaton as "the Eternal" (*der Ewige*). In the commentary accompanying Mendelssohn's German translation of the Bible (the *Bi'ur*), Mendelssohn comments on Exodus 3:14:

> In the midrash, it is written that "the Holy One, blessed be He, said to Moses: 'Say to them that I am the one who has been, I am now the same, and I will be the same in the future.'" {Our rabbis, may their memories be for a blessing, also said: "I [who] will be with them in this plight am the one who will be with them when they are subjugated to other kingdoms." The sages intended to say that}[11] since there is neither change nor fixed

> time with Him, and since not one of His days has passed, both past and future are in the present for the Creator. Therefore, with Him all times are called by one name, which includes "has been," "is," and "will be." Consequently, [*Ehyeh-Asher-Ehyeh*] indicates necessary existence, as well as perpetual providence, as if He says with this name: "I am with human beings, bestowing grace and having mercy on those on whom I will have mercy. Hence, tell Israel that I have been, I am, and I will be, ruling and exercising providence over all matters. I, I am He. I will be with them in every plight, I will be with them in this plight, and I will be with them whenever they call me." However, in German there is no word that, like this holy name, combines the teachings of eternality, necessary existence, and providence.[12] We have thus translated this name as "the Eternal (*der Ewige*)" or "the Eternal Being (*das ewige Wesen*)."[13]

The language of Necessary Existence calls to mind the interpretation of Maimonides, as Mendelssohn goes on to note. Mendelssohn also makes an original observation regarding the connection between the two names. Like Rashbam and Ibn Ezra, Mendelssohn argues that *Ehyeh asher Ehyeh* and the Tetragrammaton possess the same sense, except that *Ehyeh asher Ehyeh* is in the first person, while the Tetragrammaton is in the third person. Why then is *Ehyeh asher Ehyeh* vocalized and not the Tetragrammaton? Mendelssohn argues that God comprehends God's own essence in the most perfect way, while God is concealed from every other being. Thus God knows the vocalization of God's own first-person name, while when human beings speak about God in the third person, they cannot give a precise vocalization.[14]

A crucial chain in this history of historical and metaphysical explanations is that which begins with the influential interpretation of Saadya and concludes with Abraham Maimonides, who harmonizes the approaches of Saadya and his father Moses Maimonides. We will see that in certain passages, Saadya follows the historical approach found in rabbinic literature, which associates *Ehyeh asher Ehyeh* with God's responsiveness to historical circumstances. Saadya also associates *Ehyeh asher Ehyeh* with the notion of eternity, an approach that has classical rabbinic precedents as well. In his conception of eternity, Saadya may be moving toward a metaphysical understanding of *Ehyeh*. However, he does not arrive at the approach of Maimonides, which is purely metaphysical. In contrast to Saadya and Halevi, for Maimonides, *Ehyeh asher Ehyeh* does not point to God's historical presence or activity but to the purely abstract character of Necessary Existence. Abraham Maimonides mediates between Saadya's concept of eternity and his father's concept of Necessary Existence, adding an experiential dimension to the revelation of the divine Name. Most strikingly, both Moses and Abraham Maimonides hint at a novel connection between the two divine names: *Ehyeh asher Ehyeh* offers an explication of the Tetragrammaton.

9

Rabbinic Interpretations of *Ehyeh asher Ehyeh*

For rabbinic background, we begin with the Aramaic translations of the Torah, the Targumim. In our present version of Targum Onqelos, the name *Ehyeh asher Ehyeh* is not translated. This follows Onqelos' practice of not translating the Tetragrammaton or other divine names. However, we have one manuscript variant of Onqelos that does translate the term as *ehe ʿal ma de-ehe* ("I will be what I will be" or "I will be according to what I will be").[1] This could be a metaphysical assertion of God's eternal existence or a historical assertion that God will act according to circumstances.[2] Another Targum, Pseudo-Jonathan, explicates *Ehyeh asher Ehyeh* in a threefold way: "[I am] the one who spoke and the world came into being (*Ehyeh* #1), [He who] spoke and all came into being (*asher Ehyeh* #2)", and he said, "Thus shall you say to the children of Israel, 'I am (the One) that I am and who will be (*Ehyeh* #3)' sent me to you." Targum Jonathan thus reflects a widespread interpretation of the Tetragrammaton as "the One who spoke and the world came into being (*den de-amar ve-hava ʿalma*)." How does he derive this interpretation from the name *Ehyeh asher Ehyeh*? One possibility is that Jonathan is reading *Ehyeh* as causative; God is, as it were, the "Be-er," the One who brings things into existence.[3] In his interpretation of Exodus 3:15, Jonathan also reflects the notion of eternity: "I am (the One) that I am and who will be" sent me to you.

Rabbinic midrashim include both historical and eternal interpretations. In Midrash *Tanḥuma* (Printed Version), which probably dates to the seventh century C.E., we find an explicitly historical interpretation:[4]

> Moses said to the Holy Blessed One: "Behold, when I come to the children of Israel and I shall say to them, the God of your fathers sent me, What shall I say to them?" (Exodus 3:13) Moses pleaded with the Holy Blessed One to divulge the great name to him. He said: "If they should ask me: 'what is His name?' what shall I answer?" He answered [Moses]: "Do you want to know My name? I am called according to My actions. When I judge humankind, I am called God (*Elohim*); when I take revenge upon the wicked, I am called [Lord of] Hosts; when I suspend the sins of a person, I am called God Almighty (*El Shaddai*); and when I sit [to judge] with the quality of mercy (*yoshev bemidat raḥamim*), I am called Merciful (*raḥum*). My name is in accordance with My actions. But go and say to them: The God of Abraham, the God of Isaac, and the God of Jacob has sent me unto you; this is My name forever, and this is My memorial unto all generations" (ibid., v. 15).[5]

In this interpretation, *Ehyeh asher Ehyeh* is not a name in itself but a stand in for the names that God will be called according to the qualities God expresses in different historical circumstances. Thus the expression is not only historical but suggests that God's name is fluid, since God's activities cannot be captured by any one description. We find an almost identical tradition in *Exodus Rabbah.* While this is an early medieval compilation dated to either the tenth or eleventh century C.E., it does include and rework material from *Tanḥuma* (Printed Version).[6] This is the first interpretation offered of *Ehyeh asher Ehyeh*, which I translate from the critical edition published by Avigdor Shinan:

> *Ehyeh asher Ehyeh* (Exodus 3:14). [God] said to him: I am called according to my actions. Sometimes I am called God Almighty (*El Shaddai*), [Lord of] hosts, *Elohim*, Lord [the Tetragrammaton]. When I judge the creatures, I am called *Elohim*, when I suspend the sins of a person, I am called God Almighty (*El Shaddai*), when I make war on the wicked I am

> called [Lord of] hosts, and when I am merciful upon my world I am called Lord, for Lord is none other than the quality of mercy, as it is said: [Lord, Lord], God of mercy and graciousness (Exodus 34:6). Thus: *Ehyeh asher Ehyeh* (I will be what I will be); I am called according to my actions.[7]

A complementary interpretation is put forth next in *Exodus Rabbah* by Rabbi Isaac: "The Holy Blessed One said to Moses, Say to them, 'I am He, I am the one who was, who is now, and who will be in the future.' Thus, *Ehyeh asher Ehyeh* is written here three times." Rabbi Isaac is deriving this from the fact that Exodus 3:14a includes *Ehyeh* two times (*Ehyeh asher Ehyeh*) and Exodus 3:14b includes *Ehyeh* once ("thus shall you say to the Israelites, *Ehyeh* sent me to you"). The three *Ehyehs* thus signify the past, present, and future. One could give this a metaphysical or a historical interpretation. A metaphysical interpretation would suggest that the three *Ehyehs* symbolize the three phases of eternal being.

A more historical twist is offered next by R. Jacob bar Avina of Sepphoris:

> The Holy Blessed One said to Moses, "Say to them, 'In this tribulation I will be with you and in the tribulations to come I will be with you.'" [Moses] said to him, "And shall I say thus to them? It is enough [to mention] to them one tribulation in its time!" [God said to him], "[Granted.] Rather—thus say to the children of Israel, '*Ehyeh* sent me to you.' (Exodus 3:14b). You I inform [about the other tribulations], but not them."[8]

We find a similar version in the Babylonian Talmud (b. *Berakhot* 9a):

> *Ehyeh asher Ehyeh* (Exodus 3:14a). The Holy Blessed One said to Moses, "Go tell Israel, 'I was with them in this tribulation and I will be with them in the tribulations of the kingdoms.' [Moses] said to him, 'Master of the universe! One tribulation in its time is enough!' Then the Holy Blessed One said to him, "Say to them, 'I will be [*Ehyeh*] sent me to you' (Exodus 3:14b)."

Thus, in Exodus 3:14a, God suggests to Moses himself that God's name is *Ehyeh asher Ehyeh*—one who will be with the nation in present and future tribulations. However, in Exodus 3:15b, Moses is instructed that when he speaks to Israel, he should use the name *Ehyeh* alone, affirming that God is present with them in their current travail, thus sparing them the worry about tribulations to come.

10

The Interpretation of Saadya Gaon

Saadya Gaon parallels both sides of rabbinic interpretation, the metaphysical and the historical. In his stand-alone Arabic translation of the Torah (the *Tafsīr*), he translates *Ehyeh asher Ehyeh* as "the eternal (beginningless) that will not cease to be (*al-azalī alladhī lā yazūl*)." *Al-azalī* ("the eternal") is an adjectival noun deriving from the noun *al-azal*, which means eternal in the sense of beginning-less.[1] The noun may derive from either the Arabic root *a-z-l* or the root *z-y-l*. In the first case, the term *al-azal* would derive from the verb *azala,* to be confined, restricted, withheld, or prevented. The term thus has to do with narrowness, so that the mind is prevented by its narrowness from determining the limit of the beginning. This is contrasted with *al-abad*, everlastingness, which is derived from *ubūd*, the act of shrinking from a thing or shunning; the mind shrinks from or shuns determining the limit of the end.[2]

The other possibility offered is that the term *al-azal* is derived from the root *z-y-l*, which most often appears in the negative, in the phrase expressed as "*lā yazāl* + imperfect indicative": he does not cease from doing something. Thus, another derivation of the term *al-azal* is from the phrase *lam yazal*, meaning "he has not ceased, he has ever been," that is, that God has never been non-existent. In the second part of his translation of the phrase *Ehyeh asher Ehyeh,* Saadya uses an imperfect form of the verb *z-y-l, lā yazūl*, meaning "he does or will not cease."

Saadya thus captures some of the assonance of the Hebrew phrase *Ehyeh asher Ehyeh* by playing on the assonance of the Arabic terms *al-azalī* and *lā yazūl*. Saadya's translation has an exegetical purpose; he accounts in a direct way for the two *Ehyeh's,* and does so with a distinct theological twist. The first *Ehyeh* means "I always was," and the second *Ehyeh* means "I always will be." This parallels Rabbi Isaac's interpretation in *Exodus Rabbah* that *Ehyeh* is written three times to signal past, present, and future. Saadya, however, includes simply the past and future in his translation of this one verse, in accordance with the two mentions of *Ehyeh*. While Saadya's interpretation may be considered metaphysical, his understanding of eternity seems to refer to eternal and unchanging or everlasting physical time and is thus not purely metaphysical. It will be left to later thinkers such as Ibn Ezra and Maimonides to take the next step and affirm that the reason God always was and always will be is because God's existence is necessary rather than contingent.

In a poem attributed to Saadya, we find both metaphysical and historical interpretations: "and the fifth name is *Ehyeh asher Ehyeh* because he was and he also will be (*ki hu hayah ve-gam hu yihyeh*)."[3] This parallels the translation we have in Saadya's stand-alone translation, the *Tafsīr*: "The eternal (*al-azalī*) who will not cease," and more strikingly, in the translation accompanying Saadya's long commentary (the *Sharḥ*), which we will explore below: "who always was and always will be."[4] In the very next line, Saadya expresses the threefold interpretation we saw attributed to Rabbi Isaac in *Exodus Rabbah*, as well as the historical account of R. Jacob b. Avina and the passage from b. *Berakhot*: "He was with us in the tribulation of Egypt, he is with us in the tribulation of the kingdoms, and he will be with us in the future [redemption], as it is written, 'and God said to Moses, *Ehyeh asher Ehyeh*,' and he said, 'thus say to the children of Israel, '*Ehyeh* has sent me.'" Here, Saadya reflects upon the presence of God in the three times (past, present, and future), and also adds a historical reading.

Other comments of Saadya also reflect the historical reading. We read in Isaiah 52:6: "Therefore my people shall know my name; therefore [they shall know] on that day that I am the one who says, "Here I am (*hineni*)." Saadya comments on Isaiah 52:4–6:

> *Ehyeh asher Ehyeh* is the name that God created in accordance with the events that He wanted to occur in Egypt, and likewise He will create for us names that He will make known to us

> in accordance with the events that take place at the time of redemption, as he says, "Therefore my people will know my name" (Isaiah 52:6).[5]

And in the long commentary to Exodus 3:14, he writes:

> I will be as I will be (*akūn kamā akūn*), that is to say, I will be called by names according to my actions. When I am merciful I will be called Merciful, when I am vengeful I will be called Vengeful, when I cause death I will be called Giver of Death and when I give life I will be called Giver of Life; likewise when I make poor and when I make rich and likewise [with respect to] the other names/attributes of action.

This suggests that *Ehyeh asher Ehyeh* is not in itself a name, but a stand-in for names that will be appropriate according to the circumstances, an approach that parallels the interpretation found in Midrash *Tanḥuma*.[6] There is thus a connection between the historical approach and the fluidity of God's name. Since historical circumstances are contingent, no one name will apply in all circumstances. The historical interpretation suggests that God is present and will act appropriately in changing circumstances. This is very different from the purely metaphysical understanding of God as eternal unchanging Being.

We thus see that Saadya's historical interpretation of *Ehyeh asher Ehyeh* is rooted in classical rabbinic sources such as the traditions from *Tanḥuma* and *Berakhot*.[7] Likewise, his interpretation of this name as eternity (*hayah ve-yihyeh*) is not a philosophical innovation, but has rabbinic roots and parallels. While it is true that Rabbi Isaac's interpretation of the name as eternity is found in *Exodus Rabbah*, a medieval compilation whose final form post-dates Saadya, Saadya nevertheless may have been aware of some version of the tradition.[8] Moreover, in addition to the Targums and midrashic sources, we find sources for the interpretation of this name as eternity in early liturgical poetry. For example, in a *piyyuṭ* attributed to the poet Yannai (which probably dates to the sixth century C.E.), we find the expression, "Your name was and will be" (*shimkha hayah ve-yihyeh*); this name could be *Ehyeh* or the Tetragrammaton.[9] In another poem, of disputed attribution to Yannai, we read, "He who was and will be in his world" (*he-hayah ve-yihyeh be-ʿolamo*).[10] In a poem by

Pinḥas ha-Kohen b. Jacob of Kappara (before tenth century, perhaps c. 750–800 C.E.) for Shemini ʿAtseret, we read:

> On the eighth day there will be a gathering,
> For the seed [of Abraham], so shall it be (*le-zeraʿ koh yihyeh*)![11]
> As it says, *Ehyeh asher Ehyeh*;
> For what has been is what will be (*ma[h] she-hayah hu she-yihyeh*),
> And what has been done is what will be done, and what will be;[12]
> And by His word, He brings everything to life,
> Therefore [He], may he be blessed and sanctified, was and will be (*hayah ve-yihyeh*).[13]

These early poets thus reflect the two translations we found in the Targumim: "he who was and will be" *(Targum Onqelos),* and "he who spoke and the world came into being" *(Targum Jonathan).*

The interpretation of eternity is also reflected in the *Rosh Ha-shanah piyyuṭ* "*Ve-khol ma'aminim*" ("All believe"), which interprets *Ehyeh asher Ehyeh* as *hayah ve-yihyeh*: "He is called by [the attribute] *Ehyeh asher Ehyeh.* And all believe that he was and will be (*hayah ve-yihyeh*)." Indeed, we find a comment in the Vilna Mahzor: "this follows the approach of Rav Saadya Gaon."[14]

11

Saadya's Long Commentary to Exodus 3:13-15

The two approaches—the metaphysical and the historical—are integrated and explicated at length in Saadya's long commentary to Exodus 3:13–15. Abraham Maimonides, in his commentary to the Torah, cites Saadya's translation and a very short fragment—or, perhaps, a quotation from a paraphrase—from Saadya's long commentary. In addition to the fragmentary citation in Abraham Maimonides we do in fact possess sections from Saadya's long commentary to Exodus 3:13–15 in two as yet unpublished manuscript versions. Professor Haggai Ben-Shammai is preparing the long commentary to Exodus 3:1–20 for publication and has generously shared the original and his Hebrew translation, along with a lecture on these texts which may be published as an article.[1] With his permission, I will make some brief remarks on this long commentary, which sheds light both on Saadya's views and on Abraham Maimonides' citation.

Abraham Maimonides quotes just one translation and interpretation of *Ehyeh asher Ehyeh*. Saadya in fact offers seven interpretations. As Ben-Shammai points out, three are national-historical (2–4), and four theological (1, 5–7). Saadya's historical interpretations echo those we have seen in his commentaries to Isaiah and Genesis; as he writes in his fifth interpretation, "I will be named according to my actions."[2] Three are what we have called metaphysical, pointing to the conception of eternity (1, 5, 6); these will be our focus. In each of his interpretations, Saadya is concerned to answer why only one *Ehyeh* appears in the repetition of the name in Exodus 3:15 ("*Ehyeh* sent me to you").

Saadya introduces his discussion in his comment to Exodus 3:13 with a preface reflecting the historic interpretation:

> The attributes of action are according to the events that God creates. And since this was certain in the understanding of Moses and Israel, Moses requested that God explain to him a name corresponding to the event [of the Exodus to come], saying, "and they will say to me, what is his name?" Then God answered this saying, "*Ehyeh asher Ehyeh*." The explanation of this includes seven notions.

After this historical prologue, Saadya begins his first interpretation, which introduces a metaphysical twist:

> First is that *Ehyeh* is derived from "being" (or: existence, *kawn*). Since it is necessary that there is a distinction between the existence of the creatures, which is finite, and the existence of the Creator, which is infinite, the existence of God is termed eternity (*azaliyya*). Thus the explication of *Ehyeh asher Ehyeh* is "who has not ceased to be and will not cease to be" (*alladhī lam yazal wa-lā yazūl*) [i.e. who has never been non-existent and never will be non-existent] as the ancient ones [the Rabbis] said, "the same for what passed and for what will come" (*eḥad le-she-avar ve-eḥad le-ha-ba*). The interpretation of "*Ehyeh* sent me to you" is therefore "the eternal" (*al-azalī*), which includes the two times [past and future] together.

Saadya here suggests that *Ehyeh asher Ehyeh* in Exodus 3:14a indicates eternity in the past and the future, as we have seen in his *Tafsīr*. Thus the one term *Ehyeh* in Exodus 3:14b can be translated by the one term "the eternal" (*al-azalī*), which includes both past and future. Saadya has not yet arrived at Maimonides' notion of metaphysical necessity. His concept of eternity is concerned with the infinitude of God—stretching from the past to the future—in contrast to the finitude of creatures who come to be and pass away.

Among Ben-Shammai's most important findings is the fact that Saadya frames his discussion of God's eternal nature in terms of the *kalām* distinction between God's attributes of action and attributes of essence.[3] The name *Ehyeh asher Ehyeh* satisfies both criteria; *Ehyeh asher Ehyeh* signals that "I will do as I have done," expressing God's attributes of action, as well as "I will be consistent eternally, as that is my essential nature," reflecting God's essential attributes. In his fifth interpretation, Saadya integrates the two categories; God suggests that "even though my actions change, my essence does not change. I am always in one state (or: condition *ḥāl/matsav*)." The name *Ehyeh asher Ehyeh* in Exodus 3:14a signifies God's changing actions, while the name *Ehyeh* in Exodus 3:14b indicates that God's essence does not change.[4]

Professor Ben-Shammai notes that Saadya does not frequently quote rabbinic texts in Hebrew and must have had such a text before him in citing *eḥad le-she-avar ve-eḥad le-ha-ba* (the same for what has passed and for what will come), although Ben-Shammai has not yet uncovered the rabbinic source. This Hebrew citation confirms our intuition that Saadya is basing his concept of eternity on rabbinic precedents, although he chooses to present his conception of eternity using the new abstract philosophical term *azaliyya*.[5]

12

Abraham Maimonides on Saadya Gaon

Abraham Maimonides picks up on Saadya's abstract formulation of the notion of eternity. He agrees with Saadya that the concept of eternity (*azaliyya*) includes not only eternity in the past but eternity in the future, a linguistic point that Ben-Shammai notes was of debate in Arabic philosophical literature, in which thinkers often contrast *azaliyya* (primordiality) with the term *abadiyya* (everlastingness).[1] He suggests that while the term *azaliyya* itself often connotes eternity in the past, conceptually it includes the notion of eternity in the future.

It is not clear which version of Saadya he had before him, as he revises Saadya's vocalization to a form that we do not have attested in Saadya. Abraham asserts that Saadya translates *Ehyeh asher Ehyeh* into Arabic as *al-azalī alladhī lam yazal*, "the eternal that has not ceased."[2] However, Abraham prefers a different translation as more precise: "the eternal that will not cease" (*al-azalī alladhī lā yazāl*), a translation close to the version we have of Saadya's *Tafsīr*, with a slight change in vocalization (*al-azalī alladhī lā yazūl*).[3] The reason he prefers this translation is that in the phrase *Ehyeh asher Ehyeh*, the first *Ehyeh* should imply that God always was, and the second, that God always will be. Abraham writes:

> As is well known, Rav Saadya Gaon translates *Ehyeh asher Ehyeh*: "the eternal that has not ceased" (*al-azalī alladhī lam yazal*), while the more precise translation is "the eternal that will not cease" (*al-azalī alladhī lā yazāl*). And I found something like this

> in his long commentary. For [the first] *Ehyeh* is an indication of primordiality/eternity (*azaliyya)* without beginning (*lā awwal lahā)*, and *asher Ehyeh* is an indication (*ishāra)* of everlastingness (*abadiyya*) and continuity (*sarmadiyya)* without end (*lā ākhir lahā)*.[4] Now the notion of primordiality (*azaliyya)* necessarily involves (*talzamuhu*) everlastingness/continuity (*abadiyya)*.[5] Nevertheless, the more precise translation is the one I have indicated [i.e. the eternal that will not cease, *al-azalī alladhī lā yazāl*].

Abraham suggests that the first *Ehyeh* indicates primordiality without beginning, while *asher Eheyh* indicates everlastingness. He thus agrees with Saadya about the concept of *azaliyya*, although he makes a slight terminological qualification. For Saadya, the term *azalī* itself includes both past and future; he writes explicitly in the long commentary that *al-azalī* includes both times together. For Abraham, the term *al-azalī* itself may only indicate the past; he writes that *Ehyeh* signifies eternity (*azaliyya)* without beginning. Nevertheless, conceptually, *al-azalī* also includes the future; he explains that the notion of *azalī* necessarily involves everlastingness. Thus Abraham here seems to move Saadya's conception of eternity in the direction of metaphysical necessity. He suggests that what is primordial, without beginning, is necessarily everlasting; the eternal (*al-azalī*), that which always existed, by definition will always exist.[6] Abraham prefers a translation that makes this point explicit: that which always was (*al-azalī*) always will be (*lā yazāl*).[7]

In mentioning two possible translations, Abraham may have in mind—in addition to the formulation in Saadya's long commentary—Saadya's explication of eternity in *Kitāb al-amānāt wa'l-i'tiqādāt* II:13:

> [The soul] will rather praise him by means of the essential attributes, [such as] that he is the eternal, who has not ceased to be and will not cease to be (*al-azalī alladhī lam yazal wa-lā yazūl)*, as Scripture says: "the eternal God is a dwelling place" (Deuteronomy 33:27).[8]

In this passage, Saadya uses both forms, although he is here commenting on Deuteronomy 33:27 rather than *Ehyeh asher Ehyeh.*[9] Whichever passage of Saadya Abraham has in mind, he is concerned to show that Saadya's conception of eternity in the past includes eternity in the future.[10]

Abraham goes on to connect Saadya's interpretation of *Ehyeh asher Ehyeh*—the eternal that is beginningless and endless—to the philosophical notion of Necessary Existence, articulated by Avicenna and developed by his father Moses Maimonides:

> And there is no difference [between this] and what my father mentioned in his explication of this exalted name (*hādhā al-shem ha-nikhbad*), that it points to Necessary Existence, for Necessary Existence necessarily involves (*lāzam*) eternity (*azaliyya*), everlastingness (*abadiyya*), and perpetuity (*sarmadiyya*). And expression is restricted and confined in these exalted, divine matters.[11]

We can observe that before turning to Maimonides' concept of Necessary Existence, Abraham notes Saadya's interpretation of *Ehyeh asher Ehyeh* as pointing to eternity in the past and future; as a Biblical interpreter, he may have appreciated Saadya's interpretation of the doubling of *Ehyeh*. Abraham also shows interest in harmonizing the interpretations of Saadya and his father; he identifies Saadya's conception of eternity with his father's conception of Necessary Existence. Building upon Saadya's suggestion that eternity in the past also entails everlastingness in the future, he pushes Saadya's conception of eternity in the direction of necessity and non-contingency; Necessary Existence necessarily involves eternity, everlastingness, and perpetuity.

Indeed, in his long commentary, Saadya seems to be moving toward this purely metaphysical conception. However, Saadya does not have the conceptual vocabulary to express himself in such terms; Saadya lived a century before Avicenna had formulated his famous metaphysical proof of God's existence, which clearly articulated the contrast between God's necessity and the world's contingency.[12] Abraham's words seem to imply that had Saadya lived a century later, he would have formulated his conception of eternity in purely metaphysical Avicennian terms.[13] While Abraham attempts to equate the two interpretations, his assertion that there is "no difference" between eternity and Necessary Existence implicitly acknowledges that someone might find a difference. This suggests an awareness that he is revising Saadya's formulation in accordance with a new, more sophisticated metaphysical vocabulary.

Most strikingly, we should note that Abraham interprets *Ehyeh asher Ehyeh* through the lens of his father's explication of "this exalted name" (*hādhā al-shem ha-nikhbad*) as Necessary Existence. In the context of his exegesis of Exodus 3:14, one might naturally assume that "this exalted name" simply refers to *Ehyeh asher Ehyeh*. However, in rabbinic and medieval literature, the Hebrew phrase *ha-shem ha-nikhbad* is generally used for the Tetragrammaton; hence Abraham Maimonides seems to be identifying the two exalted names.[14] Thus, when he speaks of his father's "explication of this exalted name, that it points to necessary existence," he seems to gesture toward explication of both divine names, and perhaps to the way the names shed light upon one another. He may be echoing his father's equally ambiguous language at the end of *Guide* I:62, in which Maimonides speaks in a paragraph on the Tetragrammaton of "this name (*hādhā al-ism*), which is *Ehyeh asher Ehyeh*."[15] Maimonides, like his son, seems to identify *Ehyeh asher Ehyeh* and the Tetragrammaton. We may thus find in Abraham a key to interpreting Maimonides' own writing.

13

The Interpretation of Maimonides

a. The Tetragrammaton

Like Halevi and Ibn Ezra, Maimonides associates the name *Ehyeh asher Ehyeh* with the Tetragrammaton; in fact, in the ambiguous sentence just quoted at the end of *Guide* I:62, it appears as if he identifies the two. Unraveling the relationship between the two names requires careful reading of Maimonides' allusive writing. Maimonides is facing a two-fold halakhic prohibition. One is a prohibition against pronouncing the Tetragrammaton; the second, a prohibition against teaching in public subjects comprised in the Work of the Chariot (*ma'aseh merkavah*), which Maimonides equates with metaphysics. Maimonides interprets the divine name as pointing to the concept of Necessary Existence, clearly the subject of metaphysics.[1] Maimonides therefore cannot expound his teaching on the Tetragrammaton overtly; he must teach obliquely. He does so by hints and allusions. Through the use of deliberate ambiguity, Maimonides teaches that the name *Ehyeh asher Ehyeh* offers an explication of the Tetragrammaton.

Maimonides opens *Guide* I:61 by stating that "all the names of God that are to be found in any of the [Scriptural] books derive from actions. The only exception is the Tetragrammaton; this is the name that has been originated without any derivation, and for this reason is called the articulated [or explicit] name (*ha-shem ha-meforash*). This means that this name gives a clear, unequivocal, indication of God's essence. On the other hand, all the other great names give their indication in an equivocal way, being derived from terms signifying actions, which exist like our own actions."[2]

Maimonides adds that the Tetragrammaton is unique or particular (*murtajal*) to God. The verb *irtajala* can refer to coining a name; it can also mean "to be independent of others, with no one to share or participate."[3] It seems in this context that Maimonides is saying that the Tetragrammaton is a name that is unique and particular to God—not primarily that the name is not derived grammatically from another root or syntactically from another form, but that it is not derived from actions that God shares in common with other beings.[4] The Tetragrammaton is not derived from God's actions in the world, but points to God's essence, which is to exist necessarily, with no cause.

The term "derived" (*mushtaqq*) can refer to the grammatical derivation of a word or name from another word or name.[5] Josef Stern has explained the way al-Fārābī's use of the term *mushtaqq* sheds light on Maimonides' usage here. In Arabic logic, the term "derived" *(mushtaqq)* refers to terms like "the Merciful," adjectival nouns that are derived from verbs or names. Following al-Fārābī, Maimonides explains that adjectival nouns such as "the Merciful [One]" suggest an unstated subject.[6] Thus even if we recognize that "merciful" refers to an attribute of God's actions rather than God's essence, we can be misled to believe that there is multiplicity in God, that God is a being who possesses qualities such as mercy.

In *Guide* I:54, Maimonides emphasizes that we call God merciful when we see actions such as tender care for creation. We thus apply the term "merciful" figuratively to God. In *Guide* I:61, Maimonides adds that in contrast to names such as "the Merciful" or "the Just," the logical and syntactic form of the Tetragrammaton is simple and underived.[7] The Tetragrammaton is not derived from actions or qualities we see in this world. As Halevi noted, the Tetragrammaton cannot take the definite article *ha* ("the"). God is not "the Tetragrammaton," the one who possesses a quality of Necessary Existence. Thus we are not misled to think that God is a being who is the substratum of any attribute, even the attribute of Necessary Existence.

Likewise, Maimonides explains that even the name *Adonai*, which is said in place of the Tetragrammaton, is a derived term; it is derived from the notion of lordship. He mentions *Adonai* because among the commonly known (*mashhūra*) divine names, it is the most particularized (*akhaṣṣa*) or specific to God. Names such as the Judge, the Gracious, the Merciful, and even *Elohim* are not particular to God; they are not God's specific designation, the name that refers to God and God alone. Rather, they can be used in a general way to refer to other beings, and are derived from actions that take place in the human realm.[8]

In contrast, Maimonides asserts that there is no "commonly accepted" (*mashhūr)* derivation of the Tetragrammaton, and no other being shares in it. However, Maimonides goes on to suggest that there may indeed be an etymological and semantic derivation of the Tetragrammaton of which we are not aware. He notes that we do not know enough about the ancient Hebrew language from the Biblical examples we have, and that the Tetragrammaton might indeed signify the notion of the necessity of existence (*maʿna wājib al-wujūd*).[9] Maimonides thus draws an explicit connection between the Tetragrammaton and the concept of existence. Moreover, in asserting that this concept might be revealed by greater knowledge of Biblical Hebrew, he suggests an implicit connection with the root *hayah* or *havah.*[10]

In *Guide* I:61–62, Maimonides emphasizes the prohibition against expounding the Name in public, insisting that what was taught to the priests was not simply the pronunciation of the Name, but its meaning (*maʿna*). Thus Maimonides himself takes necessary precautions against explicating the semantic significance of the Name, and does so through hints. This is the first hint that the Name may possess a semantic significance connected with existence and hence the root *hayah.*[11]

This passage forms an interesting contrast to *Kuzari* IV:1, in which Halevi distinguishes between the Tetragrammaton, which is the personal name of God, and *Elohim*, which is a general name for divine forces.[12] Maimonides agrees with Halevi that the Tetragrammaton is unique and particular to God, but disagrees on the reason. For Halevi, the Tetragrammaton is the personal name of a personal God. He uses the specific grammatical term for a proper name—*ism ʿalam*—and compares the Tetragrammaton to the proper names Reuven and Shimʿon. In contrast, Maimonides' God is radically non-anthropomorphic; thus he would not describe the distinction between the Tetragrammaton and *Elohim* as one between a personal God and the general forces of nature. Moreover, he does not use the grammatical term "proper name" as does Halevi. His distinction is metaphysical. Since the Tetragrammaton indicates God's essential nature, it indicates that which makes God different from all other beings; the notion of Necessary Existence distinguishes God from all beings that are contingent. His concept of Necessary Existence reflects Avicenna's metaphysical proof of God's existence, the argument that all contingent beings must rest on a necessary Being. Maimonides does not say that the Tetragrammaton is God's proper name like Reuven or Shimʿon, but that it is the name that indicates God's essence, pure existence without any attribute.[13]

We can note here that all names for Maimonides as for al-Fārābī refer by way of a notion or a mental representation (*maʿna, taṣawwur*). When we contemplate the Tetragrammaton, we have some notion or representation in our minds.[14] Maimonides does not state unambiguously what that notion is; he indicates with some qualification that it may be the notion of Necessary Existence, and that greater knowledge of ancient Hebrew might clarify this notion. He likewise indicates that certain other divine names discussed in rabbinic literature—the names of twelve and forty-two letters—are called "names" even though these phrases include many words, because they refer to one notion (as, for example, the name "the White House" refers to one building, even though it includes several words).[15] Thus in Maimonides' view, the names of twelve and forty-two letters might be descriptions such as "the uncaused, necessary being." Maimonides indicates that they taught some sort of divine science and came near to representing God's essence,[16] while the Tetragrammaton "gives a clear unequivocal indication of God's essence."[17]

Maimonides goes on to indicate that the reason one is prohibited from pronouncing the Tetragrammaton is that it indicates a notion (*maʿna*) that God does not share with any other being; it points to God's essence in a unique way, in which none of the other creatures shares. All the divine names other than the Tetragrammaton indicate attributes and not God's essence alone. All other names are derivative; they point to the relation of an action to God or direct the mind to God's perfection.[18] Thus Maimonides interprets the saying "In that day God will be one and his name one" as meaning that God will be invoked by one name only, the name that indicates God's essence and does not derive from God's actions. Likewise the saying that "Before the world was created, there were only the Holy One blessed be He and his name," indicates that all the derivative names have come into being after the world has come into being, that is, they are logically dependent on expressions that apply to created beings. He argues that all these names have been laid down conventionally to correspond to actions existing in the world. However, if one envisions God's essence as it is when divested and stripped of all actions, God no longer has a derived name in any respect, but only one original name that indicates his essence. There is no non-derivative name except the articulated name, the Tetragrammaton. This name does not derive from God's actions, but represents God's essential nature, which is simple, necessary being (*Guide* I:61, p. 149). In terms borrowed from created beings, God is called the Merciful, the Just, the Lord; but God really is Necessary Existence, existence without attributes.[19]

Maimonides' view of divine names is thus parallel to his view of attributes. *Kalām* theologians distinguished two categories of divine attributes: attributes of action and essential attributes. Saadya and Baḥya Ibn Paqūda both accept this distinction, and each describes God as having three essential attributes: for Saadya, they are Living, Knowing, and Powerful; for Baḥya, One, Eternal, and Existent.[20] Maimonides, however, rejects the notion that God has essential attributes. According to Maimonides, God is not a being who is a substratum that bears various characteristics; diverse attributes would compromise God's absolute oneness. Attributes such as mercy refer to God's actions with respect to creation; they are attributes of action. For Maimonides, beyond the natural world and its processes, there is only one singular essence, the Necessary Existent.

b. *Ehyeh asher Ehyeh*

Maimonides further explicates this notion when discussing the name *Ehyeh asher Ehyeh* in *Guide* I:62–63. Maimonides throws us a rhetorical twist here, as he appears to identify *Ehyeh asher Ehyeh* with the Tetragrammaton. He writes, "all the names of God are derived except the articulated name (*shem ha-meforash*). It behooves us to speak of this name, which is *Ehyeh asher Ehyeh*, in a separate chapter as it includes the subtle notion with which we are dealing, I mean the negation of attributes."[21] The wording of these two sentences is awkward and ambiguous. According to the strict rules of Judeo-Arabic grammar and syntax, the phrase "this name, which is *Ehyeh asher Ehyeh*" *(hādhā al-ism, wa-huwa Ehyeh asher Ehyeh)* most naturally refers back to the Tetragrammaton, thereby identifying the Tetragrammaton with the phrase *Ehyeh asher Ehyeh.*[22] Yet the name that is explicitly discussed in a separate chapter (*Guide* I:63) seems to be *Ehyeh asher Ehyeh;* this fact has led some scholars to suggest that "this name," to be discussed in a separate chapter, refers exclusively to *Ehyeh asher Ehyeh.*[23] However, if Maimonides wanted to make an unambiguous contrast between the two names, he could have written that "it behooves us to speak of **the name** *Ehyeh asher Ehyeh* in a separate chapter" rather than "**this name**," which, apparently, points back to the Tetragrammaton. Through deliberate use of ambiguous language, Maimonides provokes the reader to ponder the relationship between the Tetragrammaton and the name *Ehyeh asher Ehyeh.* And indeed at the end of *Guide* I:63, which is ostensibly devoted to *Ehyeh asher Ehyeh,* he returns to the Tetragrammaton, the name originated without derivation. This suggests, in accordance with the interpretation of his son, that for Maimonides, *Ehyeh asher Ehyeh* offers an explanation of the Tetragrammaton.

This appears to be the reading of Salomon Munk (1803–67). In his French translation of the *Guide,* Munk replicates the ambiguity of the key sentence at the end of *Guide* I:62. At first reading, Munk's translation seems to separate clearly between the two names. He translates: "I return to my subject, and after having remarked that all the names of God are derived, with the exception of the *shem ha-meforash,* it is necessary that we speak, in a distinct chapter, of the name (contained/included/concealed [*renfermé*] in these words:) *Ehyeh asher Ehyeh,* "I am that which I am" (Exodus 3:14); for this relates to the subtle subject that we are occupied with here, I mean the negation of attributes." If we read Munk's added parenthetical phrase carefully, we see that perhaps Munk himself is translating in Maimonides' esoteric style, and suggesting that the name contained/included/concealed (*renfermé*) in the words *Ehyeh asher Ehyeh* is the Tetragrammaton itself.

Responding to the halakhic prohibitions of pronouncing the Name and expounding upon metaphysics publicly, Maimonides refrains from openly drawing a connection between the two names, just as Rashbam puts forth his proposal in coded language (*Atbash*). Maimonides is also taking precautions in light of the strictures of metaphysics. In *Guide* I:57, Maimonides insists that *existence* is an equivocal term. God is not a being who possesses the attribute of existence; God does not exist in the same sense as we do. Necessary Existence, existence without attributes, is unlike contingent existence. Thus although Maimonides suggests that the Tetragrammaton may signify the notion of Necessary Existence, he does not assert explicitly that the Tetragrammaton is derived from the root *hayah*; "to be" is an attribute and the Necessary Existent has no attributes. Maimonides uses circumspection in raising the question of the Biblical connection between the Tetragrammaton in Exodus 3:15 and the root *hayah* of the name *Ehyeh asher Ehyeh* in Exodus 3:14.[24] Through intentionally ambiguous language, Maimonides draws an implicit connection between the two names, alerting us to the fact that the two names indicate Necessary Existence in different and complementary ways. The Tetragrammaton does so by being syntactically simple and apparently underived; *Ehyeh asher Ehyeh* does so by its unique syntax. Hence, *Ehyeh asher Ehyeh* explicates the Tetragrammaton.

In *Guide* I:63, Maimonides turns explicitly to the name *Ehyeh asher Ehyeh*. He argues that when Moses asserts that the people will ask about God's name, they would not have been asking about the articulation or pronunciation of the name. If they already knew the name, it would be no proof of Moses' mission, since his knowledge and theirs would be equivalent. If they did not know the name, his knowledge would similarly offer them no proof of his mission.[25] Thus Maimonides asserts that Moses acts as a gentle pedagogue. He does not want to insult the people by suggesting that they do not know about the reality of the Necessary Existence, so he suggests that they are ignorant of God's name alone, rather than that which is signified by the name. Moses wants to offer the knowledge embedded in the phrase *Ehyeh asher Ehyeh*.[26]

Maimonides goes on to suggest that Moses was the first person to be addressed as a prophet with a prophetic mission. Abraham was addressed by God as an individual, not with a mission to direct a prophetic message to others. When Moses was asked to address a call to the people and convey to them his prophetic mission, he noted that the first thing they would ask was that he should offer them true knowledge of God; then he would make the claim that God has sent him. Accordingly, Moses' first intention was to convey to them "a true notion of the existence of God, which is *Ehyeh asher Ehyeh*. This is a name deriving from the verb *hayah,* which signifies existence."

Now if *Ehyeh* is derived from the verb *to be*—and *being* is a notion that applies to other beings—it is not completely equivalent to the Tetragrammaton, which Maimonides insists indicates God's essence in a way no other beings share in. At the same, *Ehyeh asher Ehyeh* works as a phrase pointing to God because no other being shares in the mode of Necessary Existence indicated by the presence of *Ehyeh* in both subject and predicate positions. This repetition pushes the verb "I am" to mean something other than its meaning applied to other beings. For other beings, "I am" is a statement of possible, contingent being; for God, it is a statement of necessary, uncaused being.

Maimonides thus moves from the verb *hayah*—to be—to the philosophical notion of existence and the abstract concept of Necessary Existence. He indicates that the key to *Ehyeh asher Ehyeh* lies in the fact that the subject and predicate are the same. There is no predicate separate from the subject; "I am" (*Ehyeh)* is identical with "I am" (*Ehyeh).* This unique syntax suggests a being who is utter simplicity rather than multiplicity.[27] Existence is not an attribute, as God has no attributes. God is not a composite being, a substratum bearing qualities. Hence God asserts as it were, "I exist in that I [must] exist"; I am a being whose essence is to be.[28] Maimonides writes: "[God] is existent not through [the attribute of] existence . . . the existent that is the existent, or the necessarily existent. This is what demonstration necessary leads to, the view that there is a necessarily existing thing that has never been and will never be not existent." As Maimonides learned from the Islamic philosopher Avicenna (c. 970–1037), God's essence is to exist necessarily, with no possibility of non-existence.[29]

Thus in *Guide* I:63, Maimonides fulfills the promise made at the end of *Guide* I:62 to devote a separate chapter to *Ehyeh asher Ehyeh*, which teaches the negation of attributes. The Necessary Existent is existent not through the attribute of existence. The only thing we can say about Necessary Existence is that it is not contingent being. This is the *via negativa,* the negation of all attributes of created being.[30]

Maimonides ends *Guide* I:63 by asserting that all divine names are derived or used equivocally, except the Tetragrammaton, which is not indicative of an attribute but of simple existence and nothing else. *Ehyeh asher Ehyeh* thus refers explicitly to Necessary Existence through logic and syntax, while the Tetragrammaton poetically alludes to simple existence, functioning as a name that is on the face of it simple and underived, but has an implicit relationship to being. By returning to the Tetragrammaton at the end of the chapter apparently explicating *Ehyeh asher Ehyeh* (*Guide* I:63), Maimonides hints once again at the connection between the two names. *Ehyeh asher Ehyeh* teaches through logical explication the meaning of Necessary Existence, implicitly alluded to by the Tetragrammaton.

We find a final confirmation that Maimonides sees *Ehyeh asher Ehyeh* as an explication of the Tetragrammaton in *Guide* I:64. Maimonides indicates that the Tetragrammaton is sometimes intended to signify the essence (*dhāt*) and true reality (*ḥaqīqa*) of God, as for instance [in the Biblical verse], "they shall say to me: what is his name?" (Exodus 3:13). In the Biblical text, the answer to this question is *Ehyeh asher Ehyeh* (Exodus 3:14). Maimonides cites a proof text on *Ehyeh asher Ehyeh* to explain the Tetragrammaton. Thus Maimonides reinforces the notion that *Ehyeh asher Ehyeh* explicates Y-H-V-H, perhaps hinting at the interpretation expressed by Ibn Ezra and Rashbam; God calls himself "I am," whereas we call God "he is."[31]

Given the prohibition against expounding the Name, Maimonides does so through hints and allusions. He ends the chapter ostensibly about *Ehyeh asher Ehyeh* by returning to the Tetragrammaton. Thus if accused of teaching the meaning of the divine Name publicly by composing a separate chapter on the Tetragrammaton, Maimonides can respond that he did not write a chapter about the Tetragrammaton, but about *Ehyeh asher Ehyeh*.[32]

At the end of *Guide* I:63, Maimonides adds that absolute existence includes that God shall always be, that is, he who is necessarily existent. Maimonides therefore makes a bridge between the notion of eternity and that of Necessary Existence.[33] This connection is made explicit by one of Maimonides' medieval commentators, R. Moses Narboni (1300–62). Narboni comments to *Guide* I:61: God "is the Necessary Existent; it is he that necessitates being *(meḥuyyav ha-heyot)*, and all that exists comes from him. Thus Y-H-V-H indicates that he is, was, will be (*hoveh, hayah, yihyeh)* and he is the substance that is Necessary Existence (*ha-ʿetsem ha-meḥuyav ha-metsiyut*)."[34] This connection between eternity and Necessary Existence is also picked up by Maimonides' son.

14

Abraham on Eternity and Relationship

Thus we return to Abraham Maimonides, who endorses Saadya's interpretation of *Ehyeh asher ehyeh*. As a Biblical interpreter, he probably appreciated the clear way Saadya explicated the text. The first *Ehyeh* accounts for eternity *a parte ante* (beginningless); the second *Ehyeh* refers to eternity in the future *a parte post* (endless). Abraham then suggests that this is no different from Necessary Existence, because Necessary Existence entails eternity. We have seen that his father himself did draw a brief bridge between Necessary Existence and eternity in the future at the end of *Guide* I:63, when he writes that absolute existence implies that God shall always be. However, while Necessary Existence entails that God always will be—since there is no possibility of non-existence—Saadya's notion of eternity does not entail that God's everlasting existence is necessary, as opposed to contingent. Moreover, Maimonides himself does not explicitly cite the notion we find in the Midrash, *piyyuṭ*, and Saadya that *Ehyeh* means *hayah* and *yihyeh* (was and will be).

Abraham then accounts for the next Biblical pronouncement of God, "Tell him that *Ehyeh* sent me to you; that is my name forever." Abraham asserts that the first pronouncement of *Ehyeh* (*Ehyeh asher Ehyeh*, Exodus 3:14a) relates to God's exalted essence, which it is difficult for language to express, while the second *Ehyeh* ("Thus say to the children of Israel, *Ehyeh* sent me to you," Exodus 3:14b) relates to service (*'ubūdiyya*) and belief (*i'tiqād*) in God's divine sovereignty, and thus Moses said to him, "After you inform them of my name that teaches my exalted essence (*dhātī al-muʿaẓẓama*), inform them of my name that points to the relation of my divinity to their patriarchs who apprehended it, and for whose sake they served me, and for whose sake I did acts of kindness; and make known my name through them and not through others."[1] Abraham thus combines the metaphysical and historical interpretations in a way that follows the two interpretations of Halevi and several interpretations we find in Saadya. The first pronouncement of *Ehyeh* refers to God's eternal existence; the second *Ehyeh* refers to the relationship of God to humanity. We can see the lucid way Abraham derives this as a Biblical commentator, because the phrase "*Ehyeh* has sent me to you" suggests that God sent Moses to Israel as an act of divine providence.[2] Abraham also appears to follow Saadya's interpretation of Exodus 3:15, in which Saadya writes that "this is my name" [points to] attributes of essence, while "this is my memorial" [points to] attributes of action.

Abraham expands upon this notion in his exegesis of Exodus 6:2: "God spoke to Moses and said to him: "I am the Lord (the Tetagrammaton). I appeared to Isaac and Jacob as *El Shaddai*, but by my name Lord I did not make myself known to them." Since God did use the Tetragrammaton in speaking to the patriarchs, how can God make this statement? This exegetical conundrum is one that Maimonides himself did not explicitly address. Maimonides only mentions Exodus 6:2 in one context; he does not delve extensively into the problem of the divine names in the verse. Rather he adduces the verse as proof that Moses' prophecy was different in kind from that of all other prophets. In *Guide* II:35, he writes:

> The proof taken from the Law as to his prophecy being different from that of all others who came before him is constituted by his saying: "and I appeared to Abraham, and so on, but by my name the Lord I did not make myself known to them." Thus it informs us that [Moses'] apprehension was not like that of the Patriarchs, but greater—nor, all the more, like that of others who came before.[3]

Maimonides' claim here is about the quality of Moses' prophecy in general, rather than about the divine Name specifically; it is not clear from this passage whether Maimonides is arguing that Moses' apprehension of the Tetragrammaton specifically is greater than that of his predecessors. Nevertheless, Abraham may have taken the passage as inspiration for his exegetical argument that Moses' knowledge of the Tetragrammaton was different in kind and superior to that of the Patriarchs.

Abraham Maimonides does explicitly take into account the solution of Abraham Ibn Ezra to the problem of Exodus 6:2. Ibn Ezra suggests that while the patriarchs knew the Tetragrammaton, they knew it as a proper noun, rather than as an adjective. As a proper noun, it indicates God's self-sufficient existence; as an adjective, it shows God as the agent of the existence of all other beings.[4] The early Biblical ancestors were not at the level of Moses, who was able to perform miracles through his knowledge of the Tetragrammaton.[5]

Abraham Maimonides rejects the view that miracles are performed by means of a particular divine Name. Rather, they are carried out by the divine will alone.[6] After noting several solutions of his predecessors such as Ibn Ezra to the problem of Exodus 6:2, Abraham offers his own solution.[7] Abraham suggests that God did not use the Tetragrammaton with the patriarchs *in the same way* as God did with Moses. Abraham explains that the divine name can express either God's essence or a relationship.[8] Whereas Moses heard the Tetragrammaton as an expression of God's essence, the patriarchs heard the explicit name of God, the Tetragrammaton, in the context of his relationship with them. God told Abraham the proper name that pointed to his action: 'I am the Lord who brought you out of Ur of the Chaldeans (Genesis15:7)." Similarly, he said to Jacob, 'I am the Lord, the God of Abraham your father and the God of Isaac (Genesis 28:13)." Speaking to Abraham, he connected the name Lord with the providential act of bringing Abraham out of Ur of Chaldeans; speaking to Jacob, he connected the name Lord with his providential relation with Abraham and Isaac. However, speaking to Moses in Exodus 6, he revealed the divine name as a name expressing God's essence, "without connection, without description, without action, and without relationship."[9]

Unlike his father, Abraham identifies the name *El Shaddai* with Necessary Existence, and suggests that the patriarchs knew the name *El Shaddai* in the same way that Moses knew the Tetragrammaton, "without connection, without description, and without relationship."[10] When God uses the name *El Shaddai* to the patriarchs, he complemented the name with actions he commanded:

> And thus he said to Abraham, "I am *El Shaddai*," and then he commanded to him commandments, that is, "Walk before me, [and be wholehearted]" (Genesis 17:1). However, the commandment has no connection with the name or with its meaning. Likewise, he said to Jacob, "I am *El Shaddai*, and again after that he gave him good tidings, "be fruitful and multiply" (Genesis 35:11). However, the tidings have no connection with the name or with its meaning; but when he said to Abraham, "I am the Lord," he completed the explanation of what was meant by that name, "who brought you out of Ur of the Chaldeans." And thus he said to him [as it were] "[this is] a proper name that points to my action, 'who took you out of Ur of the Chaldeans.'"[11]

Thus according to Abraham, when God uses *El Shaddai* to the patriarchs, he indicates his essence, Necessary Existence. After using the name *El Shaddai* to the patriarchs, he commands actions, rather than explicating the name providentially, as he did with the Tetragrammaton. Thus the patriarchs' understanding of God as *El Shaddai* was an understanding of God's essence, Necessary Existence. Their understanding of God as the Tetragrammaton is an understanding of God in relation to creation.[12] Abraham asserts that this resolves the problem of divine names presented by Exodus 6:2—which he calls a secret (*sod, sirr*) of the Torah—in a unique way.[13]

Whereas Maimonides in *Guide* I:63 interpreted *El Shaddai* as sufficiency to produce other beings, Abraham suggests that *El Shaddai* points to Necessary Existence.[14] However, he indicates that there are degrees of knowledge of Necessary Existence. The Tetragrammaton known by Moses conveys a more perfect knowledge of Necessary Existence than what Abraham, Isaac, and Jacob knew through the name *El Shaddai*.

In this context, Abraham writes that his father explained in an allusion (*ishāra*) what he understood of the notion *(maʿna)* of the explicit name *(shem ha-meforash)*, that it indicates the notion of Necessary Existence.[15] The allusion to which Abraham refers is his father's suggestion that Necessary Existence is the meaning in ancient Hebrew of the Tetragrammaton.[16] As we have seen, in *Guide* I:63–64, Maimonides suggests that both *Ehyeh asher Ehyeh* and the Tetragrammaton represent the essence and true reality of God, the highest knowledge of God attainable.[17] In contrast, Abraham indicates explicitly that the name *Ehyeh asher Ehyeh* is an intermediate stage of knowledge of Necessary Existence between *El Shaddai*, the lower level, and the Tetragrammaton, the highest level.[18] Abraham notes that the name *Ehyeh asher Ehyeh*, revealed in Exodus 3:14a, is connected to the name *Ehyeh* in Exodus 3:14b, the name Moses will communicate to Israel as part of his prophetic mission. In contrast, the Tetragrammaton in Exodus 6:2 is revealed to Moses for his own understanding—the highest, most complete understanding of Necessary Existence.

Abraham Maimonides thus loses the *sui generis* nature of the Tetragrammaton expressed by Maimonides. While he hints at the close connection between *Ehyeh asher Ehyeh* and the Tetragrammaton—one is an explication of the other—his notion that *El Shaddai* also expresses Necessary Existence softens the philosophical precision of his father. What he accomplishes as a Biblical exegete—resolving the problem of the Tetragrammaton in Exodus 6:2—softens the pristine philosophical clarity of Maimonides' identification of the Tetragrammaton and *Ehyeh asher Ehyeh* with Necessary Existence.

At the same time, Abraham adds an experiential dimension to revelation of the divine names. The names *El Shaddai, Ehyeh asher Ehyeh*, and the Tetragrammaton all offer knowledge of Necessary Existence. The Tetragrammaton does not reveal the divine essence uniquely, by its very nature. Each divine name must be received by its hearer according to the hearer's level of understanding. Thus the patriarchs learn of Necessary Existence, God's essence, from the name *El Shaddai*. When they hear the Tetragrammaton, they learn of God's providential relation to creation. By contrast, Moses hears the name *Ehyeh asher Ehyeh* as an intermediate understanding of Necessary Existence, to be transmitted to others, while he receives from the Tetragrammaton a complete understanding of Necessary Existence. It is Moses alone who receives the Tetragrammaton as a full expression of God's exalted essence (*al-dhāt al-muʿaẓẓama*).

Conclusion

We saw in Part One that Abraham Maimonides states that he seeks to harmonize two views: one in which the light of God's glory is physical and sensory, and one in which "God's glory" is a metaphor for intellectual illumination. In both his Torah Commentary and his Compendium, Abraham Maimonides speaks of attaining a glimpse of God's exalted essence or existence. While for Maimonides, light signifies conjunction with the Active Intellect, for Abraham Maimonides and his Pietist circle—as for Sufi-influenced thinkers like al-Ghazālī—light is experiential and sensory-like, offering a glimpse into a divine reality that both includes and transcends the intellect. Abraham Maimonides omits the central Maimonidean concept of the Active Intellect, and speaks in experiential terms of overflow of the lights of God's majesty. This language suggests a background in the spiritual practices attested to in the writings of his Pietist associates, and a broader, integrative theory of the human soul in its apprehension of the divine.

Abraham Maimonides draws on the concepts of created light and created word developed by Onqelos and Saadya, as well as light imagery developed by al-Ghazālī and Halevi, to describe interface between the divine and the human in several key events of divine encounter. Abraham Maimonides suggests that in the cleft of the rock, Moses may have achieved a glimpse of the divine essence. In events of collective religious experience—vision of the Glory of the Lord in the wilderness, preparation of the priests at Mount Sinai, the Sinai revelation, and the vision of the nobles—Abraham Maimonides emphasizes internal spiritual preparation and internal experience of illumination, even while the light is witnessed by all. Maimonides, too, uses the image of created light; however, his interpretation seems to bear an esoteric dimension, in which light symbolizes illumination of the Active Intellect. For Maimonides, the Sinai event takes place in what appears to be a *sui generis* vision of prophecy, and the revelation by a "voice" represents illumination of the intellect. For Abraham Maimonides, all at Sinai achieved some degree of prophecy and heard a real created voice. While both thinkers use Sufi language of contemplation, for Maimonides, contemplation and prophecy include a scientific dimension of understanding the natural order. By contrast, Abraham Maimonides is a contemplative pietist, rather than a scientist.

It is striking that in the firmly attested writings of Abraham Maimonides, he never alludes to the Active Intellect, a term central to the Avicennian-influenced thought of his Egyptian milieu. While Abraham Maimonides does use intellectual terms to depict apprehension of the divine, he seems to reject the exclusively intellectualist focus signaled by the term and concept of the Active Intellect. Likewise, while his father is careful to translate all visual language into the language of intellect, Abraham Maimonides retains the visual dimension of light imagery. Perhaps he is aware of his contemporary audience, for whom abstract Aristotelian terminology would have little significance or appeal. He also suggests an integrated model of sensory-affective and intellectual modes of apprehension. Abraham Maimonides thus shows no inclination toward Maimonides' esoteric position, which identifies the created light and Glory with the Active Intellect, shifting the focus from visual to intellectual apprehension.

At the same time, we may ask whether there is an experiential dimension to Maimonides' thought. As David Blumenthal, Shlomo Pines, and others have pointed out, *Guide* III:51 is replete with Sufi and experiential terms: being with/encountering God (*al-maqām ʿindahu*), total devotion to God (*al-inqitāʿ, al-infirād ilayhi*), closeness (*qurb*) to God, being in God's Presence (*bayna yadayhi*), solitude (*al-khalwa*), joy (*al-ghibṭa*), and passionate love (*al-ʿishq*). Blumenthal also emphasizes that the subject of this connection with God is the intellect (*ʿaql*), which Maimonides asserts is the bond (*al-wuṣla*) between humans and God. Maimonides would have absorbed such Sufi terminology from thinkers such as Avicenna and al-Ghāzālī. What he has done in *Guide* III:51 is to intellectualize this Sufi terminology, emphasizing that it is the intellect that is the bond of connection, the bond through which one attains closeness to God and passionate love for the divine. As Blumenthal suggests, "one might say that for Maimonides, intellectuality passed into a 'higher' intellectuality; thinking passed into a deep passion for God; contemplation passed into a meditative delivering of the self to God; and reflection passed into a being, or standing, before God. For Maimonides, as for his milieu, mind and religious experience were necessary complements of one another."[1]

This can certainly be described as a kind of intellectualist or philosophical mysticism, the attainment of a connection with the divine through the intellect. We should note that *Guide* III:51 is the same chapter in which Maimonides emphasizes the rigorous process of study of mathematics, physics, and metaphysics. Maimonides' passionate experience of God takes place through a heightened or inspired state of mind, which includes awe at both its exhilarating discoveries and its moments of perplexity and wonder. His apophatic moments of retreat into silence come after a studied process of philosophical negation based on rigorous logic.

Thus we see another contrast between Maimonides and his son. While Abraham Maimonides denies anthropomorphism, he does not devote himself to the rigorous philosophical process of denying positive attributes. In his Sabbath meditation, he describes an unimpeded ascension to the upper world, and does not mention silence or negation. While his father follows the Neoplatonic *via negativa*—stripping away all positive assertions and affirmations—Abraham Maimonides pursues the positive vehicle of assertion of wonder and awe at God's creation. In this respect, Abraham Maimonides is different from al-Ghāzālī, who quotes a *ḥadīth* that became a favorite Sufi epigram: "'[true] apprehension is the inability to apprehend.' Glorified is he who made no way for his creation to know him other than being unable to know him."[2]

In *Guide* I:59, Maimonides echoes this Sufi and Neoplatonic expression of the theme of learned ignorance, the notion that the ultimate level of knowledge is the realization that one does not know:

> All people, those of the past and those to come, affirm that God cannot be apprehended by the intellects (*al-'uqūl*), that none can apprehend what He is but He alone, that apprehension of Him consists in the inability to attain the farthest limit in apprehending Him (*idrākuhu huwa al-'ajzu 'an nihāyat*

> *idrākihi*). Thus all the philosophers say: We are dazzled by his beauty, and he is hidden from us because of the intensity with which he becomes manifest, just as the sun is hidden to eyes that are too weak to apprehend it.[3]

For Maimonides, apprehension of God leads one to a state of wonder, being dazzled and perplexed by the overflow of intellectual light. Abraham Maimonides is guided by love, devotion, and the desire for infusion of God's spiritual light, rather than perplexity and dazzlement.[4]

We should also note the words of Julius Guttmann:

> Despite the importance that he attaches to reason, Abraham was far removed from his father's rationalism. According to Maimonides, the link between man and God was constituted solely and exclusively of theoretical knowledge. . . . For R. Abraham, on the other hand, . . . theoretical knowledge is only one among many factors. . . . The highest religious perfection is impossible without intellectual perfection, but is not identical with it, for it contains other powers and qualities of the soul of equal value with theoretical knowledge.[5]

It is true that Abraham Maimonides defends the role of reason in religious life. He decries the anti-rationalism of those who reject causality, and as we have seen, does offer an example of Sabbath meditation contemplating the order of creation.[6] S. D. Goitein thus describes Abraham as a "paradigm of learned orthodoxy," adding that "Abraham united in his single person three spiritual trends that are usually at odds with each other: strict legalistic orthodoxy, ascetic pietism, and Greek science—sober, secular humanism."[7]

We must temper this evaluation somewhat. While Abraham does offer a Sabbath meditation on the contemplation of creation in the spirit of Maimonides' *Hilkhot Yesodei ha-Torah* 2:1–2, he does not carry out the detailed scientific investigation called for in its companion text, *Hilkhot Teshuvah* 10:6:

> When a person meditates on [God's] wondrous, majestic works and creatures, and beholds in them [God's] transcendent, boundless wisdom, he will straight-away love, praise, glorify, and passionately desire to know the Great Name, as David said:

> *My soul thirsts for God, the living God* (Psalm 42:3). (*Hilkhot Yesodei ha-Torah* 2:1–2)

> A person ought therefore to devote oneself to the understanding and comprehension of those sciences and studies which will inform one concerning his Master, as far as it lies in human faculties to understand and comprehend—as indeed we have explained in the Laws of the Foundations of the Torah. (*Hilkhot Teshuvah* 10:6)

For Maimonides, love and awe for God arise not only from contemplation of creation, but from engaging in rigorous scientific study of mathematics, physics, and biology. Abraham Maimonides' writings indicate that the deepest roots of his mystical devotion lie elsewhere.

Abraham Maimonides also shows keen awareness of the allusive language of his father, pointing toward an esoteric dimension in his father's thought. We find this awareness in Abraham Maimonides' approach to the divine names as well as to divine light. In Part Two, we saw that Abraham Maimonides cites Saadya, who translates *Ehyeh asher Ehyeh* into Arabic as "the eternal (beginningless) that will not cease to be." In his long commentary to Exodus 3:14, Saadya includes two modes of interpreting *Ehyeh asher Ehyeh.* The first is historical; *Ehyeh asher Ehyeh* is not in itself a name but a stand in for the names that will be expressed in various historical circumstances, an approach that has classical rabbinic roots. The second interprets *Ehyeh asher Ehyeh* as "the eternal (beginningless) that will not cease to be," an approach that also has pre-philosophical roots in rabbinic literature. Saadya's notion of eternity draws a contrast between the finitude of creatures and the infinitude of God, which is beginningless and endless.

Abraham Maimonides makes a conceptual identification between Saadya's interpretation of *Ehyeh asher Ehyeh* as eternity and the assertion of his father that the name *Ehyeh asher Ehyeh* signifies Necessary Existence: I exist in that I [must] exist. For Maimonides, this indicates God's mode of being, which distinguishes it from all contingent being. His interpretation reflects Avicenna's metaphysical proof of God's existence, the argument that all contingent beings must rest on a necessary Being. This is a philosophical stream that post-dates Saadya. While linguistically

Ehyeh is derived from *hayah,* Maimonides suggests that conceptually the Tetragrammaton is not derived from an attribute applied to any other being, in contrast to such names as The Merciful and even *Adonai,* which indicates lordship. However, Maimonides also draws an allusive relationship between *Ehyeh asher Ehyeh* and the Tetragrammaton, perhaps hinting at the connection between the Tetragrammaton and *hayah* which, like Rashbam, he is hesitant to openly spell out.

Abraham Maimonides also seeks to harmonize Saadya's conception of eternity and his father's conception of metaphysical necessity. Indeed, Abraham Maimonides seems to imply that had Saadya lived a century later and been exposed to Avicenna's metaphysical proof, he, too, would have formulated a purely metaphysical conception of God's eternity. In his commentary to Exodus 33:22, we saw an additional example of this impulse; he is interested in harmonizing Saadya's approach to revelation—which features the notion of the created Glory—with his father's conception of revelation as intellectual illumination. He thus does not draw philosophical boundaries as sharply as does his father. For example, he is not as concerned as his father to make a sharp distinction between the Tetragrammaton and *Ehyeh asher Ehyeh*—which uniquely express Necessary Existence—and other names such as *El Shaddai.* Perhaps he sees his role as a bridge between the philosophical and exegetical worlds of Saadya and Maimonides. At the same time, he engages in the allusive style of philosophical writing of his father, hinting through the use of ambiguous language at the bold assertion that *Ehyeh asher Ehyeh* explicates the Tetragrammaton. Abraham Maimonides can thus serve as a source both for the understanding of Maimonides' own writing and for the history of interpretation of the divine names.

In addition, Abraham Maimonides adds an experiential dimension to revelation of the divine names. The names *El Shaddai, Ehyeh asher Ehyeh,* and the Tetragrammaton all offer knowledge of Necessary Existence. The Tetragrammaton does not reveal the divine essence uniquely; each divine name is received according to one's level of understanding. Moses alone receives from the Tetragrammaton a complete understanding of Necessary Existence; he alone receives the Tetragrammaton as an expression of God's exalted essence (*al-dhāt al-muʿaẓẓama*). We can discern the shift in focus from the approach of Moses to that of Abraham Maimonides. While Abraham Maimonides reflects the intellectualist approach of his father, his focus continually turns to the experiential dimension of divine revelation.

We are thus returned to Abraham Maimonides' intriguing notion that one can glimpse the essence of the divine. Abraham Maimonides alludes to God's exalted essence or existence in three contexts. Abraham Maimonides indicates that in the cleft of the rock, Moses saw the passing by of the created light, or received a glimpse of the exalted essence (*lamḥ al-dhāt al-muʿaẓẓama*). In the Compendium, Abraham Maimonides describes the goal of arrival or attainment (*wuṣūl*) as the fruition of the special worship of the Creator, which consists in understanding God, that is, glimpsing God's exalted existence (*lamḥ wujūdihi al-ʿaẓīm*). Finally, Moses receives an understanding of the Tetragrammaton as an expression of God's exalted essence (*al-dhāt al-muʿaẓẓama*).

Both Moses and Abraham Maimonides describe a special worship that culminates in passionate love and awe. For Maimonides, this state of transcendent love and joy arises through intellectual communion with the divine, and dazzling wonder at what the intellect can and cannot fathom. For Abraham Maimonides, divine light and the divine Name offer a radiant glimpse of God's exalted being. We thus glimpse two intersecting and complementary visions of what it means to encounter the Divine.

Notes

Notes to Introduction

1 See *Iggerot ha-Rambam*, ed. I. Shailat (Jerusalem: Ma'aliyot, 1988), 530–54. The letter mentions only two Jewish thinkers, Isaac Israeli and Joseph Ibn Ṣaddīq; he dismisses Isaac Israeli and is ambiguous regarding Ibn Ṣaddīq. See Sarah Stroumsa, "Note on Maimonides' Attitude to Joseph ibn Ṣaddīq," in *Shlomo Pines Jubilee Volume*, ed. Moshe Idel, Warren Zev Harvey, and Eliezer Schweid (Jerusalem: Hebrew University, 1988–90), vol. 2, 33–38; Joel Kraemer, "Maimonides and the Spanish Aristotelian School," in *Christians, Muslims, and Jews in Medieval and Early Modern Spain—Interaction and Cultural Change*, ed. M. M. Meyerson and E. D. English (Notre Dame: University of Notre Dame Press, 1999), 62, note 24; idem, *Maimonides: The Life and World of One of Civilization's Greatest Minds* (New York: Doubleday, 2008), 590, note 75. For a recent study of this letter, see Steven Harvey, "Did Maimonides' Letter to Samuel Ibn Tibbon Determine Which Philosophers Would Be Studied by Later Jewish Thinkers?," *Jewish Quarterly Review* 83, no. 1–2 (July–October 1992), 51–70.

2 In *Guide* I:71, he alludes to a tradition of Andalusian Jews, who, he argues, all cling to the affirmations of the philosophers and do not follow the way of the theologians (*mutakallimūn*). Maimonides writes that the Andalusian thinkers have "approximately the same doctrine that we set forth in this Treatise" concerning matters inherited from ancient Jewish traditions. Resianne Fontaine has speculated that he is referring here specifically to Ibn Daud; Dov Schwartz has argued that he includes Judah Halevi in this Andalusian tradition. See *Guide of the Perplexed* (*Dalālat al-ḥā'irīn*) I:71, trans. Shlomo Pines (Chicago: University of Chicago Press, 1963), 177 (hereafter, page numbers will refer to this edition); Resianne Fontaine, "Was Maimonides an Epigone?," *Studia Rosenthaliana* 40 (2007–08): 9–26; Dov Schwartz, *The Clash of Paradigms: Between Theology and Philosophy in Medieval Jewish Thought* [Hebrew] (Jerusalem: Magnes, 2018), 109–127.

3 See Steven Harvey, "The Meaning of Terms Designating Love in Judaeo-Arabic Thought and Some Remarks on the Judaeo-Arabic Interpretation of Maimonides," *Proceedings of the Founding Conference of the Society for*

Judaeo-Arabic Studies, ed. Norman Golb (Amsterdam: Harwood Academic Publishers, 1997), 193, notes 85–86, and 195–96. For his critique of the philosophical path and caution about the danger of philosophy, see Paul Fenton, "The Doctrine of Attachment of R. Abraham Maimonides: Fragments from the Lost Section of *The Sufficient [Guide] for the Servants of God*" [Hebrew], *Da'at* 50 (2003): 115; Elisha Russ-Fishbane, *Judaism, Sufism, and the Pietists of Medieval Egypt: A Study of Abraham Maimonides and His Times* (Oxford: Oxford University Press, 2015), 210.

4 See Sarah Stroumsa, *Maimonides in His World: Portrait of a Mediterranean Thinker* (Princeton: Princeton University Press, 2009), 7; Joel Kraemer, *Maimonides: The Life and World of One of Civilization's Greatest Minds* (New York: Doubleday, 2008), 11–12.

5 Al-Fārābī lived in Baghdad, Aleppo, and Damascus; Avicenna lived in Iran. See Stroumsa, *Maimonides in His World*, 16.

6 The Aristotelian metaphysics of this tradition had been influenced by Neoplatonism through an Arabic paraphrase of Plotinus' *Enneads*—known as the *Theology of Aristotle*—and Proclus' *Elements of Theology*, as well as other Neoplatonic material. Thus scholars sometimes talk about Neoaristotelianism, or Neoplatonic Aristotelianism. See Alfred Ivry, *Maimonides'* Guide of the Perplexed*: A Philosophical Guide* (Chicago: University of Chicago Press, 2016), 38; idem, "Neoplatonic Currents in Maimonides' Thought," in *Perspectives on Maimonides*, ed. Joel Kraemer (London: Littman, 1996), 115–140; Kraemer, "Maimonides and the Spanish Aristotelian School," 45, citing Philip Merlan, *Monopsychism, Mysticism, Metaconsciousness: Problems of the Soul in the Neoaristotelian and Neoplatonic Tradition* (The Hague: M. Nijhoff, 1969).

7 Kraemer, "Maimonides and the Spanish Aristotelian School," 45.

8 Stroumsa, *Maimonides in His World*, 15.

9 See *Iggerot ha-Rambam*, 552–54.

10 See *Guide* II:9, p. 268; Stroumsa, *Maimonides in His World*, 14–15; Kraemer, "Maimonides and the Spanish Aristotelian School," 51.

11 Elisha Russ-Fishbane, *Between Politics and Piety: Abraham Maimonides and his Times* (PhD dissertation, Harvard University, 2009), 122.

12 The one other rare exception we know of was Abraham's father-in-law, R. Ḥananel ben Samuel, who develops Maimonidean philosophical interpretations of doctrines such as providence and prophecy. It is striking that R. Ḥananel devotes an extensive passage to the hierarchy of separate intellects, which he interprets in line with Avicenna's distinction between necessary and contingent existence. R. Ḥananel's philosophical views were colored by Avicennian and Sufi-influenced thought, the dominant Egyptian intellectual trend. Nevertheless, he expresses caution on the dangers of studying philosophy which can lead to the denial of the createdness of the world, God's providence, and God's knowledge of particulars. See Paul

Fenton, "A Re-Discovered Description of Maimonides by a Contemporary," *Maimonidean Studies* 6 (2008): 279-81; idem, "Maimonides—Father and Son: Continuity and Change," in *Traditions of Maimonideanism*, ed. C. Fraenkel (Leiden: Brill, 2009), 132; idem, "More on R. Ḥananel b. Samuel the Judge, Leader of the Pietists" [Hebrew], *Tarbiz* 55 (1986): 80–95, 99–101, 103–04; idem, "A Judeo-Arabic Commentary on the Haftarot by Ḥananel ben Shemu'el, Abraham Maimonides' Father-in-Law," *Maimonidean Studies* 1 (1990): 32, 39–48; Russ-Fishbane, *Between Politics and Piety*, 120; S. D. Goitein, "R. Ḥananel the Chief Judge, Son of Samuel he-Nagid, Father-in-Law of Maimonides" [Hebrew], *Tarbiz* 50 (1981): 371–95. As noted, Abraham Maimonides himself also cautions about the danger of philosophy. See above, note 3, and below, chapter 4.

13 See Paul Fenton, "Some Judaeo-Arabic Fragments by Rabbi Abraham he-Ḥasid, the Jewish Sufi," *Journal of Semitic Studies* 26, no. 1 (Spring 1981): 48; idem, "A Judeo-Arabic Commentary on the Haftarot," 28.

14 *The Complete [Guide] for the Servants [of God] (Kitāb kifāyat al-ʿābidīn)*, published in part by Samuel Rosenblatt as *The High Ways to Perfection of Abraham Maimonides* (Baltimore: Johns Hopkins Press), II:290 (hereafter, *High Ways*). On the basis of a genealogical list discovered in the Cairo Genizah, S. D. Goitein hypothesized that Abraham's mother's side of the family came from a long line of Egyptian pietists. In the genealogical list, many of the names of Abraham's maternal family were followed by the epithet "pious" (*ḥasid*). Goitein deduced that Abraham had been exposed to pietism from his mother's side of the family. Mordechai Akiva Friedman accepted this hypothesis. However, Paul Fenton and Elisha Russ-Fishbane have shown that the scribe who wrote this fragment was active at the end of the thirteenth century and that in an original more minimal list, the term *ḥasid*, which appears only once, "was a mere honorific for a pious individual and not a mark of affiliation with the movement that, at the time, was still in its infancy." See Russ-Fishbane, *Judaism, Sufism, and the Pietists of Medieval Egypt*, 51; Mordechai Akiva Friedman, "Two Maimonidean Documents: A Letter from Maimonides to the Sage, R. Samuel, and an Epistle of Congratulations to Maimonides on the Occasion of His Wedding" [Hebrew], in *Me'ah She'arim: Studies in Medieval Jewish Spiritual Life, in Memory of Isadore Twersky*, ed. E. Fleischer et al. (Jerusalem: Magnes, 2001): 206.

15 While Moses Maimonides had also absorbed Sufi vocabulary, which he knew through Avicenna, the elder Maimonides gave this Sufi vocabulary a distinct flavor of Aristotelian intellectualism. See Steven Harvey, "The Meaning of Terms Designating Love," 193, and notes 85–86; 195–96. Compare David Blumenthal, *Philosophic Mysticism: Essays in Rational Religion*, ch. 3 (Ramat Gan: Bar-Ilan University Press, 2006).

16 Abraham's father-in-law R. Ḥananel seems to have made his own integration of these trends.

17 What has come down to us of this commentary is one manuscript of Abraham's commentary to Genesis and Exodus. The Judeo-Arabic text and a Hebrew translation was published by E. Y. Wiesenberg: Abraham Maimonides, *Perush ʿal Bereshit u-Shmot,* ed. and trans. E. Y. Wiesenberg (London: Rabbi S. D. Sassoon, 1959). A new Hebrew translation of Abraham Maimonides' commentary on Genesis was recently published by Moshe Maimon (New York, 2020).

18 Russ-Fishbane, *Judaism, Sufism, and the Pietists of Medieval Egypt*, 54. For the concept of philosophical mysticism, see David Blumenthal, *Philosophic Mysticism: Studies in Rational Religion* (Ramat Gan: Bar-Ilan University Press, 2007); Gideon Freudenthal, "The Philosophical Mysticism of Maimonides" [Hebrew], *Daʿat* 64–66 (2009): 77–97.

19 Russ-Fishbane, *Between Politics and Piety*, 122ff; idem, *Judaism, Sufism, and the Pietists*, 211.

20 See Shlomo Pines, "The Philosophic Purport of Maimonides' Halachic Works," in *Maimonides and Philosophy*, ed. S. Pines and Y. Yovel (Dordrecht, the Netherlands: M. Nijhoff, 1986): 1–14.

21 See Tzvi Langermann, "The 'True Perplexity': The *Guide*, Part II, Chapter 24," in *Perspectives on Maimonides,* ed. Joel Kraemer (London: Littman, 1996): 159–174; Joel Kraemer, "Maimonides and the Spanish Aristotelian School," 50–54; as well as the issue of *Aleph* devoted to this subject, *Aleph* 8 (2008).

22 See Daniel Davies, *Method and Metaphysics in Maimonides' Guide for the Perplexed* (New York: Oxford University Press, 2011); Yair Lorberbaum, "On Contradictions, Rationality, Dialectics, and Esotericism in Maimonides' *Guide of the Perplexed,*" *The Review of Metaphysics* 55 (June 2002); Kraemer, "Maimonides and the Spanish Aristotelian School," 52–54.

23 See *Guide* I:32, p.75; *Guide* III:619, p. 619; and Steven Harvey, "The Meaning of Terms Designating Love in Judaeo-Arabic Thought and Some Remarks on the Judaeo-Arabic Interpretation of Maimonides," in *Proceedings of the Founding Conference of the Society for Judaeo-Arabic Studies*, ed. N. Golb (Amsterdam: Harwood Academic Publishers, 1997): 193–94.

24 On Maimonides' conception of receptivity to intellectual guidance from the Active Intellect, see below, chapter 5; cf. Diana Lobel, *Philosophies of Happiness: A Comparative Introduction to the Flourishing Life* (New York: Columbia University Press, 2017), 172–73.

Notes to Chapter 1

1 Nahem Ilan, "Between Mount Sinai and the Cleft of the Rock: Moses as the Ultimate Sufi in Rabbi Abraham Maimuni's Torah Commentary" [Hebrew], in *Studies in Judaeo-Arabic Culture, Proceedings of the Fourteenth Congress of the Society for Medieval Judaeo-Arabic Culture*, ed. Yoram Erder et al. (Tel Aviv: Tel Aviv University, 2014), 136; Russ-Fishbane, *Judaism, Sufism, and the Pietists of Medieval Egypt*, 230. Russ-Fishbane points out that the view that the experience at Mount Sinai is internal is present in Abraham he-Ḥasid as well.

1 On the verbal noun *khuṭūr*, see E. W. Lane, *Arabic-English Lexicon* (Cambridge: Islamic Texts Society, 1984), 764. See also *High Ways*, I:148; on *khāṭir* as mind, see ibid., I:140, II:30. I thank Eli Shaubi for the references from the *High Ways*.

2 The term *lamḥ* occurs in Saadya's commentary to *Sefer Yetsirah* I:4 (II:1). Saadya describes the generation of the universe in this way: "They [the ten infinite *sefirot*] flash like a flash (*yalmaḥu . . . ka-lamḥ*)." Warren Zev Harvey brings evidence that the Arabic editor of Ibn Gabirol's poem *Ahavtikha* ("I have loved you") writes that the poem is "an answer to one who asked him about the flash (*lamḥ*) of generation (*al-kawn*)," alluding to Saadya's comment on *Sefer Yetsirah*. See Saadya Gaon, *Commentary to Sefer Yetsirah*, ed. and trans. J. Qafiḥ (Jerusalem: American Academy for Jewish Research, 1972), 67; Warren Zev Harvey, "Philosophy and Poetry in Ibn Gabirol" [Spanish], *Anuario Filosófico* 33 (2000): 491–504; English translation in *Solomon Ibn Gabirol: Sources, Doctrines, and Influence on Medieval Philosophy*, ed. N. Polloni, M. Benedetto, and F. Dal Bo, forthcoming, 2020.

3 Or: "The first is more likely from the point of view of linguistic expression while the second is more likely from the point of view of meaning." Lane explains the distinction between *lafẓ* and *ma'na* as follows: "with respect to the word, or words, or wording, and the meaning; and with respect to the actual order of the words, and the order of the sense." Lane, *Arabic-English Lexicon*, 2667. On this distinction, see also Ilan, "Between Mount Sinai and the Cleft of the Rock," 142, note 42. Blau explains the root *q-r-b* as "to be likely." See Joshua Blau, *A Dictionary of Mediaeval Judaeo-Arabic Texts* (Jerusalem: Academy of the Hebrew Language, 2006), 537.

4 On the identity of the "requestor" as Moses, see Ilan, "Between Mount Sinai and the Cleft of the Rock," 142, note 43.

5 Abraham Maimonides, *Perush*, ed. Wiesenberg, 471–73.

6 We should note that Maimonides himself ascribes the concept of created light to the Aramaic translation of Onqelos; he never cites Saadya by name, and may have wanted to appeal to the Tannaitic (early rabbinic) authority ascribed to Onqelos, or seen Onqelos as Saadya's source. This is in keeping with the fact that Maimonides cites no medieval Jewish sources

in the *Guide*. Onqelos appears as a character in the *Guide*, one to whom Maimonides describes sophisticated philosophical positions, such as denial of knowledge of the separate intellects in *Guide* I:37 (see below, chapter 5). See Howard Kreisel, *Prophecy: The History of an Idea in Jewish Philosophy* (Amsterdam: Springer Netherlands, 2003), 214; Menachem Kellner, *Maimonides' Confrontation with Mysticism* (Oxford: Littman, 2006), 193. I thank Eli Shaubi for pointing out that Abraham Maimonides may have been thinking of Onqelos here, and Zev Harvey for noting that Onqelos is a stand-in for philosophical positions.

7 *Daniel, with the Translation and Interpretation of Rabenu Se'adyah Gaon*, ed. and trans. J. Qafiḥ (Jerusalem, 1980–81), 133–38.

8 Saadya Gaon, *Kitāb al-amānāt wa'l-i'tiqādāt* II:12, trans. J. Qafiḥ (Jerusalem: Sura Institute for Research and Publication, 1970), 110–11; English translation, *Book of Beliefs and Opinions,* trans. Samuel Rosenblatt (New Haven: Yale University Press, 1948), 130–31. Alexander Altmann explains that Saadya developed the notions of created light and created word against the background of both Mu'tazilite and rabbinic conceptions. The Mu'tazilites were wont to explain visions of God in metaphorical terms. While Saadya uses the Mu'tazilite method of allegorical explanation (*ta'wīl*) with respect to other Biblical anthropomorphisms, he generally refrains from doing so with respect to prophetic visions of God. Altmann argues that he developed the notion of the created glory from the realm of rabbinic *merkavah* mysticism, while the notion of the created word arises from the rabbinic concept of the *memra*. In the *Book of Doctrines and Beliefs*, he separates the two notions while in his commentary to *Sefer Yetsirah* he brings the two together. See Alexander Altmann, "Saadya's Theory of Revelation: Its Origin and Background," in his *Studies in Religious Philosophy and Mysticism* (Ithaca: Cornell University Press, 1969), 157–60.

For *Shekhinah* as light in rabbinic sources, see Elliot Wolfson, *Through a Speculum That Shines: Vision and Imagination in Medieval Jewish Mysticism* (Princeton: Princeton University Press, 1994), 43–44. For the glory and visionary experiences in other pre-Kabbalistic sources, see ibid., 125–87. For light in Kabbalistic sources, see Moshe Idel, *Kabbalah: New Perspectives* (New Haven: Yale University Press, 1988), 67, 83, 316–17, note 80; idem, *Studies in Ecstatic Kabbalah* (Albany: State University of New York Press, 1988), 111.

9 See, for example, Abraham Maimonides, *Perush,* ed. Wiesenberg, 383 (to Exodus 24:11) and 422 (to Exodus 28:17); cf. Ezra Labaton, *A Comprehensive Analysis of Rabenu Abraham Maimuni's Biblical Commentary* (PhD dissertation, Brandeis University, 2012), 263, where he translates *ma'na* as "the general context." In his comment to Exodus 28:17, Abraham mentions that Saadya explains the term *milleta* in accordance with context, but not with language. For Saadya's exegetical method, see Haggai Ben-Shammai,

"The Tension between Literal Interpretation and Exegetical Freedom: Comparative Observations on Saadia's Method," in *With Reverence for the Word: Medieval Scriptural Exegesis in Judaism, Christianity, and Islam*, ed. Jane Dammen McAuliffe, Barry D. Walfish, and Joseph W. Goering (New York: Oxford University Press, 2003), 33–44.

10 *High Ways*, II:382. The title of Abraham Maimonides' Compendium can be translated approximately as *The Complete [Guide] for the Servants [of God]* (*Kitāb kifāyat al-ʿābidīn*). S. D. Goitein notes that a Muslim contemporary of Abraham Maimonides in Egypt (ʿAbd al-ʿAẓīm al-Mundhirī) wrote a book with an almost identical title: *Kifāyat al-mutaʿabbid wa-tuḥfat al-matazahhid* (*Complete [Guide] for the Pious Servant of God and a Present for the Ascetic*). The word *Kifāya* literally means "sufficient," so one could also translate: *The Sufficient [Manual] for the Servants [of God]*. See S. D. Goitein, "Abraham Maimonides and his Pietist Circle," in *Jewish Medieval and Renaissance Studies*, ed. Alexander Altmann (Cambridge: Harvard University Press, 1967), 146. The term *wujūd* is a philosophical term for existence. It also has Sufi overtones of ecstatic existence, related to the Sufi use of the term *wajd* for ecstasy, finding. Thus, Michael Sells suggests in various contexts the phrases "ecstatic existentiality, found existentiality, founded existentiality." It is not clear whether these overtones of the root *w-j-d* are suggested here. See Michael Sells, trans. and ed., *Early Islamic Mysticism* (New York: Paulist Press, 1996), 68, 252–54.

11 *High Ways*, 382; see *Guide* III:51, p. 621; and Russ-Fishbane, *Judaism, Sufism, and the Pietists of Medieval Egypt*, 210, who draws attention to this passage and parallel.

12 *High Ways*, II:382. Paul Fenton has published fragments discovered in the Cairo Genizah of the missing chapter on *wuṣūl*. For the concept and term of *wuṣūl*, see Fenton, "The Doctrine of Attachment," especially 108–13. Abraham Maimonides' doctrine of prophetic attainment (*wuṣūl*) requires a separate study. For a rich and illuminating recent treatment, see Eli Shaubi, *R. Abraham Maimonides: The Process of Attaining Prophecy* (Master's Thesis, Hebrew University of Jerusalem, 2019). For Abraham Maimonides' teachings on prophetic attainment in relation to his father's conception of human perfection, see Russ-Fishbane, *Judaism, Sufism, and the Pietists of Medieval Egypt*, 189–96. See also below, chapter 4.

13 *Guide* III:51, p. 621 (with emendations). For the influence of Avicenna on Maimonides' depiction of intellectual prayer in *Guide* III:51, see Steven Harvey, "Avicenna and Maimonides on Prayer and Intellectual Worship," in *Exchange and Transmission across Cultural Boundaries: Philosophy, Mysticism, and Science in the Mediterranean World*, ed. H. Ben-Shammai, S. Shaked, S. Stroumsa (Jerusalem: Israel Academy of Sciences and Humanities, 2013), 82–105.

14 For Abraham Maimonides' one mention of "Active Intellects" (in the plural), see below, XX, note XX.

15 *Haqdamot ha-Rambam la-Mishnah,* ed. I. Shailat (Jerusalem: Ma'aliyot, 1992), 366 [Arabic], 136 [Hebrew].

16 *High Ways*, II:374–76.

17 Ibid., II:378.

18 Ibid., II:310; Russ-Fishbane, *Politics and Piety*, 117, note 69. The language of contemplating "intelligibles" is found in Avicenna and al-Ghazālī. Alexander Treiger, *Inspired Knowledge in Islamic Thought: al-Ghazālī's Theory of Mystical Cognition and Its Avicennian Foundation* (London: Routledge, 2012), 62.

19 This alludes to Maimonides' discussion in *Guide* I:1–2 and III:51, and *Hilkhot Yesodei ha-Torah* 4:8–9.

20 *High Ways*, II:224–26.

21 For *Hilkhot Yesodei ha-Torah* 7:1, see below, section 3b; for *Guide* II:12 and III:52, see below, chapter 2.

22 Russ-Fishbane, *Judaism, Sufism, and the Pietists of Medieval Egypt,* 207.

23 See Suhrawardī, *The Philosophy of Illumination*, ed. and trans. John Waldridge and Hossein Ziai (Provo: Brigham Young University Press, 1999), 159–60 (section 5:9). Ibn Ṭufayl, a twelfth-century Andalusian thinker, quotes both Ibn Bājja and Avicenna in their descriptions of spiritual ascent. As Shlomo Pines noted, the famous passage by Avicenna, cited by Ibn Ṭufayl, may have been in Maimonides' mind when, in the Introduction to the *Guide*, he describes the experience of lightning flashes. Avicenna, describing the [Sufi] "knower [of God]" writes, "Then, when by will and discipline one is carried to a limit where he catches delightful glimpses of the Truth, strokes of lightning as it were, would no sooner flash than they disappear. . . . Now, if he persists in his disciplinary practice, these static glimpses multiply. . . . Every time he glances (*lamaḥa*) at a thing, he turns toward the side of sanctity, and remembers something of that." Avicenna, *Kitāb al-ishārāt wa-l-tanbīhāt*, ed. J. Forget (Leiden: Brill, 1892), 202–03, cited by Ibn Ṭufayl, *Ḥayy ben Yaqdhān: Roman Philosophique d'Ibn Thofaïl*, ed. L. Gauthier (Beirut: Imprimerie Catholique, 1936), 17–18; English translations, *Ibn Ṭufayl's Ḥayy ibn Yaqẓān*, ed. L. Goodman (Los Angeles: Gee Tee Bee, 1983), 96; trans. George Atiyeb in *Medieval Political Philosophy*, ed. R. Lerner and M. Mahdi (Ithaca: Cornell University Press, 1963), 136–37. Pines, "Translator's Introduction" to the *Guide of the Perplexed*, ci and note 72.

24 Ghazali, *Mishkāt al-anwār*, trans. by David Buchman (Provo: Brigham Young University Press, 1998), 3, 20. The phrase "the light of lights" can be found in the *Theology of Aristotle*, ed. F. Dieterici (Leipzig, 1882), 44 and 118. See Herbert Davidson, *al-Fārābī, Avicenna, and Averroes, on Intellect* (New York: Oxford University Press, 1992), 132 and note 27.

25 Kristin Zahra Sands, *Sufi Commentaries on the Qur'ān in Classical Islam* (New York: Routeledge, 2006), 135, citing Toshihiko Izutsu, *Creation and the Timeless Order of Things* (Ashland: Whitecloud Press, 1994).

26 See Joav Avtalion, *A Comparative Study: Abraham Maimonides' Kitāb Kifāyat al-'Ābidīn and Abū Hāmid Muhammad al-Ghazālī's Ihyā 'Ulūm al-Dīn* [Hebrew] (PhD dissertation, Bar-Ilan University, 2010); Aviva Schussman, "The Question of the Islamic Sources of Abraham Maimonides' *Compendium for the Servants of God*" (Hebrew), *Tarbiz* 55 (1986): 229–51. Maimonides, too, has clearly read al-Ghazālī. See Steven Harvey, "Al-Ghazālī and Maimonides and Their Books of Knowledge," in *Be'erot Yitzhak: Studies in Memory of Isadore Twersky*, ed. J. Harris (Cambridge, MA: Harvard University Press, 2005), 99–117; Amira Eran, "Al-Ghazālī and Maimonides on The World To Come and Spiritual Pleasures," *Jewish Studies Quarterly* 8 (2001): 138–66. Scott Girdner has also shown striking parallels between al-Ghazālī's *Mishkāt al-Anwār* and Maimonides' *Shemonah Peraqim*. See Scott Girdner, "Ghazali's Hermeneutics and Their Reception in Jewish Tradition: *Mishkāt al-Anwār* (The Niche of Lights) and Maimonides' *Shemonah Peraqim* (Eight Chapters)," in *Islam and Rationality: The Impact of al-Ghazālī*, ed. Georges Tamer (Leiden: Brill, 2015), vol. 1, 253–74.

27 Ghazālī, *Mishkāt*, 27. Scholars such as Herbert Davidson and Alexander Treiger have argued that al-Ghazālī does not reject the existence of separate intellects and the Active Intellect. However, like Abraham Maimonides, al-Ghazālī prefers traditional language of angels when describing the celestial hierarchy. See Davidson, *al-Fārābī, Avicenna, and Averroes*, 132–37, 151–52; Treiger, *Inspired Knowledge in Islamic Thought*, 105–07. For Abraham Maimonides, see *High Ways*, II:58–59 (cf. II:72). In this one passage, Abraham Maimonides does describe the angels as mediums of prophecy: "know that the testimonies of the intellect and the proofs of Scripture have already established the fact that the most perfect of existing things that God, exalted be He, has created, are the angels, and the utmost that anyone other than them can attain (*al-wuṣūl*) is to reach something of their perfection . . . [As for] the prophets, their perfection and attainment (*kamāluhum wa-wuṣūluhum*) is also through them (*bi-wasāṭatihim*), as is proven by the statements of the Torah and the prophets. . . ." However, Abraham Maimonides omits the explicit language identifying the angels with the separate intellects described by the Arabic Aristotelians, an identification made by his father.

Scholars have also debated whether al-Ghazālī accepts the Neoplatonic scheme of emanation. As Lazarus-Yafeh has noted, when al-Ghazālī uses the language of emanation (here, the verb *fāḍa*), it is "only in relation to God's incessantly flowing grace. Man must be ready for the absorption and assimilation of the light of divine grace and concentration of the mind on God, and must be in a perpetual state of anticipation. Then he may be worthy of the divine light, which will light up his heart, as it lit up the hearts of the prophets and the saints." Hava Lazarus-Yafeh, "Symbolism of Light in Al-Ghazzali's Writing," in *Studies in Al-Ghazzali* (Jerusalem: Magnes, 1975), 312. Like al-Ghazālī, Abraham uses the verb *fāḍa* and the noun *fayḍ* to describe an overflowing grace from the divine, which is not necessarily intellectual. He does not use the term *fayḍ* in the technical sense of creation of the world through emanation.

28 Al-Ghazālī, *Iḥyā' ʿulūm al-dīn* (Cairo, 1937–39), vol. 2, book 21, 1370 (*bayān* 8); English translation, "The Book of the Marvels of the Heart," trans. R. J. McCarthy, in al-Ghazālī, *Deliverance from Error: An Annotated Translation of* al-Munqidh min al-Ḍalāl *and Other Relevant Works of al-Ghazālī* (Lousiville, KY: Fons Vitae, 2000), 322.

29 Al-Ghazālī, *Iḥyā' ʿulūm al-dīn*, vol. 2, book 21, 1371 (*bayān* 8); English translation, *Deliverance from Error*, 323–24. I have made one minor emendation, in accordance with the recommendations of Scott Girdner and Yonatan Negev. I thank both for their help in explicating the text.

30 The prooftext of Psalm 36:10 (*be-orekha nir'eh-or*) presents a challenge to the translator. At times it seems appropriate to translate "through your light, we see light." At other times, the translation "in your light, we see light" seems to more appropriately convey the sense of being within the presence of God's light. For the sake of consistency, I have chosen to translate "through your light, we see light" throughout.

31 *High Ways*, II:338. Similarly, he writes that the lights of God's overflow shine upon his prophets and friends (*ashraqat anwār fayḍihi ʿalā anbiyā'ihi wa-awliyā'ihi*), ibid., II:60.

32 He writes: "His special way [consists] in his reflecting on this in a detailed manner, and that there comes to his mind what the first one thinks of. And there is added to that that he reflects upon (*iʿtabara*) the totalities of existence, and what he is able to reflect upon of its particulars, from the center of the earth up to the circumference of the highest [celestial] sphere. And he reflects upon His wisdom, exalted be He, in this existence and details in his thoughts what was created on the first day, on the second, and on every one of the rest of the six days, according to what can be understood from the portion of Genesis." Ibid., I:140.

33 Ibid., I:142. I have emended the translation, following some of Russ-Fishbane's emendations in *Politics and Piety*, 168.

34 Baḥya Ibn Paqūda and al-Ghazālī drew upon a common source, Pseudo-Jāḥiẓ, in carrying out teleological proofs from the wisdom of creation to the existence of a creator. See David H. Baneth, "The Common Teleological Source of Baḥya Ibn Paqūda and al-Ghazālī" [Hebrew], in *Sefer Magnes*, ed. F. Baer et al. (Jerusalem, 1938); Diana Lobel, *A Sufi-Jewish Dialogue: Philosophy and Mysticism in Baḥya Ibn Paqūda's* Duties of the Heart (Philadelphia: University of Pennsylvania Press, 2007), 119–40; Warren

Zev Harvey, "Averroes and Maimonides on the Obligation of Philosophic Contemplation (*I'tibār*)," *Tarbiz* 58, no. 1 (1988): 75–83.

35 Baḥya Ibn Paqūda, *Kitāb al-hidāya ilā farā'iḍ al-qulūb* (*Torat ḥovot ha-levavot*) X:1, ed. and trans. J. Qafiḥ (Jerusalem, 1973), 410; English translation, *Book of Direction to the Duties of the Heart*, trans. Menahem Mansoor (London: Routledge and Kegan Paul, 1973), 427.

36 *High Ways*, II:418. I have made use of Shaubi's translation. See Shaubi, *R. Abraham Maimonides*, 42. Halevi expresses this sentiment in quite similar language in *Kuzari* III:1 regarding the servant of God, "He who would love to be at the level of Enoch, of whom it was said that 'Enoch walked [with God] (Genesis 5:24),' or at the level of Elijah (2 Kings 2:11), to be free enough to seclude himself for the company of the angels, for he would not feel lonely in solitude and seclusion (*khalwa*). On the contrary, they would be his companions (*uns*), while in the crowd he would feel lonely (*yastawḥish*) due to his being deprived of witnessing the kingdom of Heaven." *Kuzari* III:1; published as Judah Halevi, *Kitāb al-radd wa'l-dalīl fi'l-dīn al-dhalīl* (*al-Kitāb al-Khazarī*), ed. D. Baneth and H. Ben-Shammai (Jerusalem: Magnes, 1977), 90. Subsequent citations give page number in this edition, as well as part and paragraph. Translations are my own. Published translations, *Sefer ha-Kuzari: Maqor ve-targum*, trans. J. Qafiḥ (Jerusalem: Kiryat Ono, 1996–97), 90; and *The Kuzari*, trans. H. Hirschfeld (New York: Shocken, 1964), 135. Halevi goes on to argue that ascetics in his contemporary age, unlike these ancient prophets and sages, do not make contact with the divine light, which would offer them the intimate fellowship it did the sages of old (*Kuzari* III:1, p. 91; ed. Qafiḥ, 91; ed. Hirschfeld, 136); see Diana Lobel, *Between Mysticism and Philosophy: Sufi Language of Religious Experience in Judah Ha-Levi's* Kuzari (Albany: State University of New York Press, 2000), 157.

37 *High Ways*, II:418.

38 Abraham Maimonides, *Perush*, ed. Wiesenberg, 307.

39 Shaubi, *R. Abraham Maimonides*, 44, note 181.

40 We return to this point in greater detail below in Chapter 4.

41 *Guide* III:51, p. 626.

42 *High Ways*, II:158.

43 See Russ-Fishbane, *Politics and Piety*, 126 and note 103. On the term *qurb*, see al-Qushayrī, *Al-Risāla al-Qushayrīya fī 'ilm al-taṣawwuf*, ed. M. al-Mar'ashalī (Beirut, 1998), 145–48; English translation in *Early Islamic Mysticism*, trans. and ed. Michael Sells (New York: Paulist Press, 1996), 137–41.

44 See Baḥya Ibn Paqūda, *Torat ḥovot ha-levavot* VIII:3 (Tenth Way), ed. Qafiḥ, 347–348; ed. Mansoor, 369; cf. Lobel, *A Sufi-Jewish Dialogue*, 230. Note that for Maimonides, too, God's providence does engender a response of passionate love.

45 One unpublished Geniza fragment speaks of the ascent of souls from vegetable to animal to human soul, and then to the "Active Intellects, which are the root of the souls and source of the sciences and virtues, and which are near to their Lord." RNL Yevr.-Arab. I.2926, ll. 3–8; see Fenton, "The Doctrine of Attachment," 118; Russ-Fishbane, *Judaism, Sufism, and the Pietists of Medieval Egypt*, 216. Fenton identified this fragment as belonging to the lost final chapter of the *Kifāya*. However, there are several anomalies in the terminology of this passage that might cast doubt upon this attribution to Abraham Maimonides' *Kifāya*—among them, the anomalous phrase "Active Intellects." In the firmly attested works of Abraham Maimonides, we never find the term "Active Intellect" (either in the singular or the plural). He certainly does not make use of the concept of Active Intellect in the way that al-Fārābī, Avicenna, and Maimonides do.

There is one passage in Abraham's treatise *Milḥamot ha-Shem* that speaks of a union of the human intellect with the Active Intellect, but this appears to be a later addition to the text; it does not appear in the manuscript versions of the treatise. See Abraham Maimonides, *Milḥamot ha-Shem*, ed. R. Margaliot (Jerusalem: Mossad Ha-Rav Kook, 1953), 66 and Margaliot's note, 8, note 6; cf. Russ-Fishbane, *Judaism, Sufism, and the Pietists of Medieval Egypt*, 192 and note 26.

46 For example, in a comment to Exodus 34:5, where the Lord descended in the cloud, and "stood with him there [and proclaimed the name of the Lord]," Abraham writes: "A borrowing [or: allusion] and expression for the notion of attainment and intellectual apprehension (*al-wuṣūl wa'l-idrāk al-'aqlī*), similar to 'mouth to mouth' (Numbers 12:8) and 'face to face' (Exodus 33:11), and similar [expressions]."

47 See Russ-Fishbane, *Politics and Piety*, 122.

48 See *Guide* III:54, p. 635; *Hilkhot Teshuvah* 8:2–3.

49 For a contrast between intellectual and holistic modes of spirituality among medieval Jewish thinkers, see Daniel J. Lasker, "Modes of Spirituality in Medieval Jewish Philosophy," in *Jewish Spirituality and Divine Law*, ed. A. Mintz and L. Schiffman (New York: Yeshiva University Press, 2005): 163–85.

50 *Kuzari* IV:16–17, pp. 168–69; ed. Qafiḥ, 169–70; ed. Hirschfeld, 223. For an extended discussion, see Eliezer Schweid, *Ṭa'am ve-haqashah* (Ramat Gan: Bar-Ilan University Press, 1970).

51 Al-Ghazālī, *Iḥyā' 'ulūm al-dīn*, vol. 2, book 21, 1370 (*bayān* 8); English translation, *Deliverance from Error*, 322.

52 Al-Ghazālī, *al-Munqidh min al-ḍalāl*, ed. J. Saliba and K. 'Ayyad (Beirut, 1967), 101; English translation, *Deliverance from Error*, 78.

53 Ghazālī, *Mishkāt*, 37–38.

54 For recent studies, see, for example, Binyamin Abrahamov, "Al-Ghazālī's Supreme Way To Know God," *Studia Islamica* 77 (1993): 141–68; idem,

"Al-Ghazālī and the Rationalization of Sufism," in *Islam and Rationality: The Impact of al-Ghazālī*, vol. 1, ed. Georges Tamer (Leiden: Brill, 2015): 35–48; Scott Girdner, *Reasoning with Revelation: The Significance of the Qur'ānic Contextualization of Philosophy in al-Ghazālī's* Mishkāt al-Anwār (*The Niche of Lights*) (PhD dissertation, Boston University, 2009).

55 See Treiger, *Inspired Knowledge in Islamic Thought*, 50.

56 See William James, *Varieties of Religious Experience* (New York: Penguin, 1982), 380.

57 Ghazālī, *Mishkāt*, 37.

58 See Treiger, *Inspired Knowledge in Islamic Thought*, 63. In a harmonizing position, Ibn Ṭufayl suggests that syllogistic learning is an important preparatory stage to direct witness and taste:

I myself would not have [attained] the truth that I arrived at: the culmination of my intellectual efforts, without pursuing the words (arguments) of al-Ghazālī and Avicenna, checking them against one another … until finally I was able to see the truth for myself, first by way of research and speculation and now in the taste (*dhawq*) that comes in witness (*mushāhada*). (Ibn Ṭufayl, *Ḥayy ben Yaqdhān*, ed. Gauthier, 18, trans. Goodman, 102, trans. Atiyeb, 142)

Ibn Ṭufayl speaks of the experience of *dhawq* as taking place through what can only metaphorically be called a faculty. Ibn Ṭufayl, *Ḥayy ben Yaqdhān*, ed. Gauthier, 17, trans. Goodman, 96, trans. Atiyeb, 136.

59 See *Guide* II:38, pp. 376–77; Kreisel, *Prophecy*, 255–57; idem, *Judaism as Philosophy: Studies in Maimonides and the Medieval Jewish Philosophers of Provence* (Brighton, MA: Academic Studies Press, 2015), 275–78 and note 15; Binyamin Abrahamov, "Maimonides and Ibn Sīnā's Theory of *Ḥads*: A Re-Examination of the *Guide of the Perplexed* II:38," in *Proceedings of the Seventh International Conference of Judaeo-Arabic Studies*, ed. Haggai Ben Shammai, forthcoming. For a somewhat different perspective on *hads*, see Amira Eran, "Intuition and Inspiration: The Causes of Jewish Thinkers' Objection to Avicenna's Intellectual Prophecy (*Ḥads*)," *Jewish Studies Quarterly* 14 (2007): 39–71. In the *Iḥyā'*, after distinguishing between the way of learning and the way of inspiration, al-Ghazālī adds that the way of learning and mastery of the sciences protects one from false imaginings; Maimonides certainly accords with this view. *Iḥyā' 'Ulūm al-Dīn*, vol. 2, book 21, 1373 (*bayān* 8).

60 For *dhawq*, see *Rabbi Avraham ben ha-Rambam: Sefer ha-maspik le-'ovdei Hashem, Kitāb kifāyat al-'ābidīn* (part 2, vol. 2), ed. and trans. N. Dana (Ramat-Gan: Bar-Ilan University Press, 1989), 131, l. 5, 133, l. 13, and 188, note 5; Abraham Maimonides, *Perush*, ed. Wiesenberg, 83 (to Genesis 27:39); Nahem Ilan, "Secrets and their Meaning in R. Abraham Maimuni's Commentary on the Torah" [in Hebrew], *Bein Ever la-Arav* 5 (2012): 86; Fenton, "Dana's Edition of Abraham Maimuni's *Kifāyat al-'ābidīn*,"

Jewish Quarterly Review 82 (1991): 204. For *mushāhada*, see Abraham Maimonides, *Perush*, ed. Wiesenberg, 281–83 (to Exodus 16:9), and below, chapter 3. For other non-discursive ways of knowing, see *High Ways* II:218, ll. 12–13, II:60, ll. 5, and II:404, l. 3; and Russ-Fishbane, *Politics and Piety*, 122 and note 87.

We also find the term *dhawq* in the writings of Abraham he-Ḥasid. See Fenton, "Some Judaeo-Arabic Fragments," 63, note 47. As Russ-Fishbane observes, "in the thought of Abraham the Pious and Ḥanan'el b. Shemu'el, prophecy can come upon one without any intellectual or other preparation, from an unveiling whose source and inspiration are unknown;" Abraham he-Ḥasid speaks of "intuitive perceptions of the heart" (lit., "perceptions of the heart through 'taste,'" *madārik dhawqiya qalbiya*). See ibid., 63, l. 8; Russ-Fishbane, *Politics and Piety*, 121.

61 Abraham Maimonides, *Perush*, ed. Wiesenberg, 471.

62 Fenton tentatively suggests R. Abraham he-Ḥasid as the author of this treatise. See Paul Fenton, "A Mystical Treatise on Prayer and the Spiritual Quest from the Pietist Circle," *Jerusalem Studies in Arabic and Islam* 16 (1993): 141 and 156; English translation, "The Post-Maimonidean Schools of Exegesis in the East: Abraham Maimonides, the Pietists, *Tanḥūma* Yerushalmi and the Yemenite School," *Hebrew Bible / Old Testament*, vol. 1, part 2, ed. Magne Sáebø (Göttingen: Vandenhoeck & Ruprecht, 2000), 446–47. I have made emendations to the translation.

63 See Paul Fenton, "A Pietist Letter from the Geniza," *Hebrew Annual Review* 9 (1985): 161; Russ-Fishbane, *Judaism, Sufism, and the Pietists of Medieval Egypt*, 209.

64 Consider the same puzzle in a passage from Avicenna's *Glosses on the Theology of Aristotle*: "the light will come to it from God most high, a light that diverts it from all other things, and degrades [in its eye] the work of all sensible objects. He becomes joyful and delighted . . . and that joy and light stems from God through the mediation of Intellect; discursive thoughts and analogy cannot lead to [the joy and light] except to confirm it. As for its singular essence and quality, only contemplative witness (*mushāhada*) points to that." See *Arisṭū 'ind al-arab*, ed. A. Badawī (Cairo, 1947), 56.

65 See Paul Fenton, "La Pratique de la Retraite Spirituelle (*khalwa*) chez les Judéo-Soufis d'Egypte," in *Les mystiques Juives, Chrétiennes et Musulmanes dans l'Egypte* médiévale, ed. Giuseppe Cecere et al. (Cairo: Institut français d'archéologie orientale, 2013), 239; Russ-Fishbane, *Judaism, Sufism, and the Pietists of Medieval Egypt*, 116–17. For the Sufi practice, see Annemarie Schimmel, *Mystical Dimensions of Islam* (Chapel Hill: University of North Carolina Press, 1975), 103–05.

66 On this Sufi term for intuitive understanding, which is used by al-Ghazālī, see Sands, "Sufi Commentaries," 82–88.

67 Judeo-Arabic text of this letter together with the Hebrew translation published in E. Strauss-Ashtor, *History of the Jews in Egypt and Syria*

[Hebrew], vol. 3 (Jerusalem: Mossad ha-Rav Kook, 1970), 29. I thank Dr. Miriam Goldstein for her insight into the linguistic structure of this passage. See also translations of Russ-Fishbane, *Judaism, Sufism, and the Pietists of Medieval Egypt*, 116, and Fenton, "A Judeo-Arabic Commentary," 54–55.

68 See Fenton, "More on R. Ḥananel," 80; translation in Russ-Fishbane, *Politics and Piety*, 140.

69 Abraham Maimonides, *Perush*, ed. Wiesenberg, 473.

70 *Guide*, Introduction, 7. See also the passage from Avicenna cited in note 46 above.

71 *Guide* I:54, pp. 124-25.

72 However, we should note Maimonides' language of being "dazzled by [God's] beauty" because of the intensity with which God becomes manifest. For Maimonides, knowledge brings love, awe, and perplexing dazzlement. See *Guide* I:59, p. 139; and the discussion of Lobel, *Philosophies of Happiness*, 184–85. We return to this theme below in our conclusion.

73 *High Ways*, II:412.

74 For more complete exegesis of this passage, see below, chapter 4.

75 See *Guide* I:21, pp. 50–51.

76 See *Guide* II:36, p. 369.

77 Hannah Kasher suggests that this may represent a later stratum of the *Guide*, in which Maimonides chose to include more popular interpretations such as that of the created light for the less philosophically sophisticated reader. See Hannah Kasher, "Is There an Early Stratum of the Guide of the Perplexed?," in *Maimonidean Studies*, vol. 3, ed. Arthur Hyman (New York: Ktav, 1995), 121, 128.

Notes to Chapter 2

1 This view is parallel in some ways to that put forth by Menachem Kellner in *Maimonides' Confrontation with Mysticism*. See Esti Eisenmann, "The Term 'Created Light' in Maimonides' Philosophy" [Hebrew], *Da'at* 55 (200): 45–46; idem, "The Sinaitic Revelation in Maimonides' Thought" [Hebrew], *Iggud*, vol. 1, ed. B. Schwartz, A. Melamud, A. Shemesh (Jerusalem: World Congress of Jewish Studies, 2007–08), 357–67; cf. Kellner, *Maimonides' Confrontation with Mysticism*, 193–94.

2 Many of these passages are adduced by Menachem Kellner for his related thesis.

3 Maimonides, *Commentary on the Mishnah Rabbenu Moshe ben Maimon*, ed. and trans. J. Qafiḥ, 7 volumes (with Judeo-Arabic) (Jerusalem: Mossad Harav Kook, 1963–68), vol. 2, 378; 3 volumes (Hebrew alone) (Jerusalem: Mossad Harav Kook, 1963), vol. 1, 251.

4 *Guide* III:51, p. 628; see Warren Zev Harvey, "'*Ishq, ḥesheq,* and *amor Dei intellectualis*," in *Spinoza and Medieval Jewish Philosophy*, ed. S. Nadler (New York: Cambridge University Press, 2014), 105.
5 Eisenmann, "The Term 'Created Light,'" 47–48.
6 See *Guide*, Introduction, 15.
7 For other citations of this passage, see *Guide* II:41, pp. 385–86 and II:45, p. 399.
8 Cf. Kellner, *Maimonides' Confrontation with Mysticism*, 190.
9 Cf. Kellner, *Maimonides' Confrontation with Mysticism*, 203.
10 *Guide* I:5, p. 29.
11 *Guide* I:5, p. 30.
12 Eisenmann, "The Term 'Created Light,'" 42–44; cf. Kellner, *Maimonides' Confrontation with Mysticism*, 192.
13 Eisenmann, "The Term 'Created Light,'" 46. I thank Dr. Eisenmann for her generous and comprehensive e-mail explanations of how the seventh contradiction functions here; I have chosen to support her exegesis without entering into the details of the contradictions. For recent studies of Maimonides' contradictions and esotericism, see Daniel Davies, *Method and Metaphysics in Maimonides' Guide for the Perplexed* (New York: Oxford University Press, 2011); Sara Klein-Braslavy, "Maimonides and Esotericism," in her *Maimonides as Biblical Interpreter* (Brighton, MA: Academic Studies Press, 2011), 163–220; idem, *King Solomon and Philosophical Esotericism in Maimonides' Thought* [Hebrew] (Jerusalem: Magnes, 1996); Yair Lorberbaum, "On Contradictions, Rationality, Dialectics, and Esotericism in Maimonides' *Guide of the Perplexed*," *The Review of Metaphysics* 55 (June 2002): 711–50; Aviezer Ravitzky, "Maimonides: Esotericism and Educational Philosophy," in *The Cambridge Companion to Maimonides*, ed. Kenneth Seeskin (New York: Cambridge University Press, 2005), 300–23; Kenneth Seeskin, "Appendix: Esotericism and the Limits of Knowledge: A Critique of Strauss," in his *Searching for a Distant God: The Legacy of Maimonides* (New York: Oxford University Press, 2000).
14 This might also be a case of the fifth contradiction. Sensory and external light might be a kind of approximation of intellectual light, a first step toward understanding the abstract concept of intellectual or spiritual illumination.
15 *Guide* III:52, p. 629.
16 Hava Lazarus-Yafeh notes that the Arabic term *fāḍa* (emanate or overflow) originally applied to water, and later was applied by Neoplatonists to light as well. See Lazarus-Yafeh, "Symbolism of Light in Al-Ghazzali's Writing," 307.
17 See al-Fārābī, *Mabādi' ārā' ahl al-madīna al-fāḍila*, published as *al-Fārābī on the Perfect State*, ed. and trans. Richard Walzer (Oxford: Oxford University Press, 1985), 200–02.
18 *Guide* II:12, p. 280.

19 In the passage in *Guide* II:12, it is true that the light is equated with an overflow of intellect, while the overflow of being is equated with life. But Maimonides places the two side by side; there is a close connection in Maimonides between the concepts of light, life, and being in his Neoplatonic influenced conception of overflow or emanation (*fayḍ*). Note also Maimonides' use of the concept of God as the life of the world (*ḥayāt al-ʿālam / ḥei ha-ʿolam*) in *Guide* I:72, which, as Pines has shown, he derived from Saadya's commentary to *Sefer Yetsirah*. Pines writes, "Both Saadya and Maimonides designate God by way of analogy, first as 'the life of the world,' quoting in this connection the verse from Daniel in which He is called, 'the Living One of the World,' and secondly as 'the intellect of the world', a formula in which Maimonides gives an Aristotelian turn by drawing an analogy between the relation of God to the world and the relation of the acquired intellect to man." Shlomo Pines, "Points of Similarity between the Exposition of the Doctrine of the Sefirot in the Sefer Yeẓira and a Text of the Pseudo-Clementine Homilies," *Proceedings of the Israel Academy of Sciences and Humanities* 7, no. 3 (1989): Appendix III, 128.

20 See *Guide* I:1, p. 23. Tzvi Langermann suggests an alternative interpretation to the allegorical approach proposed by Esti Eisenmann and Menachem Kellner to these passages. He suggests that Maimonides may agree with Ibn Ṣaddīq that the light (*ḍaw'*) we see in this world is an accident in bodies, while celestial light (*nūr*) may be of a different nature. Langermann argues that Maimonides may hold the view that the light of the celestial sphere illuminates by a light that is not visible, and that the light we see in this world is a reduced version of that light; he adds that the light shown to prophets is called "created light" because it is created in its descent from the original non-visible light. Langermann argues that Maimonides may accept the view that there exist two forms of light corresponding to two forms of matter (heavenly and earthly) and that their distinction in luminosity corresponds to distance from God—not only metaphysical, but perhaps even spatial. See Tzvi Langermann, "Why is the Discussion of the Equivocal Term 'Light' Missing from the *Guide of the Perplexed*?," in *Masorah le-Yosef*, vol. 9, ed. Yosef Parhi, 329–38.

21 *Guide* I:10, 37.

22 Cf. Eisenmann, "The Term 'Created Light,'" 44.

23 *Guide* I:64, p. 156.

24 *Guide* II:5, p. 260.

25 *Guide* I:64, p. 157.

26 Cf. Kellner, *Maimonides' Confrontation with Mysticism*, 195–96.

27 *Moses Maimonides' Epistle to Yemen*, ed. Abraham S. Halkin, trans. Boaz Cohen (New York: American Academy for Jewish Research, 1952), ix (English), 44 (Arabic); cf. Abraham S. Halkin and David Hartman, *Crisis*

and Leadership: Epistles of Maimonides (Philadelphia: Jewish Publication Society, 1985), 109.

28 Kreisel, *Prophecy*, 207.

29 We have thus also supported Kellner's thesis that for Maimonides, glory and created light are not ontological entities, but rather represent expressions of the magnificence of God in the created world.

Notes to Chapter 3

1 Abraham introduces his discussion with a comment to Exodus 16:7:

> And in the morning you will see the glory of the Lord." According to what I understand, [the glory] is an equivocal term having three meanings. One of them is a word for God's essence, [as in] "show me your glory" (Exodus 33:18). The second is a word for the created light, [as in] "the glory of the Lord appeared in a cloud" (Exodus 16:10). And the third is a word for his miracles, [as in] "[not one of] the people who saw my glory and my signs that I have done in Egypt and in the wilderness" [because in this statement, "signs"] is an explanation/interpretation (*sharḥ*) of "my glory," as can be proved from the intention of the word without inclining to it. And [with respect to the phrase] the "glory of the Lord" here, it is possible that it has the sense of miracle, and it is possible that it has the sense of light, which, as I will explain [further], manifests to them, or [it may have the sense of] both of them. The first is more plausible. What points to this is that he alludes to the quails that fall in the evening by saying, "in the evening . . . ," that is to say, just as he will manifest for you meat in the evening, it is verified for you that he will take you out of Egypt. (Abraham Maimonides, *Perush*, ed. Wiesenberg, 281)

2 Ibid., 281–83.

3 Cf. Russ-Fishbane, *Judaism, Sufism, and the Pietists of Medieval Egypt*, 230.

4 On the term *qurb*, see al-Qushayrī, *Al-Risāla al-Qushairīya fī ʿilm al-taṣawwuf*, ed. M. al-Marʿashalī (Beirut, 1998), 145–48; English translation in *Early Islamic Mysticism*, trans. and ed. Michael Sells (New York: Paulist Press, 1996), 137–41. On the Egyptian Pietists' use of the term *maqām* for the event of standing before God at Mount Sinai, see Bernard Septimus, "*Maʿamad Har Sinai* and Other *Maʿamadot*," in *Shaʿarei Lashon: Studies in Hebrew, Aramaic, and Jewish Languages, presented to Moshe Bar Asher*, ed. A. Maman, S. E. Fassberg, and Y. Breuer (Jerusalem: Bialik Institute, 2007), vol. 1, 178–79.

5 Abraham Maimonides, *Perush*, ed. Wiesenberg, 283.

6 In his Commentary to Exodus 24:11 ("[they saw the God of Israel] and they ate and drank"), Abraham Maimonides cites Abraham he-Ḥasid who writes that at Mount Sinai, the entire community had been engaged in the

state of solitary meditation (*maqām al-khalwa*); when they returned from this spiritual state, they returned to eating and drinking. Thus Abraham he-Ḥasid reads back into the event at Mount Sinai the practice of forty-day solitary mountain retreats engaged in by his contemporary Egyptian Pietist community. See Abraham Maimonides, *Perush*, ed. Wiesenberg, 379; Russ-Fishbane, *Judaism, Sufism, and the Pietists of Medieval Egypt*, 120–21.

7 Compare the Biblical Hebrew verb *ḥ-w-l*, meaning to whirl, whirl about, or fall. In Aramaic and Mishnaic Hebrew, the root *ḥ-w-l* takes on a legal sense of resting upon one as an impending duty, perhaps of hovering over one's head. (See Marcus Jastrow, *A Dictionary of the Targumim, the Talmud Babli and Yerushalmi, and the Midrashic Literature*, 432.) In Arabic, Aramaic, and Mishnaic Hebrew, the sense of falling or resting upon was applied in a legal context. In Arabic, the verb was used to signify that a punishment alighted, or descended; it was due, or was necessitated by the requirements of justice to take effect (Lane, *Arabic-English Lexicon*, 619c). In Jewish law, we find the phrase *en issur ḥal ʿal issur*; one prohibition cannot take effect [fall] upon another. See Diana Lobel, "A Dwelling Place for the Shekhinah," *Jewish Quarterly Review* 90, nos. 1–2 (July–October 1999): 105 and note 12.

8 See Saadya Gaon, *Kitāb al-amānāt wa'l-iʿtiqādāt* II:7, ed. Qafiḥ, 95, ed. Rosenblatt, 109. In his Hebrew translation of this passage, Judah Ibn Tibbon translates *ḥulūl* with the Hebrew *ḥūl*, from the root *ḥ-w-l*. In the *Kuzari* as well, Ibn Tibbon regularly translates derivatives of the Arabic *ḥ-l-l* with Hebrew equivalents from the root *ḥ-w-l*. See *Kuzari*, Hebrew translation of Ibn Tibbon, ed. A. Zifroni (Tel Aviv: Maḥbarot le Sifrut, 1948), I:95 (p. 48), I:103 (p. 57), I:109 (p. 60), II:26 (p. 96), II:54 (p. 112), III:19 (p. 163), III:23 (pp. 170 and 172), III:53 (p. 196), V:14 (p. 303).

9 *Kuzari* II:54, p. 72, ed. Qafiḥ, 73–74, ed. Hirschfeld, 116.

10 *Kuzari* III:17, pp. 104–05, ed. Qafiḥ, 107, ed. Hirschfeld, 153.

11 *Kuzari* I:101, p. 35, ed. Qafiḥ, 35, ed. Hirschfeld, 73. Note Abraham Maimonides' identification of the dwelling (*ḥulūl*) of the *Shekhinah* in the Temple as "the created light" (*al-nūr al-makhlūq*). See *Kifāyat al-ʿĀbidīn*, ed. Dana, 86.

12 *Kuzari* III:19, p. 109, ed. Qafiḥ, 111, ed. Hirschfeld, 158. The term *maḥall* figured prominently in pre-Islamic Arabic love poetry, whose central motif is remembrance of the lost beloved. These odes tell of the beloved's journey away from her lover, focusing on her way-stations, the places of her alighting (*maḥallāt*). Upon return to these resting spots in the desert, which had been the places of the lovers' trysts, the poet meditates on his lost beloved and the secret of their relationship. Halevi absorbed this motif in both his poetry and philosophy. In his Hebrew poetry, the desert encampments that recall the Beloved become Mount Sinai and scenes from Israel's wandering in the wilderness. In the *Kuzari*, he uses the motif and the term *maḥall* to describe both the Jerusalem Temple and a person of the stature of Abraham, Moses,

Elijah, or the Messiah, "for they in themselves are a dwelling place (*maḥall*) of the *Shekhinah*." *Kuzari* III:65, p. 137; ed. Qafiḥ, 137; ed. Hirschfeld, 186. See Lobel, "Dwelling Place," 117–19.

13 Al-Fārābī, *al-Madīna al-fāḍila*, 244–45.

14 Translation (with two emendations) from Maimonides, "Laws concerning the Foundations of the Torah" 7:1 in *The Code of Maimonides* (*Mishneh Toreh: The Book of Knowledge*), trans. Bernard Septimus (New Haven: Yale Judaica Series, forthcoming

15 See Maimonides, "Laws concerning the Foundations of the Torah" 7:1, note 3, in *The Code of Maimonides,* trans. Septimus. Bernard Septimus suggests translating the term in this passage "prophecy is realized," suggesting "actualization of a potential state, when the necessary conditions are met."

16 Maimonides cites the Talmudic source in a parallel passage in the Eight Chapters, chapter 7: "Prophecy only rests upon (*shorah*) one who is wise, strong, and rich." *Haqdamot*, ed. Shailat, 246 [Hebrew], 390 [Arabic]. See also b. *Shabbat* 92a; b. *Nedarim* 38a.

17 Numbers 11:25–26.

18 "To witness what they would witness of Him (*li-yushāhidūn ma yushāhidūnahu*)." Abraham Maimonides, *Perush,* ed. Wiesenberg, 283. See below, section 5. Later in the passage, the object of the term "witness" is the created light: "in witnessing it (*mushāhadatihi*) there was undoubtedly guidance to perceive His oneness and greatness." Halevi, too, uses the term *mushāhada* for both witness of God (*Kuzari* IV:16, p. 168) and witness of images, likenesses, or forms (*Kuzari* IV:5, p. 160, and III:73, pp. 144–45). See Lobel, *Between Mysticism and Philosophy*, 114–15.

19 Saadya Gaon, *Kitāb al-amānāt wa'l-i'tiqādāt*, ed. Qafiḥ, 110, ed. Rosenblatt, 130.

20 *Kuzari* IV:3, p. 155; Lobel, *Between Mysticism and Philosophy*, 113. By spiritual forms, Halevi means images such as that of a king on a throne, as seen by Isaiah, or the chariot seen by Ezekiel. Halevi's view is that the glory may include these spiritual forms, into which God molds the subtle spiritual light.

21 See also *Kuzari* IV:3, pp. 156 and 159; ed. Qafiḥ, 157 and 159; ed. Hirschfeld, 208 and 212; *Kuzari* IV:7, p. 161; ed. Qafiḥ, 162; ed. Hirschfeld, 214; as well as *Kuzari* IV:11, p. 163; ed. Qafiḥ, 163; ed. Hirschfeld, 216–17.

22 In one passage, Abraham, too, alludes to a spiritual form (although he does not use that term); he suggests that the nobles saw the light in the form of a man, and writes that "in these imaginative perceptions in the vision of prophecy, there is indication of intellectual perception." (Abraham Maimonides, *Perush,* ed. Wiesenberg, 381 [to Exodus 24:10]) Abraham thus treats this light as a vision of prophecy which comes to teach something, in accordance with the approach of his father. See Chapter 7 below.

23 *Kuzari* IV:5–6, pp. 159–61.

24 Abraham comments to Exodus 16:10: "This points to their perfection and preparation (*ist'idadihim*) as Aaron had said to them, "Draw near before the Lord" (Exodus 16:9). Their inner beings and thoughts (*bawāṭinuhum wa-afkāruhum*) drew near, and they emptied (*akhlū*) their inner beings of everything other than God and they turned completely from their tents and dwellings (*maḥālātihim wa-manāzilihim*) [to look toward] the dwelling/descent of the holy (*maḥall al-qedusha*), and immediately the created light descended (*ḥalla*). And in witnessing it (*mushāhadatihi*) there was undoubtedly guidance to perceive His oneness and greatness. No one who did not behold and see it [with their own eyes] can understand this condition/state (*ḥāl*). And this *Kavod* was seen in the cloud and the cloud covered it just as the light clouds cover the celestial sphere a light covering that is possible to see the sphere with the eyes not a heavy covering that hides it totally such as happens with heavy clouds in the time of the winter and the rains. And in this in my opinion the two meanings are one. One is that in this *Kavod* there is radiance and light which the eyes could not see/glimpse (*talmuḥūhu*) if it were not that the cloud covered it and its radiance. And the second is an allusion to the way our matter prevents us from apprehending that which is separate [from matter] as it truly is (see *Yesodei ha-Torah* 4:7). And that is an allusion that has subtlety and mystery (*diqqa wa-sod*). Abraham Maimonides, *Perush*, ed. Wiesenberg, 283.

25 See Ilan, "Secrets," 83.

Notes to Chapter 4

1 See *Guide* I:32. Abraham Maimonides, *Perush*, ed. Wiesenberg, 311.

2 Abraham Maimonides, *Perush*, ed. Wiesenberg, 313.

3 *High Ways*, II:410–12.

4 *High Ways*, II:412.

5 See Shaubi, *R. Abraham Maimonides*, 45, note 181.

6 *High Ways*, II:338. Similarly he writes that the lights of God's overflow shine upon his prophets and friends (*ishraqat anwār fayḍihi 'alā anbiyā'ihi wa-awliyāhā*), *High Ways*, II:60.

7 For the notion of homeopathy or sympathetic magic, see the motif of Moses' copper serpent (Numbers 21:4–9), and the excursus of Jacob Milgrom, "Excursus: The Copper Snake," in *JPS Torah Commentary: Numbers* (Philadelphia: Jewish Publication Society, 1990), 459–60; cf. 173–74: "That a snake provides the therapy for snakebite is an instance of homeopathy, or sympathetic magic . . ." (459). Even the repetition of sounds in the name of the copper snake—*neḥash neḥoshet*—is probably meant to add to its homeopathic power, since the words resemble one another (174). I thank Beth O'Sullivan for suggesting the motif of homeopathy here.

8 Nahem Ilan, "Theological Assumptions and Hermeneutical Principles in Rabbi Abraham Maimonides' Commentary on the Pentateuch," in *A Word Fitly Spoken: Studies in Mediaeval Exegesis of the Hebrew Bible and the Qur'ān*, ed. Meir M. Bar-Asher, Simon Hopkins, Sarah Stroumsa, and Bruno Chiesa (Jerusalem: Ben-Zvi, 2007), 50, gives "in reality" (*bi-metsi'ut*).

9 Abraham Maimonides, *Perush*, ed. Wiesenberg, 313–15.

10 *Guide* I:5, p. 29.

11 *Guide* I:5, p. 30.

12 Schwarz notes that the context suggests that this should be in the plural, "we will then go forward." He also notes a manuscript variant, cited in Maimonides, *Dalālat al-hā'irīn*, ed. S. Munk and I. Joel (Jerusalem, 1929), 475, that the verb may be *yataqadasha* (sanctify himself), which would make sense, as it echoes the language of the prooftext, "and let the priests also, who come near to the Lord, sanctify themselves (*yitqaddashu*)." If one accepts this variant, this lessens the parallel between Abraham and Maimonides, although Abraham may still have Maimonides' interpretation of the verse in mind. See Maimonides, *The Guide of the Perplexed*, 2nd ed., trans. and ed. Michael Schwarz (Tel Aviv: Tel Aviv University Press, 2002), 39, note 12.

13 *Guide* I:5, p. 29.

14 See b. *Berakhot* 7a; *Exodus Rabbah* 3:1, *Leviticus Rabbah* 20:1, *Numbers Rabbah* 2:25; Michelle Levine, "Maimonides' Philosophical Exegesis of the Nobles' Vision (Exod. 24): A Guide for the Pursuit of Knowledge," *The Torah u-Madda Journal*, 11 (2002–03): 86, 104, note 122; Klein-Braslavy, *Maimonides as Biblical Interpreter*, 181.

15 Or: guides you to inner sanctification. See Ilan, "Theological Assumptions," 49.

16 While the Masoretic text of the Bible reads *askilah*, the variant *askilekha* does appear in manuscript. See Abraham Maimonides, *Perush*, ed. Wiesenberg, 306, note 44. I draw here in my translation partially from Eli Shaubi, *From Baḥya ibn Paqūda to Abraham Maimonides: Tracing the Role of Law in Medieval Sefardic Piety* (Near Eastern Studies Senior Honors Thesis, Cornell University, 2013), 85.

17 Abraham Maimonides, *Perush*, ed. Wiesenberg, 305–07.

18 In the remainder of his comment, Abraham expresses reservations about further aspects of R. Abraham he-Ḥasid's interpretation, which do not affect the question of preparation for the Sinaitic revelation.

19 Literally: through it [comes] the attainment of the prophets (*bi-hā wuṣūl al-anbiyā'*). *Wuṣūl* can have the connotation of attainment or arrival. See, for example, above, 57, in which Abraham uses the metaphor of walking on paths that lead to God (*al-masālik al-muwaṣṣila ilayhi*), until they arrive (*yaṣilū*).

20 *High Ways*, 382 (with emendations); cf. translation of Fenton, "Maimonides—Father and Son," 125.
21 Al-Ghazālī, *al-Munqidh min al-ḍalāl*, 106–07; English translation, *Deliverance from Error*, 81; Avtalion, *A Comparative Study*, 241–80.
22 *Guide* III:51, pp. 622–23.
23 *Guide* III:51, p. 620. See Steven Harvey, "Maimonides in the Sultan's Palace," in *Perspectives on Maimonides*, ed. Joel Kraemer (London: Littman, 1996), 47–75; idem, "Avicenna and Maimonides on Prayer and Intellectual Worship," 101–03.
24 *High Ways*, II:136.
25 Note the parallel critique expressed by his father-in-law, R. Ḥananel; see Fenton, "A Re-Discovered Description," 279; and above, see XX, note 12.
26 See RNL Yevr.-Arab. I 2924, 1a, ll. 2–22, 2a, ll. 18–19 through 2b, l. 18; cf. the translations of Fenton, "The Doctrine of Attachment," 115–16; and Russ-Fishbane, *Judaism, Sufism, and the Pietists of Medieval Egypt*, 194, 210, 224.

Notes to Chapter 5

1 *Guide* III:9, p. 437.
2 One precedent for this view is found in Saadya. In the Introduction to the *Book of Doctrines and Beliefs*, Saadya includes as the first of his four sources of knowledge the knowledge given by sense perception (*ʿilm al-shāhid*; literally, "the knowledge of the eyewitness"). He goes on in the Introduction to argue that God sent prophets conveying messages so that human beings could see with their own eyes proofs one could neither doubt nor reject. In this context, he notes the theophany at Mount Sinai, and argues that the community was immediately obliged to accept the teaching of religion because it had been proved by the evidence of the senses. He adds that its acceptance is also incumbent upon anyone to whom it had been transmitted by authentic transmission. Saadya Gaon, *Kitāb al-amānāt wa'l-iʿtiqādāt,* Introduction, section 5, ed. Qafiḥ, 14, ed. Rosenblatt, 27–28; and section 6, ed. Qafiḥ, 16, ed. Rosenblatt, 27–28. In *The Book of Doctrines and Beliefs*, ed. Alexander Altmann, in *Three Jewish Philosophers*, ed. Hans Lewy, Alexander Altmann, and Isaak Heinemann (Oxford: Phaedon Press, 1946), these sections are on pages 36 and 45–46, respectively.
3 Lane, *Arabic-English Lexicon*, 1611, citing classical lexicons such as *Lisān al-ʿarab*.
4 *The Qur'ān: A New Annotated Translation*, trans. A. J. Droge (Sheffield: Equinox, 2013), 195.
5 Ibid., 216. I thank Yonatan Negev for the sources from Qur'ān and Tafsīr.

6 One could argue that in Qur'ān 19:37, *mashhad yawm aẓīm* might signify an eschatological assembly on the great Day (for example, Arberry translates "then woe to those who disbelieve for the scene of a dreadful day"). However, the interpretation transmitted by al-Sulamī clearly states that they are *witnessing* that great *mashhad*, not that they are gathered in an assembly.

7 Note also that the phrase *al-mashhad al-aẓīm* is attributed to Ja'far al-Ṣādiq (d. 765), the sixth Shi'ite *Imām*. This may be additional evidence of Shi'ite terms and conceptions in the *Kuzari*, documented first by Shlomo Pines, and at greater length by Ehud Krinis. See Pines, "Shi'ite Terms and Conceptions in Judah Halevi's Kuzari," *Jerusalem Studies in Arabic and Islam* 2 (1980): 165–251; Ehud Krinis, *God's Chosen People:* Judah Halevi's Kuzari and the Shīʿī Imām Doctrine (Turnhout: Brepols, 2014). I thank Yonatan Negev for highlighting the Shi'ite connection here.

8 There is a further linguistic bridge between the two. Since the Islamic pilgrimage includes the "halt" or standing (*wuqūf* or *mawqif*) at Mount Arafat, there may be a natural connection to the event of standing before God at Mount Sinai (*mawqif / ma'amad har sinai*). Some scholars have noted the similarity between the two events. At Mount Sinai, there are preliminary preparations of abstaining from sexual relations (Exodus 19:15), washing of the garments (Exodus 19:10, 19:14), followed by a waiting upon God (Exodus 19:11, 19:15), standing at the foot of a holy mountain (Deuteronomy 4:10). On the Hajj, Muslims refrain from sexual relations, wear holy clothing, and stand (*waqafa*) before the deity at the foot of a holy mountain. Bernard Septimus has pointed out that Saadya's use of the term *mawqif* for an event of standing in the presence of God in fact provides a linguistic bridge to the Hebrew nominal phrase *ma'amad har Sinai*, standing [before God at] Mount Sinai. Further, Saadya also connects the event of standing at Sinai (*mawqif sinai*) with the eschatological Day of Judgement, like Islamic sources, which use the term *mawqif* for the event of standing before God on Judgement Day. See below, XX, note XX. See A. J. Wensinck, Jacques Jomier, and Bernard Lewis, "Ḥadjdj," in *Encyclopaedia of Islam*, 2nd ed., ed. P. Bearman, Th. Bianquis, C. E. Bosworth, E. van Donzel, and W. P. Heinrichs (Leiden: Brill, 1960–); Septimus, "*Ma'amad Har Sinai* and Other *Ma'amadot*," 163ff.; Shraga Abramson, "Expressions Concerning the Giving of the Torah," *Leshonenu* 58 (1994): 320–21.

9 See Reinhart Dozy, *Supplément aux Dictionnaires Arabes* (Leiden: Brill, 1967), I:794; Septimus, "*Ma'amad Har Sinai* and Other *Ma'amadot*," 161.

10 See, for example, Mordechai A. Friedman, *A Dictionary of Medieval Judaeo-Arabic* (Jerusalem: Ben-Zvi Institute, 2016), 884.

11 Moreover, the religious martyr, willing to die for the divine beloved, is called a witness (*shahīd*) to God. Sufi poets extend this sense of religious testimony by drawing on a motif from secular Arabic love poetry, that of the love-sick individual who pines away for his beloved, sometimes even dying

as a martyr of love. In the *Kuzari,* Halevi suggests that in his willingness to sacrifice his son Isaac, Abraham is a lover of God, ready to be a witness/martyr (*shahīd*) to God, because of his experience of *mushāhada*, witness of the divine. See Lobel, *Between Mysticism and Philosophy*, 92–93.

12 *Kuzari* I:87, p. 24; ed. Qafiḥ, 24; ed. Hirschfeld, 61.

13 See *Mekhilta*, ed. H. Horovitz and I. Rabin, 2nd ed. (Jerusalem, 1969–70), *Ba-ḥodesh*, 237 (no. 9), ll.1–2.

14 *Kuzari* I:87, pp. 24–25; ed. Qafiḥ, 25; ed. Hirschfeld, 61.

15 *Kuzari* I:91, p. 26; ed. Qafiḥ, 26–27; ed. Hirschfeld, 63.

16 See Lobel, *Between Mysticism and Philosophy*, 94–95.

17 See Septimus, "*Ma'amad Har Sinai* and Other *Ma'amadot*," 173; Maimonides, *Epistle to Yemen (Iggeret Teiman)*, trans. Boaz Cohen, ed. Abraham S. Halkin (New York: American Academy for Jewish Research, 1952), 26 [Arabic], vi [English]; *Hilkhot Yesodei ha-Torah* 8:1–2. Septimus notes that an echo of Halevi is especially likely in Maimonides' uncharacteristic use of the imagination in the *Epistle to Yemen*. In *Kuzari* III:5, p. 93, Halevi suggests that one should use the imaginative faculty to imagine inspiring images, including the standing (*ma'amad*) at Mount Sinai. In the *Epistle to Yemen*, Maimonides tells his readers to remember *ma'amad har Sinai* and adds: "It is incumbent upon you, our brothers, to raise your children on the imagination of that great *mashhad*." *Iggeret Teiman*, 28 [Arabic], vi [English]. See Septimus, "*Ma'amad Har Sinai* and Other *Ma'amadot*," 173, note 63.

18 It is possible that there is an echo of Halevi's rhetoric in *Guide* III:9, in Maimonides' assertion that "that great *mashhad* [at Mount Sinai]" was greater than any vision of prophecy, and beyond any *qiyās*. Ibn Tibbon translates *qiyās* as *heqesh*, but this term, too, is ambiguous: it can mean analogy or logic. Munk translates "*analogie*," Pines, "analogy," and Schwarz, "comparison (*hashva'a*)." Only Qafiḥ notes the alternative: *higayon*, "logic." There is a small possibility that Maimonides wanted to echo Halevi's contrast between things known by direct witness (*mushāhada*) and those known by logic (*qiyās*), as in *Kuzari* IV:16–17. Nevertheless, it seems from the same sentence that it is precisely the theophany at Mount Sinai that is beyond analogy and known only by witness, in contrast to other instances of knowledge of God and other prophetic experiences.

19 See Harvey, "Avicenna and Maimonides on Prayer and Intellectual Worship," 96–97. We have seen in section 3 that Abraham Maimonides does use the language of *mushāhada* for witness of God. See above, 45-46, 50.

20 There is one additional passage in which Halevi alludes to the phrase "the great *mashhad*," now in the plural. In *Kuzari* I:107, speaking of otherworldly visions, the Sage asks the Khazar King: "What is your opinion of one who witnesses those great angelic scenes (*yushāhid al-mashāhid al-aẓīma al-malakūtiyya*)?" The King replies that that person would long to remain

separate from the senses, delighting in that light. In response, the Sage argues that rather than wanting to escape this world, Jews can witness and have contact with the divine on earth, within history. *Kuzari* I:107, p. 35; ed. Qafiḥ, 36; ed. Hirschfeld, 74.

21 See *Guide* II:36, p. 369 (with emendations).

22 I thank Ehud Krinis and Zev Harvey for helping me to sharpen this formulation.

23 See *Guide* I:21, p. 48; *Guide* III:24, pp. 501–02.

24 Josef Stern offers a skeptical reading of this passage. He notes "the parabolic inner meaning of the biblical story of the Sinaitic revelation according to which the clouds surrounding the mountain mean that 'the dark matter that encompasses us and not Him' make it impossible for humans to apprehend God." In a note, Stern adds, "This interpretation is remarkable because Maimonides takes the inner meaning of the scriptural account of Sinai—the one biblical event that we would think would be the moment of complete revelation of knowledge of God—as the exemplary skeptical expression of how matter prevents knowledge of God." Josef Stern, *The Matter and Form of Maimonides'* Guide (Cambridge, MA: Harvard University Press, 2013), 246.

25 Cf. Eisenmann, "The Sinaitic Revelation," 359.

26 Cf. Alvin Reines, "Maimonides' Concept of Mosaic Prophecy," *Hebrew Union College Annual* 40 (1970): 350, note 93.

27 See Michael Sells, *Early Islamic Mysticism*, 102.

28 Septimus argues that the term *maqām* is in a certain way not appropriate to the event at Mount Sinai, "which is not seen as one step within a larger sequence." In contrast, Nahem Ilan argues that Abraham Maimonides does conceive of the spiritual state attained at Mount Sinai in Exodus 20 as a fruit of the spiritual preparation described in Exodus 19. See Septimus, "*Ma'amad Har Sinai* and Other *Ma'amadot*," 179, notes 91–92; Ilan, "Theological Assumptions," 51.

29 Septimus, "*Ma'amad Har Sinai* and Other *Ma'amadot*," 180. The poet Solomon Ibn Gabirol provides a precedent for using the term *ma'amad* for standing in the presence of God and combining it with non-sensory vision. In the poem *Keter Malkhut*, no. 27, he writes: "And here is delight without end or limit, for it is The-World-To-Come. And here are stations and seeing-places (*ma'amadot u-mar'ot*) for the standing souls." The context here is the vision of the soul in the afterlife, not the final Judgement, but it might bear some of the eschatological connotation of *mawqif* that we find in Saadya (see notes 93 and 112). Septimus writes: "Perhaps Ibn Gabirol (d. c. 1057) is using *ma'amad* in the sense of standing in God's presence and witnessing His glory. This interpretation certainly fits the context. The couplet (*ma'amadot u-mar'ot*) could then correspond to *mawāqif wa-mashāhid*, and thus presage the linkage of *ma'amad* and *mashhad* (=

mar'eh), common to Halevi, Ibn Tibbon, and Maimonides." Septimus adds that this reading is speculative but worth considering. Ibn Gabirol, "*Keter Malkhut*," no. 27, in *Shirei ha-qodesh*, ed. Dov Yarden (Jerusalem, 1977), vol. 1, 55; idem, "*Keter Malkhut*," in *Ha-shirah ha-'ivrit be-Sefarad u-ve-Provans*, ed. Ḥ. Schirmann (Jerusalem, 1961), vol. 1, 273; English translation by Israel Zangwill in *Selected Religious Poems of Solomon Ibn Gabirol*, ed. Israel Davidson (Philadelphia: Jewish Publication Society, 1923), 103. Septimus, "*Ma'amad Har Sinai* and Other *Ma'amadot*," 182.

30 *Guide* III:24, pp. 501–2; cf. Oliver Leaman, "Maimonides, the Imagination, and the Objectivity of Prophecy," *Religion* 18 (1988): 69–80.

31 Septimus, "*Ma'amad Har Sinai* and Other *Ma'amadot*," 180. The event at Mount Sinai was clearly a paradigmatic event of standing before God. In fact, Septimus, following Shraga Abramson, demonstrates that Maimonides was a key figure in the popularization of the Hebrew nominal phrase *ma'amad har Sinai*, standing [before God at] Mount Sinai. The phrase draws upon Deuteronomy 4:9–10: "only take heed, and keep your soul diligently, lest you forget the things that your eyes have seen, and lest they depart from your heart all the days of your life; make them known to your children and your children's children—how on the day that you stood (*yom asher 'amadeta*) before the Lord your God at Horeb, the Lord said to me, 'Gather the people to me, that I may let them hear my word, so that they may learn to fear me all the days that they live upon the earth, and that they may teach their children so.'" In his Arabic translation of the Torah (the *Tafsīr*), Saadya translates the Hebrew *'amadeta* (you stood) in Deuteronomy 4:10 as *waqafta*, a term used by Arabic authors to describe experiences of standing before God, whether in prayer or receiving divine address, particularly on the eschatological Day of Judgement. Saadya, too, in his commentary to Exodus 20:20, connects the Day of Judgement with the event at Mount Sinai. In the *Book of Doctrines and Beliefs* and his Commentary to *Sefer Yetsirah*, he goes on to use the nominal term *mawqif har Sinai* (or *mawqif Sinai*) to describe the event of standing before God at Sinai, and the phrase appears to have migrated to the Hebrew *ma'amad har Sinai*, used by Halevi along with other uses of the term *ma'amad* to describe several examples of standing before God (*Kuzari* III:5, p. 93), and then popularized by Maimonides in texts such as the *Mishneh Torah* (*Hilkhot Yesodei ha-Torah* 8:1–2), the *Epistle to Yemen*, and the *Guide of the Perplexed*. See Septimus, "*Ma'amad Har Sinai* and Other *Ma'amadot*," 163–73; Shraga Abramson, "Expressions Concerning the Giving of the Torah," *Leshonenu* 58 (1994): 317–22, at 320–21; *Perushei Rav Se'adyah Gaon le-Sefer Shemot*, ed. Y. Ratzaby (Jerusalem: Mossad Harav Kook, 1998), 101–02 [Hebrew], 313 [Arabic] (to Exodus 20:20, no. 200).

32 For Maimonides on miracles, see Tzvi Langermann, "Maimonides and Miracles: The Growth of a (Dis)Belief," *Jewish History* 18, nos. 2–3 (2004),

147–72; Alvin J. Reines, "Maimonides' Concept of Miracles," *Hebrew Union College Annual* 45 (1974): 243–85.

33 See Horowitz and Rabin, *Mekhilta*, *Yitro*, 216 (no. 4), ll. 15–18.

34 See b. *Makkot* 23b–24a, Song of Songs *Rabbah* 1:2. The midrashic argument that only the first two commandments were heard directly from God is given Biblical support: in the first two commandments, God speaks in the first person, while the remaining commandments are given in the third person.

35 *Guide* II:33, p. 365.

36 Jacob Levinger, "The Secret of the Created Voice in the Revelation at Mount Sinai," in his *Maimonides as Philosopher and Codifier* [Hebrew] (Jerusalem: Bialik Institute, 1989), 44, 46; cf. Colette Sirat, *A History of Jewish Philosophy in the Middle Ages* (Cambridge: Cambridge University Press, 1990), 198.

37 Septimus points out that Maimonides' suggestion that the people heard the Ten Commandments twice may be influenced by Saadya's commentary to Exodus 19:9, in which Saadya notes the discrepancy between the giving of the Ten Commandments in Exodus 20:1 and Deuteronomy 5:5. He also points out that this may reflect a reading of Horowitz and Rabin, *Mekhilta*, *Ba-Ḥodesh*, 219 (no. 4), ll. 2–4. Maimonides, "Laws concerning the Foundations of the Torah" 8:1, note 15, in *The Code of Maimonides*, trans. Septimus; *Perushei Rav Se'adyah Gaon le-Sefer Shemot*, ed. Ratzaby, 79–80 [Hebrew], 298 [Arabic].

38 On sub-prophetic phenomena, see Daniel J. Lasker, "Sub-Prophetic Inspiration in Judaeo-Arabic Philosophy" [Hebrew], in *Alei Asor: Proceedings of the Tenth Conference of the Society for Judaeo-Arabic Studies*, ed. Daniel J. Lasker and Haggai Ben-Shammai (Beer Sheva: Ben-Gurion University of the Negev, 2008), 131–49.

39 *Guide* III:24, p. 500. See the echo of this argument and the use of the phrase "the great *mashhad*" in R. Ḥananel, Abraham Maimonides' father-in-law, below, chapter 6.

40 See Levinger, "The Secret of the Created Voice," 45.

41 Ibid., 47; Kreisel, *Prophecy*, 232, note 120.

42 See Alvin J. Reines, "Abrabanel on Prophecy in the *Moreh Nebukhim*," *Hebrew Union College Annual* 33 (1962): 226–27; Kalman Bland, trans., *The Epistle on the Possibility of Conjunction with the Active Intellect by Ibn Rushd with the Commentary of Moses Narboni* (New York: Jewish Theological Seminary, 1982), 67–68; Shaul Regev, "Collective Revelation and *Ma'amad har Sinai* in Maimonides and His Commentators: Narboni, Shem Tov, and Abravanel," *Jerusalem Studies in Jewish Thought* 9 (1990): 260–65; Levinger, "The Secret of the Created Voice," 44.

43 Abravanel, commentary to *Guide* I:33; translation by Reines, "Abrabanel on Prophecy," 228. Abravanel's own position is that the people at Mount Sinai did not experience prophecy, which is intellectual and requires intellectual

preparation. Rather, they achieved sensuous perception of God's created glory, including the fire, the cloud surrounding it, and the created sound. He quotes here Maimonides' second position in *Guide* I:21 that sensory seeing can aid intellectual perception. As Reines points out, Abravanel does not realize that in *Guide* I:21, Maimonides is speaking of Moses' vision of the glory in the cleft of the rock. As we have noted above, Abraham Maimonides takes this position as his own: that sensory perception can aid intellectual apprehension. See Reines, "Abrabanel on Prophecy," 222, and note 2.

44 Abraham Maimonides makes this point in his comment to Exodus 6:2, although he suggests that there are degrees of understanding of Necessary Existence. Abraham Maimonides, *Perush,* ed. Wiesenberg, 241–43.

45 See Moses Narboni, commentary to *Guide* I:37 and *Guide* II:45; Abravanel, commentary to *Guide* II:33; Howard Kreisel, "'The Voice of God' in Medieval Jewish Philosophical Exegesis," *Da'at* 16 (1986): 36 and note 51; Reines, "Abrabanel on Prophecy," 235–37.

46 See Levinger, "The Secret of the Created Voice," 47; Kreisel, *Prophecy*, 231–35; idem, "The Voice of God," 35–36. As Eisenmann notes, Maimonides tells us explicitly that when applied to God, the words "saying" and "speaking" are metaphorical, referring to either will and volition or a notion that has been grasped by the understanding having come from God. Maimonides adds that in this case, "it is indifferent whether it has become known by means of a created voice or through one of the ways of prophecy." He then adds, "the terms in question never signified that He, may He be exalted, spoke using the sounds of letters and a voice." Eisenmann points out that in *Guide* I:45, he also defines "to hear" as an equivocal term, sometimes having the meaning "to accept." *Guide* I:45, p. 96, and I:65, pp. 158–59; Eisenmann, "The Sinaitic Revelation," 360.

47 Cf. Hannah Kasher, "Maimonides' Interpretations of the Story of the Divine Revelation in the Cleft of the Rock" [Hebrew], *Da'at* 35 (1995): 50–52; Reines, "Abrabanel on Prophecy," 351.

48 Levinger, "The Secret of the Created Voice," 46; cf. Klein-Braslavy, *Maimonides as Biblical Interpreter*, 204.

49 We can think of an analogy drawn from Avicenna and Maimonides' theories of prophecy. Moses could receive the truth in an intuitive flash, without discursive language, whereas the people needed to hear separate words. See *Guide*, Introduction, 7, and II:38.

50 *Guide* II:36–38, pp. 369–78.

51 *Guide* III:51, p. 621; *Guide* III:52, p. 629.

52 *Guide* III:51, p. 620; *Guide* I:54, pp. 123–24.

53 For example, Avicenna writes that when one attunes oneself through contemplative prayer, an emanation of understanding overflows from the highest Intelligence. Avicenna, *Risāla fī māhiyyat al-ṣalāh* (*Treatise on Prayer*), in *Traites mystiques d-Ibn Sīnā*, ed. M. A. F. Mehren (Leiden: Brill,

1889–99), 39; English translation by A. J. Arberry, in *Avicenna on Theology* (London: Murray, 1951; reprint, Westport, CT: Hyperion, 1979), 60. For Neoplatonic thinkers, the intellect is the bridge to the divine; this bridge goes back to Plato, whose philosopher contemplates the Good and engages in a "synoptic vision" of the Forms (*Republic* 537c).

54 Albert Einstein told one friend, "When I examine myself and my methods of thought, I come close to the conclusion that the gift of imagination has meant more to me than any talent for absorbing absolute knowledge. . . All great achievements of science must start from intuitive knowledge. I believe in intuition and inspiration. . . . At times I feel certain I am right while not knowing the reason." Hence his famous statement that, for creative work in science, "Imagination is more important than knowledge." See *The Expanded Quotable Einstein*, ed. Alice Calaprice (Princeton: Princeton University Press, 2000), 22, 287, 10. Cited by Michele and Robert Root-Bernstein, "Einstein On Creative Thinking: Music and the Intuitive Art of Scientific Imagination," *Imagine That!*, March 2010, https://www.psychologytoday.com/blog/imagine/201003/einstein-creative-thinking-music-and-the-intuitive-art-scientific-imagination. Tzvi Langermann, "The True Perplexity," *Aleph: Historical Studies in Science and Judaism* 8 (2008): 307–10.

55 See *Guide* II:36; cf. Langermann, "The True Perplexity," 308; Abrahamov, "Maimonides and Ibn Sina's Theory of *Ḥads*." On *ḥads* in Avicenna, see Dimitri Gutas, *Avicenna and the Aristotelian Tradition* (Leiden: Brill, 1988), 159–83. In contrast to Abrahamov, Sara Klein-Braslavy, Herbert Davidson, and Michael Schwarz, Amira Eran argues that Maimonides was ambivalent toward *ḥads,* believing the theory suggests a dangerous embrace of the imagination, which Maimonides regards as unreliable. See Amira Eran, "Intuition and Inspiration—the Causes of Jewish Thinkers' Objection to Avicenna's Intellectual Prophecy (*Ḥads*)," *Jewish Studies Quarterly* 14 (2007): 57–71, and 60 note 60. See also Kreisel, *Judaism as Philosophy*, 277–8, note 15; idem, *Prophecy*, 254–57; idem, *Maimonides' Political Thought*, 77–79, 292–93.

56 Reines, "Maimonides' Concept of Mosaic Prophecy," 325–62. Reines describes two features of prophecy: gestalt intuition and premise intuition. Maimonides comments that his understanding of the Book of Job came to him in something resembling prophetic revelation (*waḥy*). Reines suggests that this is a gestalt intuition. Maimonides had studied the book thoroughly; the meaning of the book came together in a flash of insight after a period of long study. Maimonides' interpretation "must have occurred through a flash of intuitive reasoning in which his knowledge of the text of Job and his understanding of metaphysical science suddenly coalesced into a gestalt in which the two sources were immediately structured into a coherent and integrated whole." Ibid., 339. This is precisely the way Avicenna and

Maimonides describe the process by which philosophers, who spend long hours contemplating philosophical issues, may develop prophetic insights.

57 *Guide* II:12, p. 280.

Notes to Chapter 6

1 *High Ways*, II:290; Fenton, "Some Judaeo-Arabic Fragments," 47–48.

2 Maimonides does assert that the people heard only one voice, one time. One reader of this manuscript argued that the people did not hear the first two words separately and must have asked Moses to intervene after hearing "all ten" (but not understanding anything). The reader of my manuscript argues that the people were able to derive the meaning of the first two commandments from hearing the "voice," rather than from deductive reasoning. The people understood that it was divine speech that they were hearing; this experience verified for them the truth of the first two commandments, i.e. the existence of God. Shaul Regev notes a similar interpretation by Averroes, which he suggests is compatible with Maimonides' view. See Regev, "Collective Revelation and *Ma'amad har Sinai*," 254–55; Bland, *Epistle on Conjunction*, 65–66. But this seems to be a direct contradiction to Maimonides' argument in *Guide* II:33 that the first two commandments are known by rational speculation alone; Maimonides' argument is precisely that the people did not learn them "from the voice." The divine "voice" represents the people's divine/natural knowledge of God's existence. Kreisel argues that the people did not hear the first two commandments distinctly; Levinger argues similarly that the people did not hear the first two commandments clearly, and needed them repeated by Moses. Kreisel, *Prophecy*, 232–34; Levinger, "The Secret of the Created Voice," 45.

3 Abraham Maimonides, *Perush*, ed. Wiesenberg, 325.

4 Or: referents.

5 Abraham Maimonides, *Perush*, ed. Wiesenberg, 315.

6 Labaton, *A Comprehensive Analysis*, 226; Abraham Maimonides, *Perush*, ed. Wiesenberg, 315, note 14; Fenton, "Some Judaeo-Arabic Fragments," 57.

7 Abraham Maimonides, *Perush*, ed. Wiesenberg, 321 (to Exodus 20:14), remark (*tanbīh*); cf. Ilan, "Secrets," 80.

8 Abraham Maimonides, *Perush*, ed. Wiesenberg, 247–49. See Ilan, "Secrets," 78.

9 See *Perushei Rav Se'adyah Gaon le-Sefer Shemot*, ed. Ratzaby, 21. In another suggestive passage, Abraham asserts that the divine word "arrived at one time to Moses and to Aaron, to Moses 'face to face', and to Aaron in the form of revelation (*waḥy*)." Abraham Maimonides, *Perush*, ed. Wiesenberg, 246 (to Exodus 6:13).

10 As noted above, in a fragment from Saadya's Commentary to Exodus (19:9), Saadya seeks to harmonize the two accounts of the hearing of the Ten Commandments, one in which the people heard the Ten Commandments from God (Exodus 20:1), and one in which they heard them from Moses (Deuteronomy 5:5). See *Perushei Rav Se'adyah Gaon le-Sefer Shemot*, ed. Ratzaby, 79–80 [Hebrew], 298 [Arabic].

11 Wiesenberg, in Abraham Maimonides, *Perush,* ed. Wiesenberg, cites this verse as Exodus 20:18.

12 See Ilan, "Between Mount Sinai and the Cleft of the Rock," 136, and note 16.

13 Abraham Maimonides, *Perush,* ed. Wiesenberg, 325.

14 Abraham describes Moses' experience of standing before God at Sinai as a *maqām*, a term which for the Pietists also carries the Sufi connotation of a spiritual or mystical state. Note Abraham's clever Judeo-Arabic exegesis; God tells Moses to "stand here by me," that is, to remain in the spiritual state (*maqām*) of standing before God.

15 Abraham Maimonides, *Perush,* ed. Wiesenberg, 325.

16 See Fenton, "Some Judaeo-Arabic Fragments," 66, note 53; Russ-Fishbane, *Judaism, Sufism, and the Pietists of Medieval Egypt*, 187; Gerson D. Cohen, "The Soteriology of R. Abraham Maimuni," *PAAJR* 35 (1967): 75–98; 36 (1968): 33–56, reprint in his *Studies in the Variety of Rabbinic Cultures* (New York: Jewish Publication Society, 1991), 219–20, 230.

17 Cf. Russ-Fishbane, *Judaism, Sufism, and the Pietists of Medieval Egypt*, 230–31.

18 Or: Eternal Source; see *Guide* I:16; Maimonides, "Laws concerning the Foundations of the Torah" 7:6 and note 83, in *The Code of Maimonides*, 3:7, trans. Septimus; see also notes to *Hilkhot Teshuvah* 3:7 in that edition.

19 I follow here the translation of Professor Septimus.

20 Septimus notes that in *Hilkhot Yesodei ha-Torah* 7:5, Maimonides, too, suggests that all others who attained the prophetic state at Sinai "returned to their tents," while Moses alone remained with God. Maimonides, "Laws concerning the Foundations of the Torah" 7:5, note 81, in *The Code of Maimonides*, trans. Septimus.

21 *Shāhadatumūhu,* Abraham Maimonides, *Perush,* ed. Wiesenberg, 325.

22 Fenton, "Some Judaeo-Arabic Fragments," 62 [Arabic], 66 [English], with emendations. R. Ḥananel ben Samuel, father-in-law of Abraham Maimonides, writes similarly:

And this is what it was like before [the giving of the Law]: one would strive for many years to attain [it], because it requires many introductions, preparations, and methods of reasoning, until an individual among them would attain [even] one of these principles that one should firmly hold about God, may his name be blessed, which came to that community of Israel at the day of standing at Mount Sinai (*ma'amad har Sinai*). And since this matter is the end and pillar that everything stands upon, [God] commanded that we mention it always; and that the generation that witnessed (*shāhidū*) that [event] [should] transmit [it] to their children who did not witness it (*yushāhidūhu*). And these children should transmit to their children what they inherited of these firm convictions (*i'tiqādāt*) whose proof (*dalīl*) is that great *mashhad* (*dhālika al-mashhad al-'aẓīm*).

See Fenton, "More on R. Ḥananel b. Samuel," 82 [Arabic], 86 [Hebrew]. Note here R. Ḥananel's echoing of Maimonides' language in *Guide* III:24 and the *Epistle to Yemen*. In both passages, Maimonides uses the term "that great *mashhad*" to ground the authoritativeness of Jewish tradition, as R. Ḥananel does here.

23 Shalom Rosenberg notes the somewhat counterintuitive character of the claim that prophecy communicated through a word is unmediated. He notes that "it is hard to see in Rabbi Abraham's words an explication that is faithful to the approach of Maimonides, and the uniqueness of the prophecy of Moses." Shalom Rosenberg, "On Biblical Exegesis in the Guide" [Hebrew], *Jerusalem Studies in Jewish Thought* 1 (1981): 106, note 20; Labaton, *A Comprehensive Analysis*, 234.

24 Abraham Maimonides, *Perush*, ed. Wiesenberg, 309–11; cf. Ilan, "Secrets," 84–85. Abraham adds one other interesting reference to the created voice. Commenting on the phrase "the anger of the Lord was kindled" [lit., "the Lord's nose waxed hot"] in Exodus 4:14, Abraham explains that "every [use of the expression] *ḥaron af* [the kindling of anger] that is said with reference to [God], may He be exalted, is metaphorical, while here it is possible that the borrowing is an expression for the created voice, which addressed him [harshly]." Abraham Maimonides, *Perush*, ed. Wiesenberg, 231.

25 Altmann, "Saadya's Theory of Revelation," 150.

26 Saadya Gaon, *Commentary to Sefer Yetsirah*, ed. Qafiḥ, 31, 108–109; *Commentaire sur le Séfer Yesira ou Livre de la Création*, trans. Mayer Lambert (Paris, 1891), 26–27, 94. In the Commentary to *Sefer Yetsirah*, the concept of second air brings together the glory and the created Word, which Saadya will later separate in the *Book of Doctrines and Beliefs*. Saadya interprets the revelation at Mount Sinai as a combination of visible and auditory manifestations in the glory. Altmann, "Saadya's Theory of Revelation," 159–60.

27 Saadya Gaon, *Kitāb al-amānāt wa'l-i'tiqādāt* II:10, ed. Qafiḥ, 103–104, ed. Rosenblatt, 120–121; and II:12, ed. Qafiḥ, 110–111, ed. Rosenblatt, 130.

28 See Pines, "Points of Similarity," Appendix III: "Quotations from Saadya's Commentary on *Sefer Yeẓira* in Maimonides' *Guide of the Perplexed*," 127–32; and Warren Zev Harvey, "*Sefer Yetsirah shel Liebes: bein Parmenides, Nietzsche, ve-ha-Rambam*," in *Ve-zot le-Yehudah*, ed. R. Wiehoff, R. Meroz, and Y. Garb (Jerusalem: Bialik, 2012), 24–27.

29 We should also note Maimonides' statement in *Guide* I:65 that "our people are in general agreement that the Torah is something created. That is to say,

that the word (*al-kalām*) ascribed to God is created and that it is ascribed to Him only in the sense that the word (*al-qawl*) which Moses heard was created and brought into existence by God in the same manner as he created all His other works of creation." Harry Wolfson, *Repercussions of the Kalam in Jewish Philosophy* (Cambridge, MA: Harvard University Press, 1979), 112, notes that Maimonides here suggests that the word heard by Moses at Mount Sinai, like the prophetic word heard by all other prophets, was created at the time it was heard. Maimonides does not accept the rabbinic tradition according to which the Torah was created before the existence of the world. Abraham, too, accepts the notion that the prophetic word is created at the time it is heard.

Notes to Chapter 7

1 I have chosen to translate the term *atsilim* as "nobles" for the sake of consistency, although Abraham suggests that the *atsilim* described in Exodus 24:11 are to be identified with the "elders" mentioned in Exodus 24:9.

2 Or: the likeness of a pavement of sapphire, like the very sky for purity. Nahum Sarna notes that the "Hebrew *livnat*, from *levenah*, 'brick', suggests a decorative floor area of covered bricks or tiles." Sarna adds that the Hebrew *sappir*, rendered "sapphire," is not the modern blue gemstone, which was unknown in the ancient Near East, but the widely used deep blue *lapis lazuli*, and that in the vision of Ezekiel (1:26; 10:1) God's throne is made of this material. This is relevant to Onqelos, who translates "under his feet" as "under the throne of His glory." Ibn Ezra, in his comment to Exodus 24:10, notes this verse in Ezekiel. See *The JPS Torah Commentary: Exodus*, commentary by Nahum Sarna (Philadelphia: Jewish Publication Society, 1991), 153; *Torat Ḥayyim* (Jerusalem: Mossad Harav Kook, 1988), Exodus 24:10, 73–74; *The Commentators' Bible*: *Exodus*, ed. Michael Carasik (Philadelphia: Jewish Publication Society, 2005), 220.

3 Literally: "understandings," "intellects," "perceptive faculties" (*afhām*).

4 This sentence is added for clarification by Wiesenberg; it is absent in the manuscript.

5 Abraham Maimonides, *Perush*, ed. Wiesenberg, 381. Abraham adds this after including a long interpretation of the Biblical passage by R. Abraham he-Ḥasid. He thus begins the passage with the words: "And I too will speak of this."

6 See Maimonides, *Commentary on the Mishnah*, ed. Qafiḥ, vol. 6, 395; *Haqdamot*, ed. Shailat, 390 [Arabic], 248 [Hebrew]; *Ethical Writings of Maimonides*, ed. Raymond L. Weiss and Charles Butterworth (New York: Dover, 1975), 83.

7 Abraham notes that Onqelos' identification of the *atsilei bnei Yisrael* in Exodus 24:11 as the "leaders" (*ravrevei*) is a translation according to contextual meaning (*ma'na*), while according to the language (*lafẓ*) of the verse, the term *atsilei* suggests the elders of Israel mentioned in Exodus 24:9. Abraham Maimonides, *Perush*, ed. Wiesenberg, 383 (to Exodus 24:11): "*ve-el atsilei*"; see Labaton, *A Comprehensive Analysis*, 227–28. Abraham he-Ḥasid, in his interpolated commentary, asserts that the unveiling (*mukāshafa*) was divided into three levels. The first is that of Moses, the second that of Aaron, and the third that of Nadav Avihu, and the seventy nobles. All these three levels "saw" (*ra'u*) the God of Israel. A fourth level is that of the nobles (*atsilim*) whom Abraham he-Ḥasid terms "friends of God" (*awliyā'*), who beheld (*yeḥezu*) God. He adds that "it is possible that this refers to an inner unveiling of the heart (*al-mukāshafa al-bāṭina al-qalbiya*) given to friends of God (*awliyā'*)." Abraham he-Ḥasid thus resolves the interpretive problem we saw in Maimonides. Maimonides argues that not all the people at Mount Sinai achieved the level of prophecy. Abraham he-Ḥasid's resolution is that there are degrees of prophetic inspiration—some fall under the category of full prophecy (*nubuwwa*), others under the category of friendship with God (*wilāya*). Abraham Maimonides, *Perush*, ed. Wiesenberg, 377; cf. Fenton, "Some Judaeo-Arabic Fragments," 58.

8 Abraham Maimonides, *Perush*, ed. Wiesenberg, 381.

9 *Guide* I:28, p. 60.

10 Maimonides follows Saadya in reading the Hebrew word *livnat* not as derived from *levenah*, "brick," but as derived from *lavan*, "white." Ibn Ezra argues that the stone is red, and comments: "Saadya says that sapphire is white, basing himself on the phrase *livnat ha-sappir*, but *livnah* has nothing to do with *lavan*, which means "white." *Livnah* means "brick," as it is translated in Ezekiel 4:1, 'and you, O mortal, take a brick and put it in front of you....'" See Ibn Ezra in *Torat Ḥayyim* (Jerusalem: Mossad Harav Kook, 1988), 73–74 (to Exodus 24:10); Carasik, *The Commentators' Bible*: *Exodus*, 220.

11 *Guide* I:28, p. 61. Abraham Maimonides (Abraham Maimonides, *Perush*, ed. Wiesenberg, 381) comments on "the very likeness of the heaven for purity" that it is "completely transparent," but does not introduce his father's analogy that transparency signifies matter that can take on any form. On this passage, see Alfred Ivry, *Maimonides'* Guide of the Perplexed: *A Philosophical Guide* (Chicago: University of Chicago Press, 2016), 57; on the language of transparency, see Hannah Kasher, "Maimonides' Interpretations," 32, note 6. Michelle Levine offers a comprehensive analysis and original interpretation of Maimonides' critique of this vision in the context of Maimonides' Aristotelian approach to physics and metaphysics. See Levine, "Maimonides' Philosophical Exegesis." While Maimonides discusses the transparency of matter to form in Aristotelian terms,

Abraham he-Ḥasid describes the vision of the angelic realm in decidedly non-Aristotelian language:

"Beneath his feet" is an allusion to the sacred angelic realm which encompasses the world of the angels according to their various degrees. Then [the verse alludes to the fact] that [the content of] the unveiling consists of [the heavenly world] and is seen, just as the spectacles are seen by means of the transparency of the sapphire. Because of how refined its substance is, the spectacles appear below it in a perfectly visible way.

The meaning of "work" refers to the effect of transparency in letting through the object perceived to the perceiver. This is an extraordinary simile (*tashbīh gharīb*) for, in so far as the beholder remains undetached from his bodily state, it is inconceivable that the unveiling of those spiritual worlds be perceived according to their reality. That inadequacy is likened to [sight] through the medium of that sapphire. It is indeed a vision, but unlike the vision of the beholder without an intermediary.

Abraham Maimonides, *Perush,* ed. Wiesenberg, 379–81; Fenton, "The Post-Maimonidean Schools of Exegesis in the East," 445.

12 Ezra Labaton points out that there is a contradiction between *Guide* I:4 and I:5. In I:4, Maimonides insists that all language of vision with respect to God is purely metaphorical; "seeing" means intellectual apprehension. Among the verses he quotes in this context is Exodus 24:10, "and they saw the God of Israel." By contrast, in *Guide* I:5, he criticizes the nobles for the corporeal nature of their vision, implying that they saw something physical. Abraham leaves it ambiguous as to whether the vision was sensory or purely intellectual. Labaton, *A Comprehensive Analysis*, 230, note 629.

13 Abraham Maimonides, *Perush,* ed. Wiesenberg, 383 (to Exodus 24:11): "*va-yeḥezu.*" Abraham he-Ḥasid likewise suggests that the eating and drinking refer to the return to an ordinary physical state after the spiritual state of solitary meditation: "The verse would then be an allusion to the fact that all of them were in a state of solitude (*khalwa*) which occurred on that blessed mountain, while devoting themselves to God awaiting the attainment of the perfect state of nearness to God (*qurb*) and his worship, which they had pursued, each according to his measure. This state was necessarily near to abstention from sustenance and therefore, when this condition came to an end, they partook of food and drink." As noted above, Abraham he-Ḥasid thus appears to describe the event at Mount Sinai as a prototype for the solitary mountain retreats of *khalwa* practiced by his circle of Pietists. Abraham Maimonides, *Perush,* ed. Wiesenberg, 379; Fenton, "The Post-Maimonidean Schools of Exegesis," 445–46.

14 Abraham Maimonides, *Perush,* ed. Wiesenberg, 383.

15 A third interpretive possibility is offered by Abraham he-Ḥasid, who argues that in the phrase "God did not stretch forth His hand," one should understand the term "hand" prophetically, as in passages such as "The hand

of the Lord was upon Elijah" (Kings 18:46) and "The hand of the Lord was upon me" (Ezekiel 37:1). Abraham he-Ḥasid suggests that the significance of this term is that God did not afford them God's prophetic inspiration (*waḥy*) in the manner that a majestic king stretches forth his hand to his close companion to convey to him that which he does not impart to another. Thus they are to be considered friends of God (*awliyā'*) and not prophets. Abraham Maimonides, *Perush,* ed. Wiesenberg, 377–79. (It is of note that Abravanel cites the same verse, Ezekiel 37:1, to suggest that only the nobles and not the leaders achieved prophecy.) This interpretation of Abraham he-Ḥasid is supported by an additional exegetical gloss in the margin of a Geniza manuscript (T-S Misc. 2.42): "The Pious R. Abraham of blessed memory, says that in the verse Exodus 34:1, 'To the Nobles of the children of Israel He did not stretch forth his hand,'; "To stretch forth' here signifies 'communion' and 'complete devotion' (*ittiṣāl wa-inqiṭā'*)." See Fenton, "Some Judaeo-Arabic Fragments," 58, note 39. The image of stretching forth one's hand is thus either stretching forth to strike (Maimonides and Abraham Maimonides) or the special touch that a majestic king offers a close companion, the unveiling (*kashf*) of divine secrets.

16 Maimonides, *Commentary on the Mishnah*, ed. Qafiḥ, vol. 6, 395; *Haqdamot*, ed. Shailat, 390 [Arabic], 248 [Hebrew]; Weiss and Butterworth, *Ethical Writings of Maimonides*, 83.

17 See Kasher, "Maimonides' Interpretations," 36, 45.

18 Maimonides, "Laws concerning the Foundations of the Torah" 1:10, in *The Code of Maimonides,* trans. Septimus (*Hilkhot Yesodei ha-Torah*), 1.

19 Drawing a parallel with al-Ghāzālī, Scott Girdner argues that "the true perception of God's existence, symbolized by the unveiling of God's face, is an understanding of God as belonging to a unique class of existence as the Necessary Existent." See Girdner, "Ghāzālī's Hermeneutics and Their Reception in Jewish Tradition," 259.

20 *Guide* I:38, p. 87.

21 *Guide* I:21, p. 49.

22 See Kreisel, *Prophecy*, 218–19; idem, "Judah Halevi's Influence on Maimonides: A Preliminary Appraisal," *Maimonidean Studies* 2 (1991): 110–12; Kasher, "Maimonides' Interpretations," 46–48; Shlomo Pines, "The Limitations of Human Knowledge according to al-Fārābī, ibn Bājja, and Maimonides," In *Studies in Medieval Jewish History and Literature*, vol. 1, ed. Isadore Twersky (Cambridge, MA: Harvard University Press, 1979), 102–03.

23 In her article "Is There an Early Stratum of the *Guide of the Perplexed?*," Hannah Kasher has suggested two layers in Maimonides' interpretation. Layer A includes the *Commentary to the Mishnah*, the *Mishneh Torah*, and *Guide* I:1–49. Layer B includes *Guide* I:50–end. In the three sources in Layer A, Moses makes one request, to apprehend the "true reality" of

God's existence (*ḥaqīqat wujūdihi*), and is informed by God that humans cannot know God as God is: "His apprehension, may He be blessed, in truth (*idrākuhu taʿalā ʿalā al-ḥaqīqa*)" (*Commentary on the Mishnah*); "His true existence as it is (*amittat himmatseʾo*)" (*Mishneh Torah, Yesodei Torah* 1:10); "The true reality of my existence as it veritably is (*ḥaqīqat wujūdī ʿala mā hiya ʿalayhi*)" (*Guide* I:37, p. 86). In Layer A, while Moses cannot see the "face" of God, he is granted a lesser apprehension, a view of the "back," "all the things created by God" (*Guide* I:38, p. 87), "knowledge of the acts ascribed to Him, may He be exalted, which . . . are deemed to be multiple attributes" (*Guide* I:21, p. 49). In Layer B, *Guide* I:54 and I:64, Moses asks for knowledge of God's essence and attributes, and is granted only knowledge of God's attributes of action, God in relation to creation, in contrast to knowledge of God's essence.

However, in her earlier article, "Maimonides' Interpretations of the Story of the Cleft of the Rock," Kasher acknowledges that while in the Eight Chapters and the *Mishneh Torah*, Moses appears to be granted some knowledge of God's being, in *all* the passages in the *Guide*—including those she ascribes to Layer A—Moses is only granted knowledge of creation. See Kasher, "Is There an Early Stratum of the *Guide of the Perplexed*?," 107–109; idem, "Maimonides' Interpretations," 39–47, esp. 45.

24 See above, 104, note 11.

25 On the term *talwīḥ*, Blau writes: "*remez*, symbolic exegesis of the Bible, one of the ways of biblical interpretation," and cites Maimonides' Commentary to the *Mishnah*. Blau, *A Dictionary of Mediaeval Judaeo-Arabic Texts*, 642. Herbert Davidson cites and discusses four uses of *talwīḥ* in the *Mishnah* commentary (Maimonides, *Commentary on the Mishnah,* ed. Qafiḥ): Introduction, 17, 19; *Ṭohorot* 1:1; *Ḥullin* 11:1; *Negaʿim* 6:1. See Herbert Davidson, *Moses Maimonides: The Man and His Works* (New York: Oxford University Press, 2005), 129. Maimonides also uses the term in the *Guide* to signal teaching in flashes. See *Guide* I:33, p. 72, ed. Munk and Joel, l. 24; *Guide* I:34, p. 78, ed. Munk and Joel, 53, l. 14. In verbal form: *Guide,* Introduction, 7, ed. Munk and Joel, 4, l. 6.

26 Abraham Maimonides, *Perush*, ed. Wiesenberg, 381.

27 On this passage, see Ilan, "Theological Assumptions," 51–52.

28 On the root *l-m-ḥ*, see ibid., 39, note 41.

29 *High Ways,* 382.

30 See Ilan, "Secrets."

Notes to Chapter 8

1 The explicit name (*shem ha-meforash*) is the name pronounced as it is written, in contrast to a substitute name (*kinnui*). The Tetragrammaton was

pronounced only in the Temple precinct during the priestly blessing and on Yom Kippur, while outside the Temple priests offered the priestly blessing using a substitute name. Even when pronounced in Temple, the articulated name was muffled by the chanting of other priests. See, for example, m. *Sotah* 7:6; b. *Sotah* 38a; b. *Qiddushin* 71a; y. *Yoma* 3:7; *Exodus Rabbah* 3:9; Hillel Ben Sasson and Moshe Halbertal, "The name Y-H-V-H and the Measure of Mercy" [Hebrew], in *Ve-zot li-Yehudah*, ed. Maren Nichoff, Ronit Meroz, and Jonathan Garb (Jerusalem: Mossad Bialik, 2012), 56–59; Ephraim E. Urbach, *The Sages: Their Concepts and Beliefs*, trans. I. Abrahams (Cambridge: Harvard University Press, 1987), 127–34. The distinctive, particular name (*shem-ha-meyuḥad*) shares an intimate relationship with God's essence. Ben Sasson and Halbertal, "The name Y-H-V-H and the Measure of Mercy," 57, 69. Maimonides in the twelfth century will suggest that the prohibition against pronouncing the name is connected with the inability to conceive it. *Guide* I:62, p. 150; ed. Schwarz, 124–25, ed. Munk and Joel, 77. Halevi notes that each of the letters of this name is both a vowel and a consonant, suggesting the breathy, insubstantial quality of the name. *Kuzari* IV:3, p. 147; ed. Qafiḥ, 150; ed. Hirschfeld, 201–02.

2 See Urbach, *Sages*, 735, note 17, 127–134; J. Z. Lauterbach, "Substitutes for the Tetragrammaton," *Proceedings of the AAJR* 22 (1930–31): 39–67; Ben Sasson and Halbertal, "The name Y-H-V-H and the Measure of Mercy," 59–60.

3 In rabbinic literature, we find the association of the Tetragrammaton with the quality of divine mercy, while the name *Elohim* is associated with judgment. For example, in *Sifre Devarim* (26:24), we read:

Every place in which "the Lord [Y-H-V-H]" is said, this is the quality of mercy, as it is said: "The Lord, The Lord, God of mercy and graciousness (Exodus 34:6); every place in which *Elohim* is said, this is the quality of judgment, as it is said: "The case of the two[parties] shall come before *ha-Elohim* (Exodus 22:8), and it says "You shall not revile *Elohim*" (Exodus 22:27).

Medieval Kabbalistic sources will develop this identification of the Tetragrammaton with the quality of mercy. In contrast, medieval philosophical sources tend to associate the Tetragrammaton with the character of being and presence implicit in the Hebrew root *hayah*.

4 Warren Zev Harvey, "Judah Halevi's Interpretation of the Tetragrammaton" (Hebrew), in *A Word Fitly Spoken: Studies in Mediaeval Exegesis of the Hebrew Bible and the Qur'ān*, ed. Meir M. Bar-Asher, Simon Hopkins, Sarah Stroumsa, and Bruno Chiesa (Jerusalem: Ben-Zvi Institute, 2007), 125–32.

5 *Kuzari* IV:3, p. 150; ed. Qafiḥ, 150–51; ed. Hirschfeld, 202.

6 Martin Buber, "The Burning Bush," in *On the Bible,* ed. Nahum Glatzer (Syracuse: Syracuse University Press, 2000), 44-62, at 61. Rabbi David Zvi Hoffmann notes that the connotation of *Ehyeh* as "I will be present"

is parallel to God's assurance that "I will be merciful to whom I will be merciful and I will be gracious to whom I will be gracious." See Hoffmann, *Sefer Va-yikra* (Jerusalem: Mossad Harav Kook, 1976), vol. 1, 70–76.

7 *Kuzari* IV:3, p. 150, ed. Qafiḥ, 150–51, ed. Hirschfeld, 202.

8 Abraham Ibn Ezra, *Perush 'al ha-Torah*, ed. A. Weiser (Jerusalem, 1976), 24 (to Exodus 3:15); *Torat Ḥayyim* (Jerusalem: Mossad Harav Kook, 1988), 34. See also below, Chapter 13, 146, note 11.

9 Abraham Ibn Ezra, *Sefer ha-Shem*, in *Yalquṭ Abraham Ibn Ezra,* ed. I. Levin (New York and Tel Aviv, 1985), 427; idem, *Perush 'al ha-Torah*, 25 (to Exodus 3:15); *Torat Ḥayyim*, 35.

10 R. Samuel ben Meir (Rashbam), *Perush ha-Torah,* ed. D. Rosin (Breslau, 1882), 84; *Rashbam's Commentary on Exodus: An Annotated Translation*, trans. Martin I. Lockshin (Atlanta: Scholar's Press, 1997), 36–38. See also below, Chapter 13, 146, note 11.

11 The curly brackets indicate insertions by Dubno.

12 *Das ewige, notwendige, vorsehende Wesen* ("the eternal, necessary, providential being").

13 English translation from *Moses Mendelssohn: Writings on Judaism, Christianity, and the Bible*, ed. Michah Gottlieb (Waltham, MA: Brandeis University Press, 2011), 216–17. See also the insightful discussion of Abigail Gillman, "Epilogue: *Ma Shemo?* The Name of God in the German Jewish Bible," in *A History of German Jewish Bible Translation* (Chicago: The University of Chicago Press, 2017), 251–61.

14 See commentary to Exodus 3:15, Gottlieb, *Moses Mendelssohn: Writings on Judaism*, 218–19.

Notes to Chapter 9

1 See *The Comprehensive Aramaic Lexicon Project*, http://cal1.cn.huc.edu/get_a_chapter.php?file=51002&sub=03&cset=H. The variant is from the apparatus to *The Bible in Aramaic,* ed. Alexander Sperber, vol. 1: *The Pentateuch According to Targum Onqelos* (Leiden: Brill, 1959), 93. The main text seems to be a Yemenite text in the British Library (OR. 228); the variant is the 1490 incunabulum of *Biblica Hebraica* from Hijar (Ixar). Other manuscript versions read *ehe 'im man de-ehe* ("I will be with whom I will be"). See *Targum Onqelos to Exodus*, ed. Israel Drazin (New York: Ktav, 1990), 59. This is the version we find in Nahmanides' comment to Exodus 3:14.

2 It is not clear whether the Aramaic is changing the Hebrew. The translator may simply be trying to render the phrase literally, word-for-word.

3 See *The Comprehensive Aramaic Lexicon Project*. I am indebted to Rabbi David Roth for this translation and interpretation. See also Drazin, *Targum*

Onqelos to Exodus, 59, notes 28–29. Modern Biblical scholars support the causative reading of *ehyeh* as a strong hypothesis. See for example Roland de Vaux, "The Revelation of the Divine Name YHWH," in *Proclamation and Presence: Old Testament Essays in Honor of Gwynne Henton Davies*, ed. John I. Durham and J. R. Porter (Richmond: John Knox Press, 1970), 48–75.

4 For the dating of the *Tanḥuma*, see *Maagarim, The Historical Dictionary Project* at the Academy of the Hebrew Language, http://maagarim.hebrew-academy.org.il/Pages/PMain.aspx?mishibbur=773000&mm15=000013020000, which has input the text of MS Cambridge Add 1212, considered overall the best available complete text of *Tanḥuma* (Printed Version). They date this text as "before the year 800." See also Marc Bregman, *The* Tanḥuma-Yelammedenu *Literature: Studies in the Evolution of the Versions* (Piscataway: Gorgias Press, 2000), Abstract, 3–5; Anat Reizel, *Introduction to the Midrashic Literature* [Hebrew] (Alon Shevut: Tevunot—Mikhelet Hertsog, 2010–11), 234–37; J. Z. Lauterbach, "*Tanḥuma*, Midrash," *JewishEncyclopedia.com*. In e-mail correspondence, Marc Bregman noted to me that this passage is "standard" *Tanḥuma* type material, which he describes as the "middle stratum." In *The Tanḥuma-Yelammedenu Literature*, Abstract, v, Bregman writes, "It seems clear that the standard type of Tanḥuma-Yelammedenu Literature was already a well-established Midrashic genre in Palestine before the end of the Byzantine period."

5 *Tanḥuma* (Printed Version), Exodus 20, MS Cambridge Add 1212, *Maagarim*, http://maagarim.hebrew-academy.org.il/Pages/PMain.aspx?mishibbur=773000&mm15=000013020000. Translation (with some revisions) based on Midrash Tanḥuma-Yelammedenu*: An English Translation of Genesis and Exodus from the Printed Version of* Tanḥuma-Yelammedenu *with an Introduction, Notes, and Indexes*, ed. Samuel A. Berman (Hoboken: Ktav Publishing House, 1996) 340.

6 For the dating of *Exodus Rabbah*, see Midrash Shemot Rabbah, *Chapters 1-14: A Critical Edition Based on a Jerusalem Manuscript with Variants, Commentary, and Introduction*, ed. Avigdor Shinan (Tel Aviv: Dvir, 1984), 23–24; Bregman, *The Tanḥuma-Yelammedenu Literature*, Abstract, iv; Reizel, *Introduction to the Midrashic Literature*, 117–18. In e-mail communication, Marc Bregman noted that the first part of *Exodus Rabbah*, chapters 1–14 (published in the critical edition by Shinan) is "late" (tenth century); it contains material from the Babylonian Talmud. However, it also uses material from Tanḥuma (Printed Version), which probably dates to the seventh century (see citation from *Maagarim* in previous footnote, and Bregman, *The Tanḥuma-Yelammedenu Literature*, Abstract, iv)._

7 Midrash Shemot Rabbah, *Chapters 1-14*, 127 (*Exodus Rabbah* 3:6). In one manuscript variant, this statement is attributed to R. Abba bar Memmel. The critical edition differs from the printed version in several of the attributions.

I cite here the first three of the six interpretations offered of *Ehyeh asher Ehyeh*, the three which are relevant to Saadya's discussion.

8 Midrash Shemot Rabbah, *Chapters 1–14*, 127 (*Exodus Rabbah* 3:6). As Shinan notes, in the printed edition, this is attributed to R. Jacob bar Avina in the name of R. Huna of Sepphoris.

Notes to Chapter 10

1 Lane defines *azalī* as "eternal, with respect to past time; existing from eternity; or ancient without beginning." Lane, *Arabic-English Lexicon*, 54.

2 Ibid., 54.

3 This *piyyuṭ* was published in Menahem Zulay, *Ha-askolah ha-payyeṭanit shel Rav Se'adyah Gaon* (Tel-Aviv: Schocken, 1969), 218–25.

4 Haggai Ben-Shammai explains the differences between the two forms of translation in several publications, among them, "Extra-Textual Considerations in Medieval Judaeo-Arabic Bible Translations: The Case of Saadya Gaon," *Materia Guidaica* 7 (2003): 53–59; idem, *A Leader's Project: Studies in the Philosophical and Exegetical Works of Saadya Gaon* [Hebrew] (Jerusalem: Bialik Institute, 2015), 308–14.

5 *Tafsīr Yesha'ya le-Rav Saadya,* ed. Yehuda Ratzaby (Kiryat Ono: Mekhon Mishnat ha-Rambam, 1993), 220, 331.

6 See also *Perushe Rav Saadya Gaon le-Bereishit,* ed. Moshe Zucker (New York: Jewish Theological Seminary of America, 1984), 57, 263.

7 We do not know whether Saadya used a written version of *Tanḥuma* as a literary source. However, it does seem that he may have made use of the midrashic tradition we find in *Tanḥuma* and then adapted in *Exodus Rabbah* 3:6. Solomon Buber, in the Introduction to his edition of the *Tanḥuma*, notes that Saadya cites (*Tanḥuma*)-*Yelammedenu* in a *teshuvah.* See *Midrash Tanḥuma ha-qadum ve-ha-yashan,* ed. Solomon Buber (Vilna, 1885), 87. I thank Marc Bregman for alerting me to this citation.

8 It is also possible that Saadya's interpretation of *Ehyeh asher Ehyeh* as eternity may have influenced the formulation of R. Isaac found in *Exodus Rabbah.* The historical interpretations in *Exodus Rabbah* have parallels in the early sources *Tanḥuma* and b. *Berakhot.* It is only the interpretation of eternity attributed to R. Isaac that we have not yet found attested in an earlier source; however, it might well have an early parallel that was known to Saadya. It is thus possible either that the source was in some way known to Saadya, that Saadya's interpretation influenced the source, or that these are simply two coincidentally parallel interpretations. In any event, since the interpretation of *Ehyeh asher Ehyeh* as eternity is found in early liturgical poetry, this interpretation does have classical, pre-philosophical roots.

9 *Piyyuṭe Yannai*, ed. Menaḥem Zulai (Jerusalem: Schocken, 1938), 17.

10 Ibid., 338; Z. M. Rabinovitz does not include this *piyyuṭ* in his collection of Yannai. Cf. entry for the word *Ehyeh* (pronoun), *Maagarim*, http://maagarim.hebrew-academy.org.il/Pages/PMain.aspx?koderekh=658&page=1.

11 Cf. Genesis 15:5: "So shall your descendants [seed] be (*koh yihyeh zar'ekha*)."

12 Cf. Ecclesiastes 1:9: "What has been done is what will be, and what has been done is what will be done."

13 *Piyyuṭe Rabbi Pinḥas ha-Kohen*, ed. Shulamit Elizur (Jerusalem: World Congress of Jewish Studies, 2004), 477–78.

14 The comment in full reads: "This follows the approach of Rav Saadya Gaon, who said one should only attribute to [God] two times, the past and the future. For the middle time of the present is nothing, for even a small instant of it is of the past or the future." *Perushe Rabenu Se'adyah Gaon 'al ha-Torah*, ed. Joseph Qafiḥ (Jerusalem: Mossad Harav Kook, 1963), 45. However, this comment may be reading Saadya's philosophical views about the fleeting nature of the present into his philological exegesis of *Ehyeh asher Ehyeh*.

Notes to Chapter 11

1 Haggai Ben-Shammai, "More on Commentary in Service of Theology: The Discussion of the Names of God in Rav Saadya Gaon's Commentary to Exodus 3 (in Manuscript)" [Hebrew], lecture delivered at the conference "Contexts and Polemics: Conference in Honor of Sarah Stroumsa," Hebrew University of Jerusalem, December 24–25, 2017. Ben-Shammai is publishing the commentary based on two manuscripts: MS RNL Yevr.–Arab. II: 1148, f. 103–06; MS Cambridge University Library T-S Misc. 28. 206.

2 See interpretations 2–4.

3 Ben-Shammai has thus discovered the missing explication of attributes of essence and attributes of action promised by Saadya Gaon, *Kitāb al-amānāt wa'l-i'tiqādāt* II:12, ed. Qafiḥ, 110, ed. Rosenblatt, 129. The distinction between essential and active attributes, introduced by the Mu'tazilites, was also acknowledged by some of their rivals, including al-Ash'arī (874–935) and al-Juwaynī (d. 1086), who attributes the distinction to "our master" (*sheikh*), i.e. al-Ash'arī. Haggai Ben-Shammai writes, "All Jewish *mutakallimūn* accepted the distinction between attributes of the essence of God and attributes of his actions, which was typical of most *mutakallimūn*, especially the Baṣran school," which was headed by Abū al-Hudhayl (d. 841/849), and included al-Jubbā'ī (d. 915) and Abū Hāshim, son of al-Jubbā'ī (d. 933). Claude Gilliot writes that it is in the generation after Abū al-Hudhayl that the Mu'tazilites "distinguished definitively between two types of attributes, those of essence (*ṣifāt al-dhāt*, sometimes *ṣifāt al-nafs*) and those of act (*ṣifāt al-fi'l*)." Likewise, Josef van Ess notes that Abū al-Hudhayl "did not speak of attributes of essence and attributes of act, which will become the

custom in the next generation of the Muʿtazila." Saadya (882–942) was thus picking up on a distinction that was being solidified in his lifetime and in his intellectual milieu. See al-Ashʿarī, *Maqālāt al-Islāmiyīn* (Istanbul, 1939–40), 508–509; al-Juwaynī, *al-Irshād*, ed. J. D. Luciani (Paris, 1938), 82 [Arabic], 137 [French]; Daniel Gimaret, *La doctrine d' al-Ashʿarī* (Paris: Cerf, 1990), 352; Josef van Ess, *Theology and Society in the Second and Third Centuries of the Hijra: A History of Religious Thought in Early Islam*, vol. 3, trans. Gwendolyn Goldblum (Leiden: Brill, 2018), 294; cf. ibid., 434; Claude Gilliot, "Attributes of God," in *Encyclopaedia of Islam*, 3rd ed., ed. Kate Fleet et al. (Leiden: Brill, 2007–), http://dx.doi.org/10.1163/1573-3912_ei3_COM_0163, accessed June 07, 2018; Majid Fakhry, *A Short Introduction to Islamic Philosophy, Theology, and Mysticism* (Oxford: Oneworld Publications, 1997), 19; idem, *A History of Islamic Philosophy*, 2nd ed. (New York: Columbia University Press, 1983), 60; Catarina Belo, "Muʿtazilites, Al-Ashʿarī and Maimonides on Divine Attributes," *Veritas* 52, no. 3 (September 2007): 117–31, at 122; A. S. Tritton, "The Speech of God," *Studia Islamica* 36 (1972): 5–22; Haggai Ben-Shammai, "Kalām in Medieval Jewish Philosophy," in *History of Jewish Philosophy*, ed. Daniel Frank and Oliver Leaman (New York: Routledge 2014), 104. R. M. Frank, "Al-Ashʿarī," in *Encyclopaedia of Islam*, 2nd ed., ed. P. Bearman, Th. Bianquis, C. E. Bosworth, E. van Donzel, and W. P. Heinrichs (Leiden: Brill, 1960–). On this distinction in Saadya, see Alexander Altmann, "The Divine Attributes: A Historical Survey of the Jewish Discussion," *Judaism* 15 (1966): 44–45.

4 In his sixth comment, Saadya writes, "he repeats *Ehyeh* only once (in Exodus 3:15), signifying that he is the essential existent, even when he does not do anything." Likewise, he comments to Exodus 3:15 that "this is my name" [points to] attributes of essence, while "this is my memorial" [points to] attributes of action. This point will be picked up by Abraham Maimonides (see below).

5 Ben-Shammai points out that while the abstract term *azaliyya* is common in parallel Arabic philosophical and theological texts, it is significant that Saadya chooses to support this new abstract vocabulary with a Rabbinic source. Lane defines *azaliyya* as "the quality, or attribute, of *azal* [eternity, with respect to past time, etc.]," noting that according to two classical sources "it is a forged term, not of the [genuine] language of the Arabs." Lane, *Arabic-English Lexicon*, 54.

Notes to Chapter 12

1 Nevertheless, in his formulation in the *Tafsīr*—the eternal that will not cease (*al-azalī alladhī lā yazūl)*, Saadya is clearly drawing upon the conventional sense of *al-azalī* as beginningless.

2 As we have seen, in the translation accompanying his long commentary, Saadya actually translates, "who has not ceased and will not cease," *alladhī lam yazal wa-lā yazūl*. Classical Arabic dictionaries suggest that the jussive form may be either *lam yazal* or *lam yazul*. I thank Yonatan Negev for this observation.

3 Or: the eternal that does not cease. It is not clear which meaning Abraham intends by the use of the imperfect, "will not cease" or "does not cease." While in Abraham's words, the more precise translation includes the imperfect form *lā yazāl*, in the earliest surviving (almost) full manuscript of Saadya's *Tafsīr*, written in the early eleventh century by a careful scribe (RNL Yevr. II C 1, ff. 125b–126a), Saadya's comment has the imperfect as *lā yazūl*. Lane's classical Arabic dictionary cites the *Kulliyāt of Abu-l-baqā'*, contrasting: 1. *lam yazal*, "He or it has not ceased to be," said of God, meaning "he has never been nonexistent" and 2. *lā yazāl*, said of God, "He will never be nonexistent" (Lane, *Arabic-English Lexicon*, 1278). Lane offers two possible derivations of the term *al-azal*, which he defines as "eternal in the sense of beginningless." The term *azal* has to do with narrowness, so that the mind is prevented by its narrowness from determining the limit of the beginning. Another derivation of the term *al-azal* is from the phrase *lam yazal*, meaning "he has not ceased, he has ever been" (Lane, *Arabic-English Lexicon*, 54). This would make sense of the phrase that Abraham Maimonides attributes to Saadya, and that is found in Saadya's *Kitāb al-amānāt wa'l-i'tiqādāt* II:13: "*al-azalī alladhī lam yazal*" ("the eternal that has not ceased"). I thank Haggai Ben-Shammai and David Sklare for sharing an image of RNL Yevr. II C 1, ff. 125b–126a, which has not yet been digitized, as well as pointing me to RNL Yevr.–Arab. 1:127, the famous "Leningrad Manuscript" of the *Kitāb al-amānāt wa'l-i'tiqādāt*.

4 On the term *sarmad*, see Shlomo Pines, *Nouvelles études sur awḥad al-zamān Abu-l-Barakāt al-Baghdādī* (Paris: Librairie Durlacher, 1995), 31, 62ff.

5 Abraham Maimonides, *Perush*, ed. Wiesenberg, 227 (to Exodus 3:14). See the translation of Raphael Jospe, "Naḥmanides and Arabic," in his *Jewish Philosophy: Foundations and Extensions*, vol. 2 (Lanham: University Press of America, 2008), 192–93.

6 Raphael Jospe translates the passage somewhat differently: "Rabbi Sa'adiah Ga'on translated *ehyeh asher ehyeh* ['I will be whatever I will be'] as *al-azali aladhi lam yazal*, the eternal which did not cease, whereas a more correct translation would be *al-azali aladhi la yazal*, the eternal which does not cease. I found something like this in his long commentary, that *ehyeh* ['I will be'] indicates eternity without beginning, and *asher ehyeh* indicates eternity and continuity without end, so the meaning of eternity is connected to continuity." Jospe interprets Abraham's imperfect verb *lā yazāl* as "does not cease" (a possibility I consider in the following note). He also appears to interpret the final phrase "the meaning of eternity is connected to

(*talzamuhu*) continuity" as a statement of the connection between *ehyeh* and *asher ehyeh*. This is certainly one interpretive possibility. The interpretive question hinges on the meaning of the verb *talzamuhu*. The first form of the root *l-z-m* connotes being inseparable from, necessarily belonging to something; I have translated it as "necessarily involves." It seems to me that Abraham is indicating the following. It is not just the phrase *ehyeh asher ehyeh* that connects the notions of eternity and everlastingness; the concept of eternity necessarily includes both past and future. Abraham indicates that he found this explication in Saadya's long commentary. And indeed, this is what we find in the manuscript version of Saadya's comment: "The interpretation of '*ehyeh* sent me to you' is therefore 'the eternal (*al-azalī*),' which includes the two times [past and future] together." (See above, Chapter 11, 134)

7 It is not completely clear how he is accomplishing his aim linguistically. He rejects part of Saadya's translation (the phrase *lam yazal*, "has not ceased"), perhaps because the negative and past meaning of the jussive verb is too far from the Hebrew original (*Ehyeh asher Ehyeh*). However, the jussive form is attested in certain Judeo-Arabic texts to have the same meaning as the imperfect. See Joshua Blau, *A Grammar of Mediaeval Judaeo-Arabic*, 2nd ed. (Jerusalem: Magnes, 1980), 316, addition to 142. He also apparently revises the imperfect verb we find in Saadya, *lā yazūl*, to *lā yazāl*. The form *lā yazāl* is frequently used with the meaning "one does not cease to do something." It is thus not clear whether Abraham intends by the use of the imperfect to mean "will not cease" or "does not cease." Perhaps the vocalization *lā yazūl*, "will not cease," introduces the notion of ceasing, while *lā yazāl*, which often means "does not cease," moves towards metaphysical necessity. It is also possible that Abraham simply had a different vocalization of Saadya's commentary than the manuscripts we possess. (I thank Yonatan Negev and Miriam Bronstein for their suggestions here.)

8 Our printed versions (Derenbourg and Qafiḥ) read: "That he is eternal, that he has not ceased and does not cease (*azalī alladhī lam yazal wa-lā yazūl*)." However, we would expect ***al**-azalī* (**the** eternal), as *alladhī* is almost always tied to a definite noun, and the passage continues with other attributes using the definite article, such as *al-wāḥid, al-qādir, al-ʿālim*. And indeed, the famous "Leningrad Manuscript" confirms our expectations. Although the manuscript has been somewhat damaged, one can read the definite article *al*. On the term *maʿānī* as signifying attributes, see Wolfson, *Repercussions of the Kalam*, 11, note 12.

9 See Jospe, "Naḥmanides and Arabic," 192. Note that Maimonides, too, cites Deuteronomy 33:27 as a prooftext for God's eternity. See *Guide* I:70, p. 172; and *Commentary on the Mishnah, Perek Ḥeleq*, fourth of the Thirteen Principles of Faith, in Maimonides, *Haqdamot*, ed. Shailat, 370 [Arabic],

142 [Hebrew]; English translation by Arnold J. Wolf, in *A Maimonides Reader*, ed. Isadore Twersky (Springfield: Behrman House, 1972), 418.

10 Abraham Maimonides may have in mind any of three phrases: 1. Saadya's translation in the *Tafsīr*: the eternal that will not cease to be (*al-azalī alladhī lā yazūl*); 2. the expression from *Kitāb al-amānāt*—the eternal that has not ceased to be and will not cease to be (*al-azalī alladhī lam yazal wa-lā yazūl*); 3. Saadya's explication in his long commentary. In this explication, Saadya makes three interpretive moves: 1. He translates *Ehyeh asher Ehyeh* as "who has not ceased to be and will not cease to be" (*alladhī lam yazal wa-lā yazūl*); 2. he interprets the name *Ehyeh* in Exodus 3:15 (*Ehyeh* sent me to you) as "the eternal" (*al-azalī*); 3. he describes the existence of God with the abstract term "eternity" (*azaliyya*).

11 Abraham Maimonides, *Perush*, ed. Wiesenberg, 227 (to Exodus 3:14).

12 For Avicenna's metaphysical proof, see the texts from Avicenna's *Healing* (*al-Shifā'*), *Deliverance* (*al-Najāt*), and other works, translated in George Hourani, "Avicenna on Necessary and Possible Existence," *The Philosophical Forum* 4, no. 1 (1972): 74–86; and in Arthur Hyman and James Walsh, eds., *Philosophy in the Middle Ages*, 2nd ed. (Indianapolis: Hackett Publishing Company, 1983), 241–55. See also Warren Zev Harvey, *Physics and Metaphysics in Hasdai Crescas* (Amsterdam: J. C. Giben, 1988), 73ff; Herbert Davidson, *Proofs for Eternity, Creation, and the Existence of God* (New York: Oxford University Press, 1987), 281–310; Gutas, *Avicenna and the Aristotelian Tradition*, 261–65.

13 I thank Professor Zev Harvey for this insightful suggestion, which arose in conversation.

14 E.g., in the Yom Kippur service, *Musaf*, we read, "*ve-ha-kohanim ve-ha-'am ha-'omdim be-'azarah, keshe-hayu shom'im et ha-shem ha-nikhbad ve-ha-nora*," which alludes to Deuteronomy 28:58: "*et ha-shem ha-nikhbad ve-ha-nora ha-zeh*." See *High Holiday Prayer Book*, trans. Philip Birnbaum (New York: Hebrew Publishing Company, 1951), 817. Abraham Ibn Ezra regularly uses the term *ha-shem ha-nikhbad* in the unequivocal sense of the Tetragrammaton. See, for example, long commentary to Exodus 3:13, 33:19; cf. Nahmanides' commentary to Exodus 3:14. The mix of Arabic and Hebrew in the use of definite pronouns: *hadhā al* (Arabic) and *shem ha-nikhbad* (Hebrew) is a regular feature in Judeo-Arabic texts, especially when the phrase receiving the definitive case is a special term rooted in Jewish religious and liturgical language. See Joshua Blau, *The Emergence and Linguistic Background of Judaeo-Arabic: A Study of the Origins of Neo-Arabic and Middle-Arabic* (Jerusalem: Ben-Zvi Institute for the Study of Jewish Communities, 1989), Appendix 2, seg. 4, 140–43.

15 *Guide* I:62, p. 152.

Notes to Chapter 13

1 Cf. Joseph Ibn Caspi, *Menorat Kessef,* printed in *Sheloshah qadmone mefarshe ha-Moreh* (Jerusalem: Ortsel, 1960), 65. Note, too, that in the *Mishneh Torah, Hilkhot Yesodei ha-Torah* 1:1, Maimonides begins his discussion of *ma'aseh merkavah* with the letters of the Name: ***y****esode* ***h****a-yesodot* ***v****e-'amud* ***h****a-ḥokhmot.*

2 *Guide* I:61, p. 147; ed. Schwarz, 155–56; ed. Munk and Joel, 100.

3 See Lane, *Arabic-English Lexicon,* 1044.

4 Maimonides explains in the Introduction to the *Guide* and in the *Treatise on Logic,* Chapter XIII, what he means by an equivocal term, which is when one word has different meanings. Completely equivocal terms (*mushtarika al-maḥḍat al-ishtirāk*) have only a name in common, such as *'ayin,* which means both fountain and eye. An amphibolous term (*mushakkika*), such as the term man applied to Zayd, the corpse of a man, and the picture of a man have in common the appearance or shape of a human being, but this common factor is an accidental property and does not constitute their essence. Finally, there is the metaphorical term (*musta'āra*) *aryeh,* whose first meaning refers to a lion, which is then transferred to the description of a courageous man. The term has a fixed usage in its original meaning, which is transferred to another object, in which it does not have a permanent meaning. As with amphibolous terms, the common factor is not the essences of things compared but some accidental property. See Arthur Hyman, "Maimonides on Religious Language," in *Perspectives on Maimonides,* ed. Joel Kraemer (London: Littman, 1996), 178–79; Israel Efros, "Maimonides' Treatise on Logic," *PAAJR* 8, no. 13 (1937–38): 59–60. On the notion that the *shem ha-meyuḥad* is the name that is distinctive to God, while all other names are substitutes (*kinuyyim*), see Ben Sasson and Halbertal, "The name Y-H-V-H and the Measure of Mercy," 57, 69.

5 See Lane, *Arabic-English Lexicon,* 1577.

6 In Josef Stern's formulation, "the Merciful [One]" designates that unique being X, such that X is merciful. The divine name "the Merciful" is derived from the attribute-term "is merciful" that is also applied to other creatures. See Stern, *Matter and Form,* 223; *Guide* I:61, ed. Schwarz, 155, note 1; F. W. Zimmerman, *Al-Fārābī's Commentary and Short Treatise on Aristotle's De Interpretatione* (Oxford: Oxford University Press, 1981), 230, note 4, xxiv–xxxviii.

7 See Stern, *Matter and Form,* 224.

8 *Guide* I:61, pp. 147–48; ed. Schwarz, 155–56, ed. Munk and Joel, 100.

9 *Guide* I:61, p. 148; ed. Schwarz, 156; ed. Munk and Joel, 101.

10 It is possible, for example, that in ancient Hebrew, "will be" (*yhyh*) was spelled *yhvh.* Maimonides does not mention the root *hayah* explicitly in *Guide* I:62 as he does in *Guide* I:63. Maimonides does not want to associate

necessary being with contingent being; as he notes in *Guide* I:57, existence is an accident and God possesses no accidents. However, this does not necessitate that there is no connection between the Tetragrammaton and the root connoting being. In asserting that if we knew more about the ancient Hebrew language we might discover that the Tetragrammaton indicates the notion of a Necessary Existence, Maimonides suggests a semantic significance of the name that in Hebrew must point to a three letter root. As mentioned below, Maimonides does not use the term "proper name" (*ism ʿalam*) as does Halevi, whom he certainly read.

11 Perhaps in suggesting that if we knew more about ancient Hebrew, we would know the meaning of the Tetragrammaton, Maimonides may be pointing to the interpretation of Ibn Ezra. Ibn Ezra states clearly that the two names are identical; *Ehyeh* is simply in the first person ("I will be"), while the Tetragrammaton is in the third person ("he will be"). See Ibn Ezra's commentary to Exodus 3:14–15. Rashbam makes a more explicit morphological point: "He calls himself *Ehyeh* ('I will be'), while we call him *Yihyeh* ('he will be'), Y-H-V-H, with a *vav* in place of *yod,* as in the verse '*ki meh hoveh la-adam*' (Ecclesiastes 2:22)." If the Tetragrammaton simply means "he will be," why is there a *vav* rather than a *yod*? Perhaps Maimonides is reflecting obliquely on this problem, and suggesting that if we knew more about ancient Hebrew, we would find that the morphological form of the Tetragrammaton might signify Necessary Existence. (For example, perhaps—and this is purely speculative—the middle *vav* might act as an intensifier. This possibility, along with that in note 10 that "will be" might have originally been spelled *yhvh*, arose in conversation with Professor Zev Harvey.)

12 *Kuzari* IV:1–2, pp. 147–148; ed. Qafiḥ, 147–48; ed. Hirschfeld, 198–99.

13 *Guide* I:61, p. 149; ed. Schwarz, 157; ed. Munk and Joel, 102; *Guide* I:63, p. 156; ed. Schwarz, 164; ed. Munk and Joel, 107.

14 Josef Stern notes that this does not necessarily mean that we understand the representation. He stresses that for Maimonides, representation is an inner language, and we often use words in a language without understanding what we are saying. Stern, personal communication and *Matter and Form*, 193–98, 222.

15 Cf. Moshe Halbertal and Avishay Margalit, *Idolatry* (Cambridge: Harvard University Press, 1992), 156. See also the very interesting comment of Kasher, "Maimonides' Interpretations," 58.

16 *Guide* I:62, p. 151; ed. Schwarz, 160; ed. Munk and Joel, 103. See also Pines, "The Limitations of Human Knowledge," 82–109.

17 *Guide* I:61, p. 147; ed. Schwarz, 155; ed. Munk and Joel, 100. On Maimonides' critique of the magical use of divine names, see Kellner, *Maimonides' Confrontation with Mysticism*, 173–75.

18 *Guide* I:61, p. 148; ed. Schwarz, 157; ed. Munk and Joel, 101.

19 Indeed, Aquinas interprets Maimonides as agreeing with him that God's proper name is "Being." See the illuminating discussion of Mercedes Rubio, *Aquinas and Maimonides on the Possibility of the Knowledge of God: An Examination of the* Quaestio de Attributis (Dordrecht: Springer, 2006), 110–33.

20 However, note that conceptually, Baḥya's essential attributes, which are wholly metaphysical, point toward the conception of Necessary Existence that we find in Avicenna and Maimonides. Maimonides is simply uncomfortable with the language of essential attributes, with its danger of introducing multiplicity into the divine. See Saadya Gaon, *Kitāb al-amānāt wa'l-i'tiqādāt* II:4, ed. Qafiḥ, 98–99; Baḥya Ibn Paqūda, *Torat ḥovot ha-levavot* I:10, ed. Qafiḥ, 73, 76; ed. Mansoor, 132–34; Lobel, *A Sufi-Jewish Dialogue*, 103–06.

21 *Guide* I:62–63, pp. 152.

22 In e-mail communication, Professors Haggai Ben-Shammai and Joshua Blau explained that the phrase *hadhā al-ism* refers to a/the preceding word/phrase, which is the Tetragrammaton. Theoretically, in Judeo-Arabic *hadhā al-ism* could refer to a following word. It is *wa-huwa* which makes this option impossible. This word introduces an "explanatory addition" which ties the Tetragrammaton and *ehyeh* as a kind of synonym of one and the same entity. The reading proposed by Yossi Schwarz and Hillel Ben-Sasson (see following note) artificially cuts apart one sentence into two disconnected units. In the one complete sentence, *wa* in *wa-huwa* functions as a relative pronoun, like *alladhī*, and therefore refers to the preceding word/phrase and not the following one, i.e. *ehyeh*. It thus seems that in this way Maimonides equates the Tetragrammaton with *ehyeh*.

23 See Yossi Schwarz,"Ben shelilah le-shetikah: ha-Rambam be-ma'arav ha-latini," Iyyun 45, no. 4 (October 1996): 391; Hillel Ben-Sasson, *The Divine Name YHWH: Its Meanings in Biblical Rabbinic and Medieval Jewish Thought* (PhD dissertation, Hebrew University, 2013), 185–94; cf. Menahem Lorberbaum, *Dazzled by Beauty: Theology as Poetics in Hispanic Jewish Culture* [Hebrew] (Jerusalem: Ben-Zvi Institute, 2011), 93–98, 106. In contrast, Alexander Altmann identifies the Tetragrammaton and *Ehyeh asher Ehyeh.* See Altmann, "Essence and Existence in Maimonides," in his *Studies in Religious Philosophy and Mysticism* (Ithaca: Cornell University Press, 1969), 110; cf. Alfred Ivry, *Maimonides'* Guide of the Perplexed: *A Philosophical Guide* (Chicago: University of Chicago Press, 2016), 62. Halbertal and Margalit, *Idolatry*, 157, suggest that *Ehyeh Asher Ehyeh* hints at the Tetragrammaton. Stern, *Matter and Form,* 221–26, argues that the Tetragrammaton, *Ehyeh asher Ehyeh* and the Arabic term *'anniyya* (or *'inniyya*) represent three ways that Maimonides circumvents what he calls the syntactic problem of divine attributes.

24 See Ben-Sasson, *The Divine Name YHWH*, 193–94.

25 See also Nahmanides, commentary to Exodus 3:13.

26 This could also be knowledge of the Tetragrammaton, as suggested by the formulation we will see at the end of the chapter. See *Guide* I:63, p. 156; ed. Schwarz, 164; ed. Munk and Joel, 107.

27 As he puts it, the secret of this name consists in the repetition as a predicate of the word that indicates existence ("I am" / *Ehyeh*); the relative pronoun ("that, who, what" / *asher*) indicates that the subject (I am / *Ehyeh*) is identical with the predicate (I am / *Ehyeh*). Josef Stern has identified Maimonides' syntactic analysis of *Ehyeh asher Ehyeh* as a resolution to the syntactic problem of divine attributes. Thus he argues that what Maimonides is negating is not simply particular attributes but the syntactic category of attributes, picking up on al-Fārābī's attention to syntax. Stern, *Matter and Form*, 218–25, and personal communication.

28 I thank Professor Bernard Septimus for suggesting to me the formulation "I exist in that I [must] exist."

29 Avicenna, *Shifā': Ilāhiyyāt* 8:6:2–3. See *The Metaphysics of the Healing: A Parallel English-Arabic Text of al-Ilāhiyyāt min al-Shifā'*, trans. Michael Marmura (Provo: Brigham Young University Press, 2005), 283. At the end of *Guide* I:62, Maimonides suggested that the term *Ehyeh asher Ehyeh* teaches the negation of attributes. The Necessary Existent is existent not through the attribute of existence. Necessary Existence negates all contingent being.

30 See Warren Zev Harvey, "Maimonides and Aquinas on Interpreting the Bible," *PAAJR* 55 (1988): 65–66. For a resolution of the tension between Maimonides' negative theology and his description of God as self-cognizing intellect, see Hannah Kasher, "Self-Cognizing Intellect and Negative Attributes in Maimonides' Theology," *Harvard Theological Review* 87, no. 4 (1994): 461–72.

31 See also above, notes 10, 58–59.

32 I thank Professor Zev Harvey for this suggestion, which arose in conversation.

33 We can see a precedent for this connection in Baḥya Ibn Paqūda, who asserts that absolute existence includes the notion of eternity. See Baḥya Ibn Paqūda, *Torat ḥovot ha-levavot* I:10; ed. Qafiḥ, 74; ed. Rosenblatt, 133. This is implicit in Avicenna's notion; absolute existence has no possibility of non-existence. As I note below, while Necessary Existence entails eternity, eternity does not entail Necessary Existence.

34 Moses Narboni, *Perush ʿal Moreh ha-Nevukhim,* in *Sheloshah qadmone mefarshe ha-Moreh* (Jerusalem, 1960), 10b.

Notes to Chapter 14

1 Abraham Maimonides, *Perush,* ed. Wiesenberg, 227 (to Exodus 3:14). On the three meanings of *sod* in his passages, see now the penetrating discussion in Ilan, "Secrets," 86–89.

2 We see this twofold dimension of God in the thought of Baḥya Ibn Paqūda, who distinguishes between God in God's essence and God in relation to creation. Baḥya Ibn Paqūda I:10, *Torat ḥovot ha-levavot*, ed. Qafiḥ, 73–74; ed. Rosenblatt, 132. In Abraham's formulation, God in God's essence is the Necessary Existent; God is not caused. However, God is also a presence that acts providentially, sending messengers and allowing God's name to be known historically. Baḥya himself takes a different approach to the divine names; he contrasts *Ehyeh asher Ehyeh* of Exodus 3:14 with "The Lord, the God of your fathers": "If the people cannot understand the word and its meaning through their reason, tell them I am the One they know by way of the tradition of their ancestors." Baḥya Ibn Paqūda, *Torat ḥovot ha-levavot*, 81–82 (I:10); idem, *Duties of the Heart*, 141.

3 *Guide* II:35, p. 367.

4 Abraham Ibn Ezra, long commentary to Exodus 3:15; see his *Perush,* ed. Weiser, 25; and *Torat Ḥayyim*, 35; long commentary to Exodus 6:3; see his *Perush,* ed. Weiser, 47, *Torat Ḥayyim*, 67; *Sefer ha-Shem,* chapter 8, in *Yalquṭ Abraham Ibn Ezra,* ed. I. Levin (New York and Tel Aviv, 1985), 427. For a lucid explication, see Raphael Jospe, *Jewish Philosophy in the Middle Ages* (Brighton, MA: Academic Studies Press, 2009), 208–09.

5 Judah Halevi argues that the early Biblical ancestors were on the same level as Moses, but they did not need to perform miracles, because the people of that time had utmost faith (*īmān*) and purity of heart. Abraham Maimonides does not mention Halevi's interpretation. See *Kuzari* II:2, 44-45; ed. Qafiḥ, 46-47; ed. Hirschfeld, 86.

6 Ibn Ezra accepts, while Maimonides and Abraham Maimonides reject, what Aviezer Ravitzky has termed "the anthropological theory of miracles," the view that communion with the All through the Tetragrammaton enables one to perform miracles. See Aviezer Ravitzky, "The Anthropological Theory of Miracles in Medieval Jewish Philosophy," in *Studies in Medieval Jewish History and Literature*, vol. 2, ed. Isadore Twersky (Cambridge, MA: Harvard University Center for Jewish Studies, 1984), 238–39 and note 20.

7 Abraham Maimonides cites Ibn Ezra's wording in reverse from the text we have. The text as we have it reads: "There is no doubt that the patriarchs knew this name, which is a proper noun, but they did not know this name as an adjective." Abraham Maimonides' version of Ibn Ezra reads: "There is no doubt that the patriarchs knew this name, which is an adjective, but they did not know this name as a proper noun." Abraham's view is that Moses knew this name as a noun, as we see in what follows. Thus on this point,

he thinks he disagrees with Ibn Ezra, while he in fact agrees. What he does reject is the view that one can perform miracles through knowledge of the Tetragrammaton.

8 As Wiesenberg notes (Abraham Maimonides, *Perush,* ed. Wiesenberg, 238, note 23), Abraham seems to be drawing upon Maimonides' discussion of attributes and accidents in Guide I:51–52. However, he introduces slight changes in terminology with respect to the terms *nisba* and *iḍāfiyya.*

9 Abraham Maimonides, *Perush,* ed. Wiesenberg, 240–41 (to Exodus 6:2); Labaton, *A Comprehensive Analysis*, 221.

10 Abraham Maimonides, *Perush,* ed. Wiesenberg, 241 (to Exodus 6:2); Labaton, *A Comprehensive Analysis*, 231.

11 Abraham Maimonides, *Perush,* ed. Wiesenberg, 240–41 (to Exodus 6:2); Labaton, *A Comprehensive Analysis*, 221.

12 See above, note 2 for the precedent in Baḥya Ibn Paqūda.

13 Labaton offers a survey of contexts in which Abraham uses the Hebrew term *sod* and its Arabic equivalent *sirr.* He concludes that he uses these terms "in metaphysical contexts (dealing with the nature of God, His name, revelation to mankind, divine messengers or in areas relating to spiritual perfection) or verses that raise difficult questions—when understood on their simple level." Labaton, *A Comprehensive Analysis*, 300. See also the insightful analysis in Ilan, "Secrets."

14 In *Guide* I:63 Maimonides writes that the name *Y-ah* refers to the notion of the eternity of existence (*azaliyya al-wujūd*), whereas *Shaddai* derives from the word *day* meaning sufficiency. This signifies that God needs no other being than himself; his existence suffices to bring others into existence. Cf. *Guide* I:58, p. 136; Shlomo Pines, "Dieu et L'etre selon Maimonide: Exegese d'Exode 3, 14 et doctrine connexe," in *Celui qui est: Interpretations juives et chretiennes d'Exode 3, 14*, ed. Alain de Libera and Emilie Zum Brunn (Paris: Cerf, 1986), 15–24.

15 Abraham Maimonides, *Perush,* ed. Wiesenberg, 240 (to Exodus 6:2).

16 *Guide* I:61, p. 148.

17 *Guide* I:63–64, pp. 155–56.

18 Abraham Maimonides, *Perush,* ed. Wiesenberg, 240–43 (to Exodus 6:2); Labaton, *A Comprehensive Analysis*, 221–22.

Notes to Conclusion

1 See David R. Blumenthal, "Maimonides' Intellectualist Mysticism and the Superiority of the Prophecy of Moses," in his *Philosophic Mysticism: Essays in Rational Religion*, ch. 3 (Ramat Gan: Bar-Ilan University Press, 2006); cf. Pines, "The Philosophic Purport of Maimonides' Halachic Works," 9–10.

2 Al-Ghazālī, *Iḥyā' 'ulūm al-dīn*, book 35, 2498 (*bayān* 2). Cf. Lobel, *A Sufi-Jewish Dialogue*, 39.

3 *Guide* I:59, p. 139.

4 For a skeptical interpretation of the theme of dazzlement, as well as its character as a state of worship, see Stern, *Matter and Form*, 244–47; for a Neoplatonic reading, see Alexander Altmann, "Maimonides on Intellect and the Scope of Metaphysics," in his *Von der Mittelalterlichen zur Modernen Aufklärung* (Tübingen: J. C. B. Mohr, 1987), 121–22; Julius Guttmann, *Philosophies of Judaism* (New York: Schocken, 1973), 180–85; Lobel, *Philosophies of Happiness,* 184–85; idem, "Silence is Praise to You: Maimonides on Negative Theology, Looseness of Expression, and Religious Experience," *American Catholic Philosophical Quarterly* 76, no. 1 (Spring 2002): 43–49; idem, "Being and the Good: Maimonides on Ontological Beauty," *Journal of Jewish Thought and Philosophy* 19, no. 1 (2011): 9, 43-45.

5 Guttmann, *Philosophies of Judaism*, 219–20.

6 *High Ways* II:130–32; I:140–42.

7 Goitein, *A Mediterranean Society*, vol. 4: *Daily Life* (Los Angeles: University of California, 1983), 475, 481.

Bibliography

Primary Sources

Abraham Ibn Ezra. *Perush ʿal ha-Torah*. Edited by Avraham Weiser. Jerusalem: 1976. Also in *Torat Ḥayyim*. Jerusalem: Mossad Harav Kook, 1988.

———. *Sefer ha-Shem*. In *Yalquṭ Abraham Ibn Ezra*. Edited by Israel Levin. New York and Tel Aviv, 1985.

Arisṭū ʿinda al-Arab. Edited by ʿAbd al-Raḥmān Badawī. Cairo, 1947.

al-Ashʿarī. *Maqālāt al-Islāmiyīn*. Istanbul, 1939–40.

Avicenna (Ibn Sīnā). *Kitāb al-ishārāt wa-l-tanbīhāt*. Edited by Jacques Forget. Leiden: Brill, 1892.

———. *The Metaphysics of the Healing: A Parallel English-Arabic Text of al-Ilāhiyyāt min al-Shifāʾ*. Translated by Michael Marmura. Provo: Brigham Young University Press, 2005.

Baḥya Ibn Paqūda. *The Book of Direction to the Duties of the Heart*. Translated by Menahem Mansoor. London: Routledge and Kegan Paul, 1973.

———. *Kitāb al-hidāya ilā farāʾiḍ al-qulūb* (*Torat ḥovot ha-levavot*). Edited and translated by Joseph Qafiḥ. Jerusalem, 1973.

The Commentators' Bible: The JPS Miqraʾot Gedolot: Exodus. Edited and translated by Michael Carasik. Philadelphia: Jewish Publication Society, 2005.

Comprehensive Aramaic Lexicon Project. Hebrew Union College-Jewish Institute of Religion, Cincinnati, USA. http://cal.huc.edu. Accessed November 23, 2019.

Early Islamic Mysticism. Edited and translated by Michael Sells. Mahwah, New Jersey: Paulist Press, 1996.

al-Fārābī, Abū Naṣr. *Al-Fārābī on the Perfect State*. Edited and translated by Richard Walzer. Oxford: Oxford University Press, 1985.

al-Ghazālī. *Ihyāʾ ʿulūm al-dīn*. Cairo, 1937–39.

———. *Mishkāt al-anwār*. Translated by David Buchman. Provo: Brigham Young University Press, 1998.

———. *Deliverance from Error: An Annotated Translation of* al-Munqidh min al-ḍalāl *and Other Relevant Works of Al-Ghazālī*. Edited and translated by Richard J. McCarthy. Louisville: Fons Vitae, 2000.

———. *Al-Munqidh min al-ḍalāl.* Edited by Jamal Saliba and Kamil 'Ayyad. Beirut: Dar al-Andalus, 1981.

High Holiday Prayer Book. Translated by Philip Birnbaum. New York: Hebrew Publishing Company, 1951.

The Historical Dictionary Project. The Academy of the Hebrew Language. https://en.hebrew-academy.org.il/ historical-dictionary-project/. Accessed November 23, 2019.

Hoffmann, David Tzvi. *Sefer Va-yikra*, vol. 1. Jerusalem: Mossad Harav Kook, 1976.

Ibn Gabirol, Shlomo. "*Keter Malkhut*." In *Shirei ha-qodesh*, edited by Dov Yarden, vol. 1, 55. Jerusalem, 1977.

———. "*Keter Malkhut*." In *Ha-shirah ha-'ivrit be-Sefarad u-ve-Provans (Hebrew Poetry in Spain and Provence)*, edited by Ḥayyim Schirmann, vol. 1, 273. Jerusalem, 1961.

———. "*The Royal Crown*." In *Selected Religious Poems of Solomon Ibn Gabirol*, edited by Israel Davidson, translated by Israel Zangwill, 82–123. Philadelphia: Jewish Publication Society, 1923.

Ibn Kaspi, Joseph. *Menorat Kessef.* Printed in *Sheloshah qadmone mefarshe ha-Moreh.* Jerusalem: Ortsel, 1960.

Ibn Ṭufayl. *Ḥayy ben Yaqdhān: Roman Philosophique d'Ibn Thofaïl.* Edited by Leon Gauthier. Beirut: Imprimerie Catholique, 1936.

———. *Ḥayy ibn Yaqẓān.* Translated by Lenn Evan Goodman. Los Angeles: Gee Tee Bee, 1983.

———. *Ḥayy the Son of Yaqẓān.* Translated by George Atiyeb. In *Medieval Political Philosophy*, edited by Ralph Lerner and Muhsin Mahdi, 134-62. Ithaca: Cornell University Press, 1963.

The JPS Torah Commentary: Exodus. Edited and translated by Nahum Sarna. Philadelphia: Jewish Publication Society, 1991.

Judah Halevi. *Kitāb al-radd wa'l-dalīl fī'l-dīn al-dhalīl* (*al-Kitāb al-Khazarī*). Edited by David Baneth and Haggai Ben-Shammai. Jerusalem: Magnes, 1977.

———. *The Kuzari.* Translated by Hartwig Hirschfeld. New York: Schocken, 1964.

———. *Sefer ha-Kuzari.* Translated by Judah Ibn Tibbon. Edited by Avraham Zifroni. Tel Aviv: Maḥbarot le-sifrut, 1948.

———. *Sefer ha-Kuzari: Maqor ve-targum.* Translated by Joseph Qafiḥ. Kiryat Ono: Mekhon Mishnat ha-Rambam, 1996.

al-Juwaynī. *al-Irshād.* Edited by J. D. Luciani. Paris, 1938.

Maimonides, Abraham. *The High Ways to Perfection of Abraham Maimonides*, 2 vols. Edited and translated by Samuel Rosenblatt. Baltimore: Johns Hopkins Press, 1938.

———. *Milḥamot ha-Shem.* Edited by R. Margaliot. Jerusalem: Mossad Ha-Rav Kook, 1953.

———. *Perush 'al Bereshit u-Shmot.* Edited and translated by Ephraim Yehuda Wiesenberg. London: Rabbi S. D. Sassoon, 1959.

———. *Perush ha-Torah le-Rabbenu Avraham ben Ha-Rambam: Sefer Bereshit*. Edited by Moshe Maimon. Monsey, NY: Ha-makhon le-ḥeqer Torat ha-qadmonim, 2019.

———. *Rabbenu Avraham ben ha-Rambam: Milḥamot Ha-shem*. Edited by Reuven Margaliot. Jerusalem: Mossad Ha-Rav Kook, 1953.

———. *Rabbi Avraham ben ha-Rambam: Sefer ha-maspik le-ʿovdei Hashem, Kitāb kifāyat al-ʿābidīn*, part 2, vol. 2. Edited and translated by Nissim Dana. Ramat-Gan: Bar-Ilan University Press, 1989.

Maimonides, Moses. *The Code of Maimonides (Mishneh Toreh: The Book of Knowledge)*. Translated by Bernard Septimus. New Haven: Yale Judaica Series, forthcoming.

———. *Dalālat al-ḥāʾirīn*. Edited by Salomon Munk and Issachar Joel. Jerusalem, 1929.

———. *The Eight Chapters of Maimonides on Ethics (Shemonah Peraḳim): a Psychological and Ethical Treatise*. Edited and translated by Joseph Gorfinkle. New York: Columbia University Press, 1912.

———. *Epistle to Yemen (Iggeret Teiman)*. Translated by Boaz Cohen, edited by Abraham S. Halkin. New York: American Academy for Jewish Research, 1952.

———. *Ethical Writings of Maimonides*. Edited by Raymond Weiss and Charles Butterworth. New York: Dover, 1975.

———. *The Guide of the Perplexed*. Translated by Shlomo Pines. Chicago: University of Chicago Press, 1963.

———. *Haqdamot ha-Rambam la-Mishnah*. Edited by Isaac Shailat. Jerusalem: Maʿaliyot, 1992.

———. *Iggerot ha-Rambam*. Edited by Isaac Shailat. Jerusalem: Maʿaliyot, 1988.

———. *A Maimonides Reader*. Edited by Isadore Twersky. Springfield: Behrman House, 1972.

———. "Maimonides' Treatise on Logic." Edited and translated by Israel Efros. *PAAJR* 7 (1937–38): 1-65 (English section); 1–136 (Hebrew section).

———. *Mishnah im Perush Rabbenu Moshe ben Maimon*. Edited and translated by Joseph Qafiḥ. 7 volumes (with Judeo-Arabic). Jerusalem: Mossad Harav Kook, 1963–68. 3 volumes (Hebrew alone). Jerusalem: Mossad Harav Kook, 1963.

———. *Moreh Nevukhim*, 2nd ed. Edited and translated by Michael Schwarz. Tel Aviv: Tel Aviv University Press, 2002.

Mekhilta, 2nd ed. Edited by H. S. Horovitz and I. A. Rabin. Jerusalem, 1969–70.

Midrash Shemot Rabbah, *Chapters 1–14: A Critical Edition Based on a Jerusalem Manuscript with Variants, Commentary, and Introduction*. Edited by Avigdor Shinan. Tel Aviv: Dvir, 1984.

Midrash Tanḥuma, "MS Cambridge Add 1212." In *Maagarim: The Historical Dictionary Project at the Academy of the Hebrew Language*. http://maagarim.hebrew-academy.org.il/Pages/PMain.aspx?mishibbur=773000&mm15=000013020000. Accessed November 27, 2019.

Midrash Tanḥuma ha-qadum ve-ha-yashan. Edited by Solomon Buber. Vilna, 1885.

Midrash Tanḥuma-Yelammedenu: *An English Translation of Genesis and Exodus from the Printed Version of* Tanḥuma-Yelammedenu *with an Introduction, Notes, and Indexes*. Edited by Samuel A. Berman. Hoboken: Ktav Publishing House, 1996.

Narboni, Moses. *The Epistle on the Possibility of Conjunction with the Active Intellect by Ibn Rushd with the Commentary of Moses Narboni*. Edited and translated by Kalman P. Bland. New York: Jewish Theological Seminary of America, 1982.

———. *Perush ʿal Moreh ha-Nevukhim*, in *Sheloshah qadmone mefarshe ha-Moreh*. Jerusalem, 1960.

The Pentateuch According to Targum Onqelos. Edited by Alexander Sperber. Vol. 1 of *The Bible in Aramaic*. Leiden: Brill, 1959.

Piyyuṭe Rabbi Pinḥas ha-Kohen. Edited by Shulamit Elizur. Jerusalem: World Congress of Jewish Studies, 2004.

Piyyuṭe Yannai. Edited by Menahem Zulai. Jerusalem: Jewish Publishing Company: Schocken, 1938.

The Qur'an: A New Annotated Translation. Translated by A. J. Droge. Sheffield: Equinox, 2013.

al-Qushayrī. *Al-Risālah al-Qushayrīyah fī ʿilm al-taṣawwuf*. Edited by M. al-Marʿashalī. Beirut: 1998.

Saadya Gaon. *Book of Beliefs and Opinions*. Translated by Samuel Rosenblatt. New Haven: Yale University Press, 1948.

———. *Commentary to Sefer Yetsirah*. Edited and translated by Joseph Qafiḥ. Jerusalem: American Academy for Jewish Research, 1972.

———. *Commentaire sur le Séfer Yesira ou Livre de la Création*. Translated by Meyer Lambert. Paris: É. Bouillon, 1891.

———. *Daniel, with the Translation and Interpretation of Rabenu Seʿadyah Gaon*. Edited and translated by Joseph Qafiḥ. Jerusalem, 1980–81.

———. *Kitāb al-mukhtār fī'l-amānāt wa'l-iʿtiqādāt*. Edited and translated by Joseph Qafiḥ. Jerusalem: Sura Institute for Research and Publication, 1970.

———. *Perushei Rav Seʿadyah Gaon le-Sefer Shemot*. Edited by Yehuda Ratzaby. Jerusalem: Mossad Harav Kook, 1998.

R. Samuel ben Meir (Rashbam). *Perush ha-Torah*. Edited by David Rosin. Breslau: 1882.

———. *Rashbam's Commentary on Exodus: An Annotated Translation*. Translated by Martin I. Lockshin. Atlanta: Scholars' Press, 1997.

Suhrawardī. *The Philosophy of Illumination*. Edited and translated by John Waldridge and Hossein Ziai. Provo: Brigham Young University Press, 1999.

Targum Onqelos to Exodus. Edited by Israel Drazin. New York: Ktav, 1990.

Theology of Aristotle. Edited by Friedrich Dieterici. Leipzig: 1882.

Torat Ḥayyim. Jerusalem: Mossad Harav Kook, 1988.

Secondary Sources

Abrahamov, Binyamin. "Al-Ghazālī's Supreme Way To Know God." *Studia Islamica* 77 (January 1993): 141–68.

———. "Al- Ghazālī and the Rationalization of Sufism." In *Islam and Rationality: The Impact of al-Ghazālī*, vol. 1, edited by George Tamer, 35–48. Leiden: Brill, 2015.

———. "Maimonides and Ibn Sina's Theory of *Hads*: A Re-Examination of the *Guide of the Perplexed* II:38." In *Proceedings of the Seventh International Conference of Judaeo-Arabic Studies*, edited by Haggai Ben Shammai. Forthcoming.

Abramson, Shraga. "Expressions Concerning the Giving of the Torah" [Hebrew]. *Leshonenu* 58, no. 4 (1994): 317–22.

Altmann, Alexander, ed. *The Book of Doctrines and Beliefs*. In *Three Jewish Philosophers*, edited by Hans Lewy, Alexander Altmann, and Isaak Heinemann. Oxford: Phaedon Press, 1946.

———. "The Divine Attributes: and Historical Survey of the Jewish Discussion." *Judaism* 15 (1966): 40–60.

———. "Essence and Existence in Maimonides." In his *Studies in Religious Philosophy and Mysticism*, 108–27. Ithaca: Cornell University Press, 1969.

———. "Saadya's Theory of Revelation: its Origin and Background." In his *Studies in Religious Philosophy and Mysticism*, 140–60. Ithaca: Cornell University Press, 1969.

———. "Maimonides on Intellect and the Scope of Metaphysics." In his *Von der Mittelalterlichen zur Modernen Aufklärung*, 60–129. Tübingen: J. C. B. Mohr, 1987.

Avtalion, Joav. "Comparative Study: Abraham Maimonides—*Kitāb Kifāyat al-'Ābidīn and Abū Hāmid Muhammad al-Ghazāli—Ihyā 'Ulūm al-Dīn*" [Hebrew]. PhD dissertation, Bar-Ilan University, 2010.

Baneth, David H. "The Common Teleological Source of Baḥya Ibn Paqūda and al-Ghazālī" [Hebrew]. In *Sefer Magnes*, edited by Fritz Baer et al. Jerusalem, 1938.

Belo, Catarina. "Mu'tazilites, Al-Ash'arī and Maimonides on Divine Attributes." *Veritas* 52, no. 3 (September 2007): 117–31.

Ben Sasson, Hillel. *The Divine Name YHWH: Its Meanings in Biblical Rabbinic and Medieval Jewish Thought*. PhD dissertation, Hebrew University, 2013.

———, and Moshe Halbertal, "The name Y-H-V-H and the Measure of Mercy" [Hebrew]. In *Ve-zot le-Yehudah*, edited by Maren Nihoff, Ronit Meroz and Jonathan Garb, 56–59. Jerusalem: Mossad Bialik, 2012.

Ben-Shammai, Haggai. "Extra-Textual Considerations in Medieval Judaeo-Arabic Bible Translations: The Case of Saadya Gaon." *Materia Guidaica* 7 (2003): 53–59.

———. "Kalām in Medieval Jewish Philosophy." In *History of Jewish Philosophy*, edited by Daniel Frank and Oliver Leaman. Routledge, 2014.

———. *A Leader's Project: Studies in the Philosophical and Exegetical Works of Saadya Gaon* [Hebrew]. Jerusalem: Bialik Institute, 2015.

———. "More on Commentary in Service of Theology: The Discussion of the Names of God in Rav Saadya Gaon's Commentary to Exodus 3" [Hebrew]. Lecture delivered at Contexts and Polemics: Conference in Honor of Sarah Stroumsa, Hebrew University of Jerusalem, December 24–25, 2017. (Ben-Shammai is publishing the Commentary based on two manuscripts: MS Russian National Library Yevr.-Arab. II: 1148, f. 103-106; MS Cambridge University Library T-S Misc. 28. 206.)

———. "The Tension between Literal Interpretation and Exegetical Freedom: Comparative Observations on Saadia's Method." In *With Reverence for the Word: Medieval Scriptural Exegesis in Judaism, Christianity, and Islam*, edited by Jane Dammen McAuliffe, Barry D. Walfish, and Joseph W. Goering, 33–44. New York: Oxford University Press, 2003.

Bland, Kalman, trans. *The Epistle on the Possibility of Conjunction with the Active Intellect by Ibn Rushd with the Commentary of Moses Narboni.* New York: Jewish Theological Seminary of America, 1982.

Blau, Joshua. *A Dictionary of Mediaeval Judaeo-Arabic Texts.* Jerusalem: Academy of the Hebrew Language, 2006.

———. *The Emergence and Linguistic Background of Judaeo-Arabic: A Study of the Origins of Neo-Arabic and Middle-Arabic* [Hebrew]. Jerusalem: Ben-Zvi Institute for the Study of Jewish Communities, 1989.

———. *A Grammar of Mediaeval Judaeo-Arabic*, 2nd edition [Hebrew]. Jerusalem: Magnes, 1980.

Blumenthal, David R. "Maimonides' Intellectualist Mysticism and the Superiority of the Prophecy of Moses." In his *Philosophic Mysticism: Studies in Rational Religion.* Ramat Gan: Bar-Ilan University Press, 2006.

Bregman, Mark. *The* Tanḥuma-Yelammedenu *Literature: Studies in the Evolution of the Versions.* Piscataway: Gorgias Press, 2000.

Buber, Martin. "The Burning Bush." In *On the Bible*, edited by Nahum Glatzer, 44–62. Syracuse: Syracuse University Press, 2000.

Carasik, Michael, ed. and trans. *The Commentators' Bible: The JPS Miqra'ot Gedolot: Exodus.* Philadelphia: Jewish Publication Society, 2005.

Cohen, Gerson D. "The Soteriology of R. Abraham Maimuni." *Proceedings of the American Academy for Jewish Research (PAAJR)* 35 (1967): 75–98; 36 (1968): 33–56. Reprinted in his *Studies in the Variety of Rabbinic Cultures*, 209–42. New York: Jewish Publication Society, 1991.

Davidson, Herbert. *Alfarabi, Avicenna, and Averroes, on Intellect: Their Cosmologies, Theories of the Active Intellect, and Theories of Human Intellect.* New York: Oxford University Press, 1992.

———. *Moses Maimonides: The Man and His Works*. New York: Oxford University Press, 2005.

———. *Proofs for Eternity, Creation, and the Existence of God.* New York: Oxford University Press, 1987.

Davies, Daniel. *Method and Metaphysics in Maimonides' Guide for the Perplexed.* New York: Oxford University Press, 2011.

de Vaux, Roland. "The Revelation of the Divine Name YHWH." In *Proclamation and Presence: Old Testament Essays in Honor of Gwynne Henton Davies,* edited by John I. Durham and J. R. Porter, 48–75. Richmond: John Knox Press, 1970.

Dozy, Reinhart. *Supplément aux dictionnaires Arabes.* Leiden: Brill, 1967.

Eisenmann, Esti. "The Term 'Created Light' in Maimonides' Philosophy" [Hebrew]. *Da'at* 55 (2005): 41-47.

———. "The Sinaitic Revelation in Maimonides' Thought" [Hebrew]. In *Iggud*, vol. 1, edited by B. Schwartz, A. Melamud, and A. Shemesh, 357–67. Jerusalem: World Congress of Jewish Studies, 2007–08.

Freudenthal, Gad, ed. *Aleph* 8 (2008).

Eran, Amira. "Al-Ghāzalī and Maimonides on The World To Come and Spiritual Pleasures," *Jewish Studies Quarterly* 8 (2001): 138–166.

———. "Intuition and Inspiration: The Causes of Jewish Thinkers' Objection to Avicenna's Intellectual Prophecy (*Ḥads*)." *Jewish Studies Quarterly* 14 (2007): 39–71.

Fakhry, Majid. *A History of Islamic Philosophy*, 2nd ed. New York: Columbia University Press, 1983.

———. *A Short Introduction to Islamic Philosophy, Theology, and Mysticism*, Oxford: Oneworld Publications, 1997.

Frank, R. M. "Al-Ash'arī." In *Encyclopedia of Islam*, 2nd ed, edited by P. Bearman, Th. Bianquis, C. E. Bosworth, E. van Donzel, and W. P. Heinrichs. Leiden: Brill, 1960–.

Fenton, Paul. "The Doctrine of Attachment of R. Abraham Maimonides: Fragments from the Lost Section of *The Sufficient* [Guide] *for the Servants of God*" [Hebrew]. *Da'at* 50 (2003): 107–119.

———. "A Judeo-Arabic Commentary on the Haftarot by Hanan'el ben Shemu'el, Abraham Maimonides' Father-in-Law." In *Maimonidean Studies,* vol. 1, edited by Arthur Hyman, 27–56. New York: Yeshiva University Press, 1990.

———. "Maimonides—Father and Son: Continuity and Change." In *Traditions of Maimonideanism*, edited by Carlos Fraenkel, 103–37. Leiden: Brill, 2009.

———. "More on R. Hananel b. Samuel the Judge, Leader of the Pietists" [Hebrew]. *Tarbiz* 55 (1986): 77–107.

———. "A Mystical Treatise on Prayer and the Spiritual Quest from the Pietist Circle." *Jerusalem Studies in Arabic and Islam* 16 (1993): 137–75.

———. "A Pietist Letter from the Geniza." *Hebrew Annual Review* 9 (1985): 159–67.

———. "The Post-Maimonidean Schools of Exegesis in the East: Abraham Maimonides, the Pietists, Tanḥūma Yerushalmi and the Yemenite School." In *Hebrew Bible / Old Testament: The History of Its Interpretation*, vol. 1, part 2, edited by Magne Sáebø, 433–55. Göttingen: Vandenhoeck & Ruprecht, 2000.

———. "La pratique de la retraite spirituelle (*khalwa*) chez les Judéo-Soufis d'Égypte." In *Les Mystiques Juives, Chrétiennes et Musulmanes dans l'Égypte* Médiévale, edited by Giuseppe Cecere et al., 211–52. Cairo: Institut français d'archéologie orientale, 2013.

———. "A Re-Discovered Description of Maimonides by a Contemporary." *Maimonidean Studies* 6 (2008): 267–91.

———. Review of Dana's edition of Abraham Maimuni's *Kifāyat al-'ābidīn*. *Jewish Quarterly Review* 82 (1991): 194–206.

———. "Some Judaeo-Arabic Fragments by Rabbi Abraham he-Hasid, the Jewish Sufi." *Journal of Semitic Studies* 26, no. 1 (Spring 1981): 47–72.

Fontaine, Resianne. "Was Maimonides an Epigone?" *Studia Rosenthaliana* 40 (2007–08): 9–26.

Friedman, Mordechai Akiva. *A Dictionary of Medieval Judaeo-Arabic*. Jerusalem: Ben-Zvi Institute, 2016.

———. "Two Maimonidean Documents: A Letter from Maimonides to the Sage, R. Samuel, and an Epistle of Congratulations to Maimonides on the Occasion of His Wedding" [Hebrew]. In *Me'ah She'arim: Studies in Medieval Jewish Spiritual Life, in Memory of Isadore Twersky*, edited by Ezra Fleischer et al., 191–221. Jerusalem: Magnes, 2001.

Freudenthal, Gideon. "The Philosophical Mysticism of Maimonides" [Hebrew]. *Da'at* 64–66 (2009): 77–97.

Gilliot, Claude. "Attributes of God." In *Encyclopaedia of Islam*, 3rd ed., edited by Kate Fleet et al. Leiden: Brill, 2007–. Accessed June 07, 2018. http://dx.doi.org/10.1163/1573-3912_ei3_COM_0163.

Gillman, Abigail. "Epilogue: *Ma Shemo?* The Name of God in the German Jewish Bible." In her *A History of German Jewish Bible Translation*, 251–61. Chicago: The University of Chicago Press, 2017.

Gimaret, Daniel. *La doctrine d' al-Ash'arī*. Paris: Cerf, 1990.

Girdner, Scott. *Reasoning with Revelation: The Significance of the Qur'anic Contextualization of Philosophy in Al-Ghazali's* Mishkāt al-Anwār (*The Niche of Lights)*. PhD dissertation, Boston University, 2009.

———. "Ghazali's Hermeneutics and Their Reception in Jewish Tradition: *Mishkāt al-Anwār* (The Niche of Lights) and Maimonides' *Shemonah Peraqim* (Eight Chapters)." In *Islam and Rationality: The Impact of al-Ghazali*, vol. 1, edited by Georges Tamer, 253–74. Leiden: Brill, 2015.

Goitein, S. D. "Abraham Maimonides and his Pietist Circle." In *Jewish Medieval and Renaissance Studies*, edited by Alexander Altmann. Cambridge, MA: Harvard University Press, 1967.

———. *A Mediterranean Society*, vol. 4: *Daily Life*. Los Angeles: University of California, 1983.

———. "R. Hananel the Chief Judge, Son of Samuel he-Nagid, Father-in-Law of Maimonides" [Hebrew]. *Tarbiz* 50 (1981): 371–95.

Gottlieb, Michah. *Moses Mendelssohn: Writings on Judaism, Christianity, and the Bible.* Waltham, MA: Brandeis University Press, 2011.

Gutas, Dimitri. *Avicenna and the Aristotelian Tradition.* Leiden: Brill, 1988.

Guttmann, Julius. *Philosophies of Judaism.* New York: Schocken, 1973.

Halbertal, Moshe, and Avishay Margalit. *Idolatry.* Cambridge, MA: Harvard University Press, 1992.

Halkin, Abraham S., and David Hartman. *Crisis and Leadership: Epistles of Maimonides.* Philadelphia: Jewish Publication Society, 1985.

Harvey, Steven. "Alghazali and Maimonides and Their Books of Knowledge." In *Be'erot Yitzhak: Studies in Memory of Isadore Twersky*, edited by Jay M. Harris, 99–117. Cambridge, MA: Harvard University Press, 2005.

———. "Avicenna and Maimonides on Prayer and Intellectual Worship." In *Exchange and Transmission across Cultural Boundaries: Philosophy, Mysticism, and Science in the Mediterranean World*, edited by Haggai Ben-Shammai, Shaul Shaked, and Sarah Stroumsa, 82–105. Jerusalem: Israel Academy of Sciences and Humanities, 2013.

———. "Did Maimonides' Letter to Samuel Ibn Tibbon Determine Which Philosophers Would Be Studied By Later Jewish Thinkers?" *Jewish Quarterly Review* 83, no. 1–2 (July–October 1992): 51–70.

———. "The Meaning of Terms Designating Love in Judaeo-Arabic Thought and Some Remarks on the Judaeo-Arabic Interpretation of Maimonides." In *Proceedings of the Founding Conference of the Society for Judaeo-Arabic Studies*, edited by Norman Golb, 175–96. Amsterdam: Harwood Academic Publishers, 1997.

Harvey, Warren Zev. "Averroes and Maimonides on the Obligation of Philosophic Contemplation (*I'tibār*)" [Hebrew]. *Tarbiz* 58, no. 1 (1988): 75–83.

———. "*'Ishq*, *ḥesheq*, and *amor Dei intellectualis*." In *Spinoza and Medieval Jewish Philosophy*, edited by Steven Nadler, 96–107. New York: Cambridge University Press, 2014.

———. "Judah Halevi's Interpretation of the Tetragrammaton" [Hebrew]. In *A Word Fitly Spoken: Studies in Mediaeval Exegesis of the Hebrew Bible and the Qur'ān*, edited by Meir M. Bar-Asher, Simon Hopkins, Sarah Stroumsa, and Bruno Chiesa, 125–32. Jerusalem: Ben-Zvi Institute, 2007.

———. "Maimonides and Aquinas on Interpreting the Bible." *PAAJR* 55 (1988): 59–77.

———. "Philosophy and Poetry in Ibn Gabirol" [Spanish]. *Anuario Filosófico* 33 (2000): 491–504. English translation in *Solomon Ibn Gabirol: Sources, Doctrines, and Influence on Medieval Philosophy*, edited by Nicola Polloni, M. Benedetto, and Federico Dal Bo. Forthcoming, 2020.

———. *Physics and Metaphysics in Hasdai Crescas.* Amsterdam: J. C. Giben, 1988.

———. "*Sefer Yetsirah shel Liebes: bein Parmenides, Nietzsche, ve-ha-Rambam*" [Hebrew]. In *Ve-zot le-Yehudah*, edited by Maren Nichoff, Ronit Meroz and Jonathan Garb, 17–27. Jerusalem: Bialik, 2012.

Hourani, George. "Avicenna on Necessary and Possible Existence." *The Philosophical Forum* 4, no. 1 (1972): 74–86.

Hyman, Arthur, and James Walsh, eds. *Philosophy in the Middle Ages*, 2nd ed. Indianapolis: Hackett Publishing Company, 1983.

Hyman, Arthur. "Maimonides on Religious Language." In *Perspectives on Maimonides*, edited by Joel Kraemer, 178–79. London: Littman, 1996.

Idel, Moshe. *Kabbalah: New Perspectives*. New Haven: Yale University Press, 1988.

———. *Studies in Ecstatic Kabbalah*. Albany: State University of New York Press, 1988.

Ilan, Nahem. "Between Mount Sinai and the Cleft of the Rock: Moses as the Ultimate Sufi in Rabbi Abraham Maimuni's Torah Commentary" [Hebrew]. In *Studies in Judaeo-Arabic Culture, Proceedings of the Fourteenth Congress of the Society for Medieval Judaeo-Arabic Culture*, edited by Yoram Erder et al., 133–53. Tel Aviv: Tel Aviv University Press, 2014.

———. "Secrets and their Meaning in R. Abraham Maimuni's Commentary on the Torah" [Hebrew]. *Bein Ever la-Arav* 5 (2012): 76–93.

———. "Theological Assumptions and Hermeneutical Principles in Rabbi Abraham Maimonides' Commentary on the Pentateuch" [Hebrew]. In *A Word Fitly Spoken: Studies in Mediaeval Exegesis of the Hebrew Bible and the Qur'ān*, edited by Meir M. Bar-Asher, Simon Hopkins, Sarah Stroumsa, and Bruno Chiesa, 31–70. Jerusalem: Ben-Zvi, 2007.

Ivry, Alfred. *Maimonides'* Guide of the Perplexed*: A Philosophical Guide*. Chicago: University of Chicago Press, 2016.

———. "Neoplatonic Currents in Maimonides' Thought." In *Perspectives on Maimonides: Philosophical and Historical Studies*, edited by Joel L. Kraemer, 115–140. London: Littman, 1996.

Izutsu, Toshihiko. *Creation and the Timeless Order of Things*. Ashland: Whitecloud Press, 1994.

James, William. *Varieties of Religious Experience*. New York: Penguin, 1982.

Jastrow, Marcus. *A Dictionary of the Targumim, the Talmud Babli and Yerushalmi, and the Midrashic Literature*. New York: G. P. Putnam's Sons, 1886.

Jospe, Raphael. *Jewish Philosophy in the Middle Ages*. Brighton, MA: Academic Studies Press, 2009.

———. "Naḥmanides and Arabic." In his *Jewish Philosophy: Foundations and Extensions*, vol. 2, 192–93. Lanham: University Press of America, 2008.

Kasher, Hannah. "Is There an Early Stratum of the *Guide of the Perplexed*?" In *Maimonidean Studies*, vol. 3, edited by Arthur Hyman, 105–129. New York: Ktav, 1995.

———. "Maimonides' Interpretations of the Story of the Divine Revelation in the Cleft of the Rock." *Da'at* 35 (1995): 29–66 [Hebrew].

———. "Self-Cognizing Intellect and Negative Attributes in Maimonides' Theology." *Harvard Theological Review* 87, no. 4 (1994): 461–72.

Kellner, Menachem. *Maimonides' Confrontation with Mysticism*. Oxford: Littman, 2006.

Klein-Braslavy, Sara. "Maimonides and Esotericism." In her *Maimonides as Biblical Interpreter*, 163–220. Boston: Academic Studies Press, 2011.

———. *King Solomon and Philosophical Esotericism in Maimonides' Thought* [Hebrew]. Jerusalem: Magnes, 1996.

Kraemer, Joel. "Maimonides and the Spanish Aristotelian School." In *Christians, Muslims, and Jews in Medieval and Early Modern Spain—Interaction and Cultural Change*, edited by M. D. Meyerson and E. D. English, 40–68. Notre Dame: University of Notre Dame Press, 1999.

———. *Maimonides: The Life and World of One of Civilization's Greatest Minds*. New York: Doubleday, 2008.

———, ed. *Perspectives on Maimonides: Philosophical and Historical Studies*. London: Littman, 1996.

Kreisel, Howard. "Judah Halevi's Influence on Maimonides: A Preliminary Appraisal." *Maimonidean Studies*, no. 2 (1991): 95–121.

———. *Maimonides' Political Thought: Studies in Ethics, Law, and the Human Ideal*. Albany: State University of New York Press, 1999.

———. *Prophecy: The History of an Idea in Jewish Philosophy*. Amsterdam: Springer Netherlands, 2003.

———. "'The Voice of God' in Medieval Jewish Philosophical Exegesis (Hebrew)," *Da'at* 16 (1986): 29–38.

Krinis, Ehud. *God's Chosen People:* Judah Halevi's Kuzari and the Shi'i Imam Doctrine. Turnhout: Brepols, 2014.

Labaton, Ezra. *A Comprehensive Analysis of Rabenu Abraham Maimuni's Biblical Commentary*. PhD dissertation, Brandeis University, 2012.

Lane, Edward William. *Arabic-English Lexicon*. Cambridge: Islamic Texts Society, 1984.

Langermann, Tzvi. "Maimonides and Miracles: The Growth of a (Dis)Belief." *Jewish History* 18, nos. 2–3 (2004): 147–72.

———. "Why is the Discussion of the Equivocal Term 'Light' Missing from the *Guide of the Perplexed?*" In *Masorah le-Yosef*, ed. Yosef Parhi, 9:329–38.

Lasker, Daniel J. "Modes of Spirituality in Medieval Jewish Philosophy." In *Jewish Spirituality and Divine Law*, edited by Alan Mintz and Lawrence Schiffman, 163–85. New York: Yeshiva University Press, 2005.

———. "Sub-Prophetic Inspiration in Judaeo-Arabic Philosophy" [Hebrew]. In *Alei Asor: Proceedings of the Tenth Conference of the Society for Judaeo-Arabic Studies*, edited by Daniel J. Lasker and Haggai Ben-Shammai, 131–49. Beer Sheva: Ben-Gurion University of the Negev, 2008.

Lauterbach, Jacob Z. "Substitutes for the Tetragrammaton." *Proceedings of the AAJR* 22 (1930–1931): 39–67.

———, and Wilhelm Bacher. "*Tanḥuma*, Midrash." JewishEncyclopedia.com. Accessed October 10, 2019. http://jewishencyclopedia.com/articles/14236-tanhuma-midrash.

Lazarus-Yafeh, Hava. "Symbolism of Light in Al-Ghazzali's Writing." In her *Studies in Al-Ghazzali*. Jerusalem: Magnes, 1975.

Leaman, Oliver. "Maimonides, the Imagination, and the Objectivity of Prophecy." *Religion* 18 (1988): 69–80.

Levine, Michelle. "Maimonides' Philosophical Exegesis of the Nobles' Vision (Exodus 24): A Guide for the Pursuit of Knowledge." *The Torah u-Madda Journal* 11 (2002–03): 61–106.

Levinger, Jacob. "The Secret of the Created Voice in the Revelation at Mount Sinai" [Hebrew]. In his *Maimonides as Philosopher and Codifier*, 39–48. Jerusalem: Bialik Institute, 1989.

Lobel, Diana. "Being and the Good: Maimonides on Ontological Beauty." *Journal of Jewish Thought and Philosophy* 19, no. 1 (2011): 1–45.

———. *Between Mysticism and Philosophy: Sufi Language of Religious Experience in Judah Ha-Levi's* Kuzari. Albany: State University of New York Press, 2000.

———. "A Dwelling Place for the Shekhinah." *Jewish Quarterly Review* 90, nos. 1, 2 (July–October 1999): 103–125.

———. *Philosophies of Happiness: A Comparative Introduction to the Flourishing Life.* New York: Columbia University Press, 2017.

———. "Silence is Praise to You: Maimonides on Negative Theology, Looseness of Expression, and Religious Experience." *American Catholic Philosophical Quarterly* 76, no. 1 (Spring 2002): 25–51.

———. *A Sufi-Jewish Dialogue; Philosophy and Mysticism in Baḥya Ibn Paqūda's* Duties of the Heart. Philadelphia: University of Pennsylvania Press, 2007.

Lorberbaum, Menahem. *Dazzled by Beauty: Theology as Poetics in Hispanic Jewish Culture* [Hebrew]. Jerusalem: Ben-Zvi Institute, 2011.

Lorberbaum, Yair. "On Contradictions, Rationality, Dialectics, and Esotericism in Maimonides' *Guide of the Perplexed*." *The Review of Metaphysics* 55 (June 2002): 711–750.

Merlan, Philip. *Monopsychism, Mysticism, Metaconsciousness: Problems of the Soul in the Neoaristotelian and Neoplatonic Tradition*. The Hague: M. Nijhoff, 1969.

Pines, Shlomo. "Dieu et L'etre selon Maimonide: Exegese d'Exode 3, 14 et doctrine connexe." In *Celui qui est: Interpretations juives et chretiennes d'Exode 3, 14*, edited by Alain de Libera and Emilie Zum Brunn, 15-24. Paris: Cerf, 1986.

———. "The Limitations of Human Knowledge according to Al-Farabi, ibn Bajja, and Maimonides." In *Studies in Medieval Jewish History and Literature*, vol. 1, edited by Isadore Twersky, 82–109. Cambridge, MA: Harvard University Press, 1979.

———. *Nouvelles Etudes sur Awḥad al-Zamān Abu-l-Barakāt al-Baghdādī.* Paris: Librairie Durlacher, 1995.

———. "The Philosophic Purport of Maimonides' Halachic Works." In *Maimonides and Philosophy: Papers Presented at the Sixth Jerusalem Philosophical Encounter, May 1985*, edited by Shlomo Pines and Yirmiyahu Yovel, 1–14. Dordrecht: Martinus Nijhoff Publishers, 1986.

———. "Points of Similarity Between the Exposition of the Doctrine of the Sefirot in the Sefer Yeẓira and a Text of the Pseudo-Clementine Homilies." *Proceedings of the Israel Academy of Sciences and Humanities* 7, no. 3 (1989).

———. "Shiʿite Terms and Conceptions in Judah Halevi's Kuzari." *Jerusalem Studies in Arabic and Islam* 2 (1980): 165–251.

———. "Translator's Introduction." In *The Guide of the Perplexed*, translated by Sholmo Pines. Chicago: University of Chicago Press, 1963.

Ravitzky, Aviezer. "Maimonides: Esotericism and Educational Philosophy." In *The Cambridge Companion to Maimonides*, edited by Kenneth Seeskin, 300–23. New York: Cambridge University Press, 2005.

———. "The Anthropological Theory of Miracles in Medieval Jewish Philosophy." In *Studies in Medieval Jewish History and Literature*, vol. 2, 231–72. Cambridge, MA: Harvard University Center for Jewish Studies, 1984.

Regev, Shaul. "Collective Revelation and *Maʿamad har Sinai* in Maimonides and His Commentators: Narboni, Shem Tov, and Abravanel" [Hebrew]. *Jerusalem Studies in Jewish Thought* 9 (1990): 251–65.

Reines, Alvin J. "Abrabanel on Prophecy in the *Moreh Nebukhim*." *Hebrew Union College Annual* 33 (1962): 221–58.

———. "Maimonides' Concept of Mosaic Prophecy." Hebrew Union College Annual 40 (1970): 325–62.

———. "Maimonides' Concept of Miracles." *Hebrew Union College Annual* 45 (1974): 243–85.

Reizel, Anat. *Introduction to the Midrashic Literature* (Hebrew). Alon Shevut: Tevunot—Mikhelet Hertsog, 2010–11.

Rosenberg, Shalom. "On Biblical Exegesis in the Guide" [Hebrew]. *Jerusalem Studies in Jewish Thought* 1 (1981): 85–157.

Rubio, Mercedes. *Aquinas and Maimonides on the Possibility of the Knowledge of God: AN Examination of the* Quaestio de Attributis. Dordrecht: Springer, 2006.

Russ-Fishbane, Elisha. *Judaism, Sufism, and the Pietists of Medieval Egypt.* Oxford: Oxford University Press, 2015.

———. *Between Politics and Piety: Abraham Maimonides and His Times*. PhD dissertation, Harvard University, 2009.

Sands, Kristin Zahra. *Sufi Commentaries on the Qur'an in Classical Islam*. New York: Routeledge, 2006.

Schimmel, Annemarie. *Mystical Dimensions of Islam*. Chapel Hill: University of North Carolina Press, 1975.

Schwartz, Dov. *The Clash of Paradigms: Between Theology and Philosophy in Medieval Jewish Thought* [Hebrew]. Jerusalem: Magnes, 2018.

Schwarz, Yossi. "Ben shelilah le-shetikah: ha-Rambam be-ma'arav ha-latini." *Iyyun* 45, no. 4 (October 1996): 389–406.

Schweid, Eliezer. *Ṭa'am ve-haqashah* [Hebrew]. Ramat Gan: Bar-Ilan University Press, 1970.

Seeskin, Kenneth. "Appendix: Esotericism and the Limits of Knowledge: A Critique of Strauss." In his *Searching for a Distant God: The Legacy of Maimonides*, 177–188. New York: Oxford University Press, 2000.

Sells, Michael, ed. and trans. *Early Islamic Mysticism*. Mahwah, New Jersey: Paulist Press, 1996.

Septimus, Bernard. "*Ma'amad Har Sinai* and Other *Ma'amadot*." In *Sha'arei Lashon: Studies in Hebrew, Aramaic, and Jewish Languages, Presented to Moshe Bar Asher*, vol. 1, edited by Aharon Maman et al., 160–184. Jerusalem: Bialik Institute, 2007.

Shaubi, Eli. *From Bahya ibn Paquda to Abraham Maimonides: Tracing the Role of Law in Medieval Sefardic Piety*. Near Eastern Studies Senior Honors Thesis, Cornell University, 2013.

———. *R. Abraham Maimonides: The Process of Prophetic Attainment*. Master's Thesis, Hebrew University of Jerusalem, 2019.

Schussman, Aviva. "The Question of the Islamic Sources of Abraham Maimonides' *Compendium for the Servants of God*" [Hebrew]. *Tarbiz* 55 (1986): 229–51.

Sirat, Colette. *A History of Jewish Philosophy in the Middle Ages*. Cambridge: Cambridge University Press, 1990.

Stern, Josef. *The Matter and Form of Maimonides'* Guide. Cambridge, MA: Harvard University Press, 2013.

Strauss-Ashtor, Eliyahu. *History of the Jews in Egypt and Syria*, vol. 3 [Hebrew]. Jerusalem: Mossad ha-Rav Kook, 1970.

Stroumsa, Sarah. "Note on Maimonides' Attitude to Joseph ibn Ṣaddīq." In *Shlomo Pines Jubilee Volume*, edited by Moshe Idel, Warren Zev Harvey, and Eliezer Schweid, vol. 2, 33–38. Jerusalem: Hebrew University, 1988–90.

———. *Maimonides in his World: Portrait of a Mediterranean Thinker*. Princeton: Princeton University Press, 2009.

Sviri, Sara. "Spiritual Trends in Pre-Cabbalistic Judeo-Spanish Literature: The Cases of Baḥya Ibn Paqūda and Judah Halevi." *Donaire* 6 (1996): 78–84.

Treiger, Alexander. *Inspired Knowledge in Islamic Thought: Al-Ghazali's Theory of Mystical Cognition and Its Avicennian Foundation*. London: Routledge, 2012.

Tritton, A. S. "The Speech of God." *Studia Islamica* 36 (1972): 5–22.

Urbach, Ephraim E. *The Sages: Their Concepts and Beliefs*. Translated by Israel Abrahams. Cambridge, MA: Harvard University Press, 1987.

van Ess, Josef. *Theology and Society in the Second and Third Centuries of the Hijra: A History of Religious Thought in Early Islam*, vol. 3, translated from German by Gwendolyn Goldblum. Leiden: Brill, 2018.

Wensinck, A. J., Jacques Jomier, and Bernard Lewis. "Ḥadjdj." In *Encyclopaedia of Islam*, 2nd ed., edited by P. Bearman, Th. Bianquis, C. E. Bosworth, E. van Donzel, and W. P. Heinrichs. Leiden: Brill, 1960–.

Wolfson, Elliot R. *Through a Speculum that Shines: Vision and Imagination in Medieval Jewish Mysticism*. Princeton: Princeton University Press, 1994.

Wolfson, Harry. *Repercussions of the Kalam in Jewish Philosophy*. Cambridge, MA: Harvard University Press, 1979.

Zimmerman, F. W. *Al-Fārābī's Commentary and Short Treatise on Aristotle's De Interpretatione*. Oxford: Oxford University Press, 1981.

Zulay, Menahem. *Ha-askolah ha-payyeṭanit shel Rav Se'adyah Gaon* [Hebrew]. Tel-Aviv: Schocken, 1969.

Index

Hebrew Bible,
- Genesis, 27, 104, 123–124, 136n17, 142n32, 143n3, 175n11
- Exodus, xiii, xvi–xix, 3, 5–44, 46–54, 59, 63, 68–75, 78, 80–81, 84–85, 89, 92–93, 96–98, 102, 104–106, 110, 116–117, 119, 121–125, 130–131, 136n17, 138n9, 144n46, 150n1, 150n6, 153n24, 156n8, 158n28, 159n31, 160n37, 161n44, 163n10–11, 164n11, 165n24, 166n1–2, 167n7, 168n12, 169n15, 171n3, 176n4, 179n10, 184n2
- Numbers, 49, 52, 144n46, 152n17, 153n7
- Deuteronomy, 20, 31–32, 54–55, 64, 68–69, 73–75, 108, 156n8, 159n31, 160n37, 164n10, 178n9, 179n14
- Judges, 55
- 2 Kings, 143n36
- Isaiah, 26, 101–102, 104, 152n20
- Jeremiah, 29–30
- Ezekiel, 30, 55, 152n20, 166n2, 167n10, 169n15
- Daniel, 6, 149n19
- Psalm, 10–11, 13–17, 23–26, 29–31, 43–45, 47, 50–51, 55, 66, 85, 130, 142n30
- Proverbs, 85
- Job, 6, 162n56
- Ecclesiastes, 48, 175n12, 181n11
- I Chronicles, 8

Talmud,
- Babylonian Talmud, xvii, 98, 173n6
- *Berakhot*, 98, 101–102, 174n8
- *Ḥagigah,* 26, 43

***

Aaron, 26, 34–35, 46, 69–72, 78, 153n24, 163n9, 167n7
Abraham, 18, 59, 92, 97, 117, 122–124, 151n12
Abrahamov, Binyamin, 162n55
Abramson, Shraga, 159n31
Abravanel, Isaac, 61, 63–64, 160–161n43, 169n15
Active Intellect, xiii, xv–xvi, 9, 11, 17, 22, 24–32, 37–38, 57–59, 61, 65–66, 126–127, 136n24, 140n14, 141n27, 144n45
- And created light, xvi, 24
- And revelation 26, 30–31, 60–61, 66
- And the created voice, xvi, 65, 127
- And the Glory, xv–xvi, 26, 28, 30, 32–33, 127
- And the Voice at Mount Sinai, 61–65
- And the Voice of God, 27, 64–65
- As reception from the divine intellect, 24
- Brings intellect from potentiality to actuality, according to Maimonides, 29, 65
- Identified with created light by Maimonides, xv, 24–30, 32, 126–127
- In Maimonides' cosmology, xiii, xv–xvi, 9, 11, 17, 22, 24–32, 37–38, 58–59, 61, 65–66, 126–127
- In Sufi thought, 25, 126
- Never discussed by Abraham Maimonides, xiii, xv, 9, 11, 17

Allegorical interpretation, 27, 40, 138n8, 149n20
al-Andalus, xii
al-Ghazālī, xi, 11–14, 17–19, 23–25, 51, 126–128, 140n18, 141–142n26–27, 142n34, 145n58–59, 146n66, 169n19
- *Mishkāt al-anwār* (*The Niche of Lights*), 12, 18, 141n26

al-Munqidh min al-ḍalāl (*Deliverer from Error*), 18, 51
Iḥyā' 'ulūm al-dīn (*Revival of Religious Sciences*), 12, 18, 51, 145n59
al-Fārābī, xi, xiii, xvi, 24, 28–29, 36–37, 58, 112, 114, 134n5, 144n45, 169n22, 183n27
al-Hudhayl, Abū, 175n3
al-Jubbā'ī, 175n3
al-Qushayrī, 35
al-Ṣādiq, Ja'far, 56, 156n7
al-Sulamī, 56, 156n6
Alexander of Aphrodisias, xi–xii
Allah, 56, 71
Altmann, Alexander, 76, 138n8, 182n23
Andalusian philosophical tradition, xi–xiv, 133n2, 140n23
Angels, 10, 12, 28, 38, 71–72, 74, 76–77, 84, 141n27, 143n36, 157n20, 168n11
Conscious, interpreting beings, according to Abraham Maimonides, 71–72, 74, 76–77
Representative of the separate intellects, according to Maimonides, 10, 12, 28, 38, 141n27
Anthropomorphism, 7, 80, 113, 128, 138n8
Apprehension, xvi, xvii, xix, 5–6, 8–9, 22–24, 26–28, 31, 39, 41, 45, 47–49, 52, 54, 58–59, 69–70, 78–84, 122, 126–129, 144n46, 161n43, 168n12, 170n23
Divine, 45, 54, 58, 126–129
Intellectual, xvi, 6, 8–9, 22–24, 26–28, 39, 41, 52, 65, 78, 127, 144n46, 161n43, 168n12, 170n23
Sensory-affective, 78, 127
Understanding, 31
Visual, 24
Aquinas, 182n19
Arafat, Mount, 156
Aristotle, Aristotelianism, Aristotelian language, xi–xiv, 17–18, 31, 77, 83–84, 127, 134n6, 135n15, 141n27, 149n19, 167–168n11
Metaphysics, 18
Aristotelian tradition, 134n6
Arabic Aristotelians, 134n6
Attributes, Divine, 23–24, 64–65, 83–84, 102–103, 105–106, 108, 112, 114–119, 122, 128, 170n23, 175n3, 180n6, 182n20, 182n23, 183n27, 183n29, 185n8
Attributes of essence and attributes of action, 23–24, 65, 83–84, 102–103, 105–106, 108, 112, 115, 122, 170n23, 175n3, 182n20
Negation of divine attributes (Maimonides), 64, 114–119, 128, 182n23, 183n27, 183n29
Negative attributes (Maimonides), 118, 183n30
Positive attributes or essence (God's glory), 115, 180n6
Averroes (Ibn Rushd), xi–xiii
Avicenna (Ibn Sīnā), xi–xii, xiv, 9, 12, 18–19, 58, 93, 109, 114, 118, 127, 130–131, 134n5, 134n12, 135n15, 139n13, 140n18, 140n23, 144n45, 145n58–59, 146n64, 161n49, 161n49, 161n53, 162n56, 179n12, 182n20, 183n33
Glosses on the Theology of Aristotle, 146n64
Avihu, 47, 70, 78, 167n7

Being, 9–10, 14, 16, 18, 20, 22, 30–31, 34–37, 40, 42–48, 51–52, 77, 82–84, 91, 93–94, 96, 98, 102–103, 105, 112, 114–115, 118–120, 128, 130–131, 142n30, 149n19, 153n24, 170n23, 171n36 176n3, 178n6, 180n6, 181n10, 182n19, 183n29, 185n14
Ben Azzai, 42–43
ben Ḥofni, Samuel, xi, xv
Ben-Sasson, Hillel, 182n22
Ben-Shammai, Haggai, 104–107, 138n9, 174n4, 175n1, 175n3, 176n5, 177n3, 182n22
Blau, Joshua, 137n3, 170n25, 182n22
Blumenthal, David, 127
Bregman, Marc, 173n4, 173n6, 174n7
Buber, Martin, 92–93
Buber, Solomon, 174n7

Cairo Genizah, 21, 74, 135n14, 139n12
Christianity, Christians, 32, 36
Cloud, the, 5–7, 23, 30, 34–40, 44, 50, 52, 54–55, 58–59, 62–63, 69, 72, 144n46, 150n1, 153n24, 158n24, 161n43
Allegorical for Maimonides, 40, 44, 54–55, 58–59, 62–63, 158n24, 161n43

Physical for Abraham Maimonides, 5, 7, 34, 39–40, 50, 52, 69, 144n46, 150n1,153n24
Cleft of the rock, theophany at, xv, 3, 5–25, 34, 39, 41, 43–44, 49, 61, 65–66, 79, 83, 126, 132, 161n43
Collective religious experience, xv, 3, 27, 38, 55–57, 60, 126
Contemplation, xvi, 10, 14, 17, 20–21, 38, 41–42, 45, 52–53, 58, 65, 93, 114, 127–130, 140n18, 146n64, 161–162n53, 163n56
Created light, xiii, xv–xvii, 1, 3, 5–35, 37, 39–54, 61, 65, 77–86, 89, 126–127, 132, 137n6, 138n8, 147n77, 149n20, 150n29, 150n1, 151n11, 152n18, 153n24
And God's Glory at cleft of the rock, xiii
And *Shekhinah*, 30, 32, 80, 138n8, 151n11
Didactic function, for Abraham Maimonides, 39
Symbol of the Active Intellect, for Maimonides, xiii, xv–xvi, 3, 8, 24–34, 54, 65, 126–127
Visual and physical dimensions, for Abraham Maimonides, xiii, xv, 3, 5–7, 25, 34, 39–41, 49, 54, 77–78, 126
Created word, xiii, xv–xvii, 3, 25, 67–77, 89, 126, 138n8, 165n26
And the Ten Words, 67–68, 73–75, 77
Apprehended by sensory and intellectual faculties, for Abraham Maimonides, xiii, xv, 25, 67–77, 126
Maimonides' view: as Active Intellect, 25
Rabbi Abraham ibn Abī'l-Rabī' he-Ḥasid's view, 67–71, 73–75
Saadya's view, xiii, 71–72, 76, 89, 126, 165n26
Creation, xvi, 14, 31, 52–53, 65, 83–84, 112, 115, 124–125, 128–130, 142n27, 142n34, 166n29, 170n23, 184n2

Davidson, Herbert, 141n27
Day of Judgement, 55–56, 156n8, 158n29, 159n31
Divine encounter, 24, 55, 59–61, 67, 72, 81, 126–127, 132
Divine names, xiv–xv, xvii–xix, 18, 89, 92–96, 110–115, 119, 122–125, 130–132, 180n6, 181n17, 184n2
Abraham Maimonides' attempt to harmonize approach of Saadya and Maimonides, xiv, 89, 94
Adonai, 91, 112–113, 131
All names but the Tetragrammaton derive from actions of God, according to Maimonides, xviii, 111–115
Connection between the two divine names, *Ehyeh asher Ehyeh* and the Tetragrammaton, for rabbinic thinkers, 92
Divine names are adjectival nouns derived from verbs, according to Maimonides, 112
Each divine name must be received by its hearer according to the hearer's level of understanding, according to Abraham Maimonides, 125
El Shaddai, xix, 97, 122–125, 131
Elohim, 18, 97, 113, 171n3
Experiential dimension of the divine names, for Abraham Maimonides, xix, 95, 125, 131
Historical approach of classical rabbinic literature and in Saadya, 89, 94, 102
Identification of *Ehyeh asher Ehyeh* and the Tetragrammaton for Maimonides, 125
Metaphysical approach of Saadya and Abraham Maimonides, xvii–xviii, 89, 94–95, 100–105, 108–110, 114
"The Merciful," 65, 97–98, 102, 112–113, 115, 131, 180n6
When God uses the name *El Shaddai* with the patriarchs, God indicates his essence, 123–125, 130–131
Divine protection, 5, 7, 23, 43–44
Divine essence, xv, xix, 5, 7, 10, 17, 22–25, 58, 78–79, 83–85, 91, 94, 106, 112, 114–115, 118–119, 121–126, 131–132, 146n64, 150n1, 170n23, 171n1, 175n3, 176n4, 184n2
And Necessary Existence, 125, 131

Can be glimpsed, according to Abraham Maimonides, xv, xix, 8, 10, 25, 84–85, 126, 132
Cannot be apprehended, according to Maimonides, 128
Exalted essence or existence, for Abraham Maimonides, xv, xix, 5, 8, 10–11, 14–15, 20, 22–23, 25, 44, 51–52, 84–85, 109–110, 121, 125–126, 131–132, 141n27, 165n24
Divine mercy, 13, 94, 97–98, 112, 115, 171n3
Divine Presence, 9, 20–21, 36, 48–49, 61, 63, 91, 95, 101, 118, 127, 142n30, 156n8, 158n29, 158n29, 184n2
Eternal and dynamic interpretations, 91–92, 97
Historical and metaphysical interpretations, xvii, 97–98, 100–102, 104, 122
Dwell, to (*ḥ-l-l*), 36–40, 151n11, 153n24
Dwelling place (*maḥall*), 36, 108, 152n12

Egypt, xi–xiii, 11–12, 21–22, 35, 67, 73–74, 101, 127, 134n12, 135n14, 139n10, 150n1, 150n4, 151n6
Egyptian Pietists, xii–xiii, 11–12, 21–22, 35, 67, 73–74, 127, 134n12, 135n14, 150n4, 151n6
Ehyeh ("I am"), xviii–xix, 92–93, 95–96, 98–99, 101–102, 105–109, 118, 121–122, 125, 171n6, 173n3, 175n10, 176n4, 177–178n6, 179n10, 181n11, 182n22, 183n27
Interpretation of three Ehyehs of Exodus 3:14 to represent past, present, and future, 96–98, 101
Represents contingent being for beings other than God, for whom it represents uncaused, necessary being, 118
The name Moses will communicate to Israel as part of his prophetic mission, according to Abraham Maimonides
Ehyeh asher Ehyeh, xiv–xv, xvii–xix, 89, 91–111, 115–119, 121, 124–125, 130–131, 174n7, 174n8, 175n14, 177–178n6–7, 179n10, 182n23, 183n27, 183n29, 184n2
And Maimonides' account of God's Necessary Existence, for Abraham Maimonides, xiv, 95, 121, 123–125, 130–131
And the divine Presence, 91–92, 95, 97, 101
As explication of the Tetragrammaton, for Maimonides, 95, 110–111, 119
Classical rabbinic interpretations: names used in historical circumstances; and as the eternal, beginningless and ceaseless, xvii–xviii, 94, 97, 100, 102, 130
Eternity without beginning and without end, for Abraham Maimonides, 108, 177n6
Expressive of God's relationship to humanity, according to Abraham Maimonides, xix, 122, 130
Historical and metaphysical interpretations synthesized by Saadya, xvii–xviii, 89, 100–102, 104–105, 130
Moses' desire to offer to the people the knowledge embedded in *Ehyeh asher Ehyeh*, according to Maimonides, 117
Moses' request to know what name he should tell the people, 117
Not a name in itself but a stand in for the qualities expressed in God's historical actions, xvii–xviii, 97, 130
Purely metaphysical interpretation (of Avicenna and Maimonides), 95, 109, 131
Saadya's translations, xvii–xviii, 100–101, 104–110, 121–122, 124–125, 130–131, 174n7, 174n8, 175n14, 177–178n6–7, 179n10
Seven interpretations of *Ehyeh* by Saadya, 104
Signifies Necessary Existence, for Maimonides, xiv, 130
Sits in intermediate stage of knowledge of Necessary Existence between *El Shaddai*, the lower level, and the Tetragrammaton,

the highest level, according to Abraham Maimonides, 125
Three interpretations: historical, metaphysical, and a synthesis of the two, 109, 122
Einstein, Albert, 162n54
Eisenmann, Esti, 26–30, 32, 61, 148n13, 149n20, 161n46
Elijah, 143n36, 152n12, 169n15
El Shaddai, *see* Divine names
Emanation, 6, 24, 26, 28, 30, 59, 65, 76, 141–142n27, 148n16, 149n19, 161n53
Intellectual, 24, 28, 30, 59, 65
Prophetic, 6, 24, 26
Enoch, 143n36
Eran, Amira, 162n55
Esau, 32
Esoteric approach, xv, 3, 24–33, 54, 61, 116, 126–127, 130, 148n13
Abraham Maimonides on Maimonides' esoteric approach, 126–127, 130
Abraham Maimonides's esoteric interpretation of the connection of *Ehyeh asher Ehyeh* and the Tetragrammaton, 116
Maimonides on plain and hidden meanings in scripture, 27–28, 31, 60
Of Maimonides in the *Guide*, 24–32, 54, 61
To avoid prohibitions on speaking of God directly, according to Maimonides in the Introduction to the *Guide*, 116
Eternal, the, xiv, xvii–xix, 21, 91, 93–94, 96–98, 100–109, 115, 119–125, 130–131, 172n12, 174n1, 174n8, 176n1, 177n3, 177–178n6, 178n8, 179n10
Abraham Maimonides on *al-azalī* as without beginning and everlasting, 108
Abraham Maimonides on why the eternal, that which has always existed, by definition will always exist, 108
Abraham Maimonides on Saadya's translations of *Ehyeh asher Ehyeh* and *al-azalī*, xviii, 107–109, 121–122, 130–131
And Necessary Existence, 94, 109, 119–120
As infinite, existing in past and future, for Saadya: beginningless and everlasting, xviii, 101, 105, 108, 178n6
As never been non-existent and will never cease, for Saadya, 100, 105
Classical rabbinic views of, xvii, 94, 96–98, 102, 130, 174n8
Eternity of *Ehyeh asher Ehyeh*, xviii–xix, 94, 96, 101–109, 121, 130–131, 174n8, 177n3, 177–178n6, 179n10
Eternity, the concept of (*azaliyya*), xviii, 105–109, 176n5, 179n10, 185n14
Saadya on the Eternal's "beginninglessness" (*Al-azalī*), xviii, 100–101, 105, 107–108, 176n1, 177n3, 177–178n6, 179n10
Exegesis, xi, xiii, xv, 6, 26, 43–44, 66, 89, 101, 110, 122–123, 125, 131, 138n9, 147n74, 148n13, 164n14, 169n15, 170n25, 175n14
Abraham Maimonides as exegete, xi, xiii, xv, 6, 43–44, 89, 110, 122–123, 125, 164n14
Exodus Rabbah, xvii, 97–98, 101–102, 173n6, 174n7–8

Face and back of the Divine, 5–7, 13, 74, 79, 81–85, 169n19, 169–170n23
"Back" represents a lower apprehension of God, which God grants Moses, 79
"Face" represents true reality of God, which Moses cannot see, 79, 81, 83, 169–170n23
Moses granted partial apprehension of God's nature (back) after he requests to apprehend the true reality of God (face), according to Maimonides in *Eight Chapters* and *Mishneh Torah*, 81, 169–170n23
Vision of the Back as representing apprehension of God's attributes of action and created things, including the separate intellects, in the *Guide*, 83–84, 170n23

Vision of the Back of God gave Moses the greatest possible apprehension of the divine, according to Abraham Maimonides, 84
Feet, under God's, 78–80, 84, 166n2, 168n11
Fenton, Paul, 20, 70, 74, 135n14, 139n12, 144n45, 146n60
"A Mystical Treatise on Prayer and the Spiritual Quest," 20
Flash of the divine, 5, 7–8, 19, 22, 66, 85, 137n2, 140n23, 161n49, 162n56, 170n25
Fontaine, Resianne, 133n2
Friedman, Mordechai Akiva, 135n14

Girdner, Scott, 141n26, 142n29, 169n19
Glory, the, xiii, xv–xvi, 3, 5, 7, 10, 15–16, 21–28, 30–35, 39–41, 43–46, 55, 61, 72, 76–77, 80, 83, 85, 126–127, 131, 138n8, 150n29, 150n1, 152n20, 154n24, 158n29, 161n43, 165n26, 166n2
And the cloud, for Abraham Maimonides, 5, 7, 34, 40, 44, 55, 72
As created light, xiii, 26–27, 41
As intuitive flash of the divine essence, for Abraham Maimonides, 7, 85
As prophetic emanation of the Active Intellect, for Maimonides, 26
As splendor, 10, 15, 32, 45–46
At the cleft of the rock, xv, 7, 34, 39, 41, 161n43
For Halevi, 39
For Saadya, xiii, 7, 39, 76, 131, 138n8
Physical sight of, for Abraham Maimonides, 7, 25, 39–40, 126
Preparation for, *see* Prophecy
God, *passim*
Honoring of, 30–31, 33, 58
Incorporeality of, 28
Unity of, 17, 20, 62–64
Worship of, 8–9, 51–52, 132, 168n13, 186n4
God's essence, *see* Divine essence
Goitein, S. D., 129, 135n14, 139n10
Goldstein, Miriam, 147n67
Guttmann, Julius, 129
Ḥads (intuition), 19, 66, 145n59, 162n55
Hajj, 156n8
Halevi, Judah, xi, xvi, xviii, 3, 18, 23, 33, 36–39, 55–58, 63, 71, 92–93, 95, 111–114, 122, 126, 133n2, 143n36, 151n12, 152n18, 152n20, 156n7, 157n17–18, 157n20, 159n29, 159n31, 171n1, 181n10, 184n5
Kuzari, 36–37, 39, 55, 58, 113, 143n36, 151n8, 151n12, 156n7
Hand of the Lord, 5–7, 23, 43–44, 78, 80, 168–169n15
Ḥananel ben Samuel, R., xii, 21–22, 134n12, 136n16, 155n25, 160n39, 164–165n22
Hāshim, Abū, 175n3
Hayah (to be), 92–93, 101–103, 113, 117–118, 120–121, 131, 171n3, 180n10
Ḥalla (to descend), 35–38, 153n24
ḥ-l-l (dwelling), *see* Dwell, to
he-Ḥasid, Abraham ibn Abī'l-Rabī', xii, xvi–xvii, 20–21, 35, 50, 60, 67–75, 84, 137n1, 146n60, 146n62, 150–151n6, 154n18, 166n5, 167n7, 168n11, 168n13, 168–169n15
Hoffmann, David Zvi, 171n6
Horeb, 159n31
Hosea, 92
Huna of Sepphoris, R.m 174n8

Ibn Aflaḥ, Jābir, xii
Ibn Bājja, xi–xiii, 140n23
Ibn Daud, Abraham, xi, 133n2
Ibn Ezra, Abraham, xi, xv, xviii, 50, 93–94, 101, 111, 119, 123, 166n2, 167n10, 179n14, 181n11, 184–185n6–7
Ibn Gabirol, Solomon, 137n2, 158n29
Keter Malkhut, 158n29
Ibn Paqūda, Baḥya, 14, 17, 34, 115, 142n34, 183n33, 184n2
Duties of the Heart, 34
Ibn Rushd, *see* Averroes
Ibn Ṣaddīq, Joseph, 133n1, 149n20
Ibn Tibbon, Judah, 151n8, 159n29
Ibn Tibbon, Samuel, xi–xii
Ibn Ṭufayl, xii, 12, 23, 140n23, 145n58
Ignorance, 117, 128
And intellectual perplexity, 128–129
Ilan, Nahem, 3, 158n28
Illumination, xiv–xvi, xix, 6–26, 29–30, 34–35, 39–41, 45–46, 54–55, 59, 66, 69, 85, 126–127, 131, 148n14

Illuminative perception (Abraham Maimonides), xv, xix, 7–26, 46
Inner, 16, 24, 26, 45–46, 55, 126
Intellectual, xiv–xv, 7, 11, 17, 20, 25, 29, 40, 54, 65, 126–127, 131
Physical and sensual, xv, 20, 25, 39, 46
Spiritual, xvi, 35, 55, 126, 148n14
Imagination, 9, 24, 28, 58, 60, 76, 78–79, 152n22, 157n17, 162n54, 162n55
Imaginative faculty (Maimonides), 24, 58, 157n17
Inspiration (*ilhām*), 13, 18, 57, 85, 122, 145n59
Intellect, xiii–xvi, 9–11, 13, 16–19, 21–32, 37–38, 51–52, 57–59, 61, 65–66, 70, 75, 77–78, 81–82, 126–128, 132, 136n24, 141n27, 144n45, 146n64, 149n19, 162n53, 183n30
Active Intellect, *see* Active Intellect
And bond between humans and God, 11, 16–17, 29, 65, 127
Doctrine of Active Intellect appears to be rejected by Abraham Maimonides, xiii, xv, 9, 11, 17
Intellectual apprehension, *see* Intellectual apprehension
Intellectual dazzlement, 17
Intellectual understanding, xvi, 25, 29, 34, 46, 49, 53, 78–79
Intuitive intellect (*ḥads*), *see Ḥads*
Pure intellect, 10
Scientific intellect, 10, 19
Separate intellects, according to Arabic Aristotelean tradition and Maimonides, xv, 30, 77, 83–84, 134n12, 138n6
Speculative intellect, 10, 17, 22
Intellectual apprehension, xvi, 6, 8–9, 22, 24, 26–28, 39, 41, 52, 65, 78–79, 127, 144n46, 161n43, 168n12
Interpretation of Scripture, *passim*
Allegorical interpretation, 27, 40, 138n8, 149n20
Metaphorical interpretation, 29, 55, 64, 70, 79, 165n24
Philosophical interpretation of Maimonides, xv–xvi, xix, 19, 58, 80, 118, 125, 128, 134n12, 138n6
Plain-sense interpretation of Abraham Maimonides, xv
Intuition, xix, 7, 19–21, 66, 85, 106, 146n60, 146n66, 161n49, 162n54, 162n56
Isaac, 59–60, 92, 97, 122–124, 157n11
Isaac, Rabbi, 98, 101–102, 174n8
Ishmael, 32
Islam, Islamic, Muslim, xi, xiii, 15, 18, 31–32, 55–56, 93, 118, 156n8
Israeli, Isaac, 133n1
Israelites, *see* People, the

Jacob bar Avina of Sepphoris, R., 98, 101, 174n8
Jacob, 92, 97, 122–124
James, William, 19
Jospe, Raphael, 177n6

Kalām, xii, 76, 106, 115
Kasher, Hannah, 147n77, 169–170n23
Kellner, Menachem, 77, 147n1–2, 149n20, 150n29
Klein-Braslavy, Sara, 162n55
Knowledge, 9, 12–13, 18–23, 28, 37, 48–49, 52, 58, 64, 71, 75, 83–85, 113–114, 117, 123–125, 128–129, 131, 134n12, 138n6, 147n72, 155n2, 157n18, 158n24, 162n54, 162n56, 163n2, 170n23, 183n26, 185n7
Discursive, 20
Intellectual, 18
Prophetic, 19, 66
Sensory-affective (Abraham Maimonides), 20, 127
Syllogistic, 19
Kraemer, Joel, xii
Kreisel, Howard, 27, 32, 61, 163n2
Krinis, Ehud, 156n7, 158n22
Kulliyāt of Abu-l-baqā', 177n3

Labaton, Ezra, 70, 168n12, 185n13
Lane, 137n3, 174n1, 176n5, 177n3
Langermann, Tzvi, 149n20
Lazarus-Yafeh, Hava, 141–142n27, 148n16
Leningrad Manuscript, 178n8
Levine, Michelle, 167n11
Levinger, Jacob, 27, 61–64, 163n2
Light, xiii, xv–xvii, 1, 3–9, 11–17, 20–55, 59, 61, 65, 66, 77–81, 83, 85, 89, 104, 110, 112, 117, 126–127, 129–130, 132, 137n6, 138n8, 140n24, 141–142n27,

142n30, 143n36, 146n64, 147n77, 148n14, 148n14, 148n16, 149n19–20, 150n29, 150n1, 151n11, 152n18, 152n20, 152n22, 153n24, 158n20
Created, *see* Created Light
Heavenly vs. earthly, 149n20
Inner (Abraham Maimonides), 15–16, 44–46
Light of lights (al-Ghazālī), 12
Of God's Glory, xiii, xvi, 7, 16, 25, 35, 45–46, 126
Overpowering light, 42
Perpetual, 30, 55, 59
Protection from spiritual-intellectual light, 44
Spiritual vision, 11, 17, 48
Lord, the (*Adonai*), xiii, xvi, 12, 14, 16, 18, 20, 23, 26–27, 30, 32, 34, 41–50, 52–53, 55, 62–65, 67–69, 71–72, 81, 85, 91–92, 97–98, 112–113, 115, 122–124, 126, 131, 144n45, 144n46, 150n1, 153n24, 154n12, 159n31, 165n24, 169n15, 171n3, 184n2
And divine names, 18, 92, 123. *See also* Divine names
And proper names, 113–114, 123–124, 181n10, 182n19
Love, 8–9, 16–17, 19–20, 127, 129–130, 132, 143n44, 147n72, 156–157n11
Intellectual, 17
Of God, 8–9, 16

Mahzor, Vilna, 103
Maimon, Moshe, modern translator, 136n17
Maimon, R. 68-69
Maimonides, Abraham, *passim*
Compendium (the *Kifāya*), xv, 8, 10, 12, 14, 23–25, 43–44, 51–52, 84–85, 126, 132, 139n10, 144n45
Milḥamot ha-Shem, 144n45
Torah Commentary, xi, xiii, xv, xviii, 7, 23, 25, 44, 48–49, 51, 68, 70–74, 80, 85, 89, 104, 126, 136n17, 150n6
Maimonides, Moses, *passim*
Hilkhot Teshuvah, 129–130
Shemonah Peraqim, 141n26
Treatise on Logic, 180n4
Epistle to Yemen, 31, 157n17, 159n31
Guide of the Perplexed, *passim*
Hilkhot Yesodei ha-Torah, 11, 22, 37, 129–130, 140n19, 140n21, 159n31, 164n20, 180n1
Commentary to the Mishnah (*Pereq Ḥeleq*), 9, 22, 81, 169n23, 170n25
Mishneh Torah, 22, 37, 62, 82–84, 159n31, 169–170n23, 180n1
Maqām, 50, 59–61, 69, 73–75, 81, 150n4, 158n28, 164n14
As encounter with the divine at Sinai (Maimonides), 59–61, 81
As standing before God at Sinai, 60, 150n4, 158n28, 164n14
Mashhad (vision/theophany/witness), xvi, 54–58, 61, 63, 68, 156n6–7, 157n17–18, 157n20, 158n29, 160n39, 165n22
Matter, 13, 40, 50, 54, 58, 73, 80–84, 94, 149n20, 153n24, 167n11
Celestial, 13, 40, 50, 84, 94, 149n20
Material (*also* Dark), 54, 58, 80–83, 94, 149n20, 153n24, 158n24, 167n11
Mecca, 55–56
Medieval Jewish thought, xii, xvii, 18, 36, 97, 102, 110, 119, 137n6, 144n49, 171n3
Meditation, 15–16, 20, 22, 42, 45–46, 51–52, 128–129, 151n6, 151n12, 168n13
Mekhilta, 61
Memmel, R. Abba bar, 173n7
Mendelssohn, Moses, 93–94
Metaphysical proof of God's existence (Avicenna), 109, 114, 130–131, 179n12
Metaphysics, xiii–xiv, xvii–xviii, 49, 52–53, 84, 89, 93–96, 98, 100–102, 104–105, 108–111, 114, 116–117, 122, 128, 130–131, 134n6, 149n20, 162n56, 167n11, 178n7, 179n12, 182n20, 185n13
Knowledge of, for Maimonides, 49, 52–53, 84, 128
Of the philosophers, 17, 109, 114, 130–131, 134n6, 167n11, 178n7, 179n12, 182n20, 185n13
Prohibition on pronouncing on publicly (i.e. the account of the Chariot), 111, 116–117

Metaphysical necessity, xiii–xiv, xviii, 105, 108, 131, 178n7
Midrash Tanḥuma, xviii, 97, 102, 173n4, 173n6, 174n7–8
Miracles, 31, 59, 62, 123, 150n1, 184n5–6, 185n7
Miriam, 26
Moses, xv, xix, 6–8, 22–26, 28–30, 35, 39, 41, 43–44, 47, 49–51, 56–57, 59, 61–65, 67–84, 92–93, 97–98, 101, 105, 117, 121–126, 131–132, 151n12, 153n7, 161n43, 161n49, 163n2, 163n9, 164n10, 164n14, 164n20, 165n23, 166n29, 167n7, 169–170n23, 184n5, 184n7
  And Voice at Sinai, 24, 61–65, 67, 75, 77
  First prophet and person given prophetic mission, according to Maimonides, 117
  Gained greatest possible intellectual apprehension of God but not of God's essence, according to Maimonides, 22
  Great intellectual apprehension, according to Maimonides, 6, 8, 22, 24
  Level of preparation, according to Maimonides, 59, 63
  Moses alone receives from the Tetragrammaton a complete understanding of Necessary Existence, according to Abraham Maimonides, 125, 131
  Prophecy not mediated by a conscious, interpreting intermediary, 76
  Prophetic powers, 63
  Speech of God heard by, 166n29
  Stated mission to offer the people true knowledge of God, according to Maimonides, 117
  Understanding of the Tetragrammaton, 132
Mount Sinai, theophany at, xv–xvii, 3, 15, 26–27, 30–32, 36, 40, 44, 50, 53–77, 89, 126, 137n1, 150n4, 150–151n6, 151n12, 155n2, 156n8, 157n17–18, 158n28, 159n31, 160n43, 164n22, 165n26, 166n29, 167n7, 168n13
  Allegorical interpretation of Maimonides, 27, 40
  As collective religious experience, for Halevi and Abraham Maimonides, 3, 55, 126
  As event of inner, prophetic illumination for Moses, according to Maimonides, 26, 55
  As overflow from the Active Intellect to Moses, according to Maimonides, 65
  As visual, physical event, for Abraham Maimonides, xv, 3, 7, 25, 34, 39–40, 42, 54, 79, 126–127
  Greater than any vision of prophecy and beyond any analogy, for Maimonides, 54, 58–59
  Maqām, *see Maqām*
  Truth of understood purely intellectually by Moses, for Maimonides, 64
Mushāhada (witnessing of the Divine), 18–19, 35, 55–58, 63, 145n58, 146n64, 152n18, 153n24, 157n11, 157n18–20
  Collective witness, 55–57
  For Abraham Maimonides, 19, 35, 153n24, 157n19
  For Halevi, 18, 55–58, 157n18
  For Maimonides, 19, 55, 57–58, 63
  Individual, 56, 58
Mu'tazilites, 138n8, 175n3
Muhammad, 31, 56
Munk, Salomon, 116
Mysticism, xiv, xix, 128, 138n8
  Intellectualist (Maimonides), 128
    Sufi, *see* Sufi tradition

Nadav, 47, 70, 78, 167n7
Nahmanides, 172n1
Narboni, Moses, 61, 63–64, 119
Naturalism, 65
  Naturalist account of prophecy (Maimonides), 65
Necessary Existence, xiii–xiv, xviii–xix, 64, 94–95, 109–112, 114–115, 117–121, 123–125, 130–131, 161n44, 181n10–11, 182n20, 183n29, 183n33
  Absolute existence implies that God will always be, is eternal, according to Maimonides, 119, 121
  And Being, 112, 114–115, 117–120, 130
  And eternity, *see* Eternal, the

As involving eternity, everlastingness, and perpetuity, for Abraham Maimonides, 109
Avicenna's metaphysical proof of God's existence, 109, 114, 130–131
Degrees of knowledge of Necessary Existence, according to Abraham Maimonides, 124
El Shaddai also expresses Necessary Existence, according to Abraham Maimonides, xix, 123–124, 131
God's essence is to exist necessarily, with no possibility of non-existence, according to Avicenna and Maimonides, 118, 121, 183n33
Indicated by the Tetragrammaton and *Ehyeh asher Ehyeh*, according to Maimonides, 94–95, 112, 117–119, 181n10–11
In Maimonides, xiii–xiv, xviii–xix, 64, 94–95, 109–112, 114–115, 117–120, 123–124, 130, 181n10–11, 182n20, 183n29
In Saadya as beginningless (*azaliyya*), xviii, 109
Maimonides' doctrine of Necessary Existence as God's essence, 112, 114–115, 118
Necessary existence and existence without attributes, 115, 117
Necessary existence of God and the contingent existence of the world, 64, 117, 134n12
Necessary Existent, xvi, 65, 115, 117–119, 169n19, 183n29, 184n2
Negative attributes, 64, 118, 128
Divine negation of all attributes of created beings, according to Maimonides, 64, 118. *See also* Attributes, Divine
Via negativa, 118, 128
Negev, Yonatan, 142n29, 155n5, 156n7, 177n2
Neoplatonism, xii, 134n6

O'Sullivan, Beth, 153n7
Onqelos, xiii, xvii, 6–7, 24–25, 31, 33, 42, 43, 71, 78, 80–81, 83–84, 96, 103, 126, 137–138n6, 166n2, 167n7
Overflow (*fayḍ*), 11, 13–14, 25, 29–30, 43, 45, 55, 59, 66, 126, 129, 142n27, 149n19, 153n6
And prophecy, for Maimonides, 55, 58, 153n6
Depicted as light, 11, 13, 29–30, 45, 55, 59, 126, 153n6
Depicted as water, 29
Divine, 19, 25, 30, 43, 45, 55, 59, 126
Of being, 30, 43, 45
Of divine grace, 30, 142n27
Of light, 14, 25, 45, 129
Of the intellect, 11, 29–30, 66, 129, 149n19

People, the (Israelites), xvi–xvii, 3, 26, 34–36, 38–39, 41, 46–50, 53, 55–56, 59–64, 67–75, 77, 78, 92, 98, 101–102, 117, 128, 150n1, 159n31, 160n36, 160n43, 161n49, 163n2, 164n10, 165n29, 167n7, 184n2, 184n5
Philosophy, xi, 17, 52–53, 134n3, 134n12, 135n12, 151n12
Piety, 16–17, 24
Pines, Shlomo, 127, 140n23, 149n19, 156n7
Pinḥas ha-Kohen b. Jacob of Kappara, 103
Plato, xi–xii, 162n54
Plotinus, 134n6
Enneads, 134n6
Praise, 21, 31, 50, 108, 129
Prayer, 9, 20–21, 36, 51, 58, 65, 91, 139n13, 159n31, 161n53
Preparation, xvi, 3, 15, 24, 34–35, 38–53, 60, 64, 70–72, 74, 80–81, 126, 146n60, 153n24, 154n18
By Moses, 35, 39, 41–44, 47, 49, 51, 70–72, 74–75, 80
For prophecy, 35, 38, 40, 41–53
Intellectual, for Maimonides, 24
Spiritual and moral, for Abraham Maimonides, 15, 24, 34, 80, 126
Presence, divine, *see* Divine Presence
Priests, 41–44, 46–50, 81, 113, 126, 154n12, 171n1
At Sinai, 42–44, 46–50, 126
Proclus, 134n6

Elements of Theology, 134n6
Prophecy, xvi–xvii, 6, 10–11, 18–19, 24–25, 27–32, 37–39, 42, 45, 50–51, 53–55, 57–67, 69–80, 117, 122, 125, 127, 134n12, 138n8, 139n12, 141n27, 146n60, 152n15–16, 152n22, 157n18, 160n43, 161n46, 161n49, 162–163n56, 164n20, 165n23, 166n29, 167n7, 169n15
Achieved by all the people in weak sense at Mount Sinai, for Maimonides, 59–60, 69–71, 73, 77, 167n7
And moment of gestalt, 162n56
And the Active Intellect, 11, 24–32, 57–59, 61, 65–66
As an overflow overflowing from God to the Active Intellect, for Maimonides, 58
Mosaic, 58, 65
Preparation for, xvi, 3, 15, 38–53
Prophecy only necessary for what cannot be known by intellect alone, for Maimonides, 77
Prophetic intuition, xix, 7, 19–21, 85, 161n49, 162n56. *See also Ḥads*
Prophetic knowledge
Prophetic perception, non-sensory or quasi-sensory, 3, 46, 60
Prophetic revelation (*waḥy*), 24, 57, 60, 162n56, 163n9, 169n15
Prophetic spirit, 18–19
Prophetic state of receptivity, 65
Prophetic vision, *see* Vision
Prophetic witness, 57, 60–61
Prophet's mind, 28, 66
Psychological theory of Maimonides, 57–58
Sub-prophetic visual and auditory phenomena, for Maimonides, 58–61, 63, 76
Transmitted to the people through Moses, 70, 72
Providence, xix, 16–17, 94, 122, 134n12, 143n44
Proximity, spiritual (*Qurb*), 17, 35, 39, 127, 168n13
Pseudo-Jāḥiẓ, 142n34
Ptolemaic astronomy, xiv

Qafiḥ, 157n18
Qur'ān, 55–56, 155n5, 156n6

Rashbam, 93–94, 117, 119, 131, 181n11
Ravitzky, Aviezer, 184n6
Rabbinic literature, 68, 89, 91, 94, 114, 130, 171n3
Reason, 10–11, 19, 37, 48, 66, 81, 101, 107, 111, 113–114, 129, 162n54, 162n56, 163n2, 164n22, 184n2
Reception of prophecy, xvii, 24, 27, 71, 73
Of the Active Intellect, for Maimonides, 27, 30
Sensory-auditory, for Halevi and Abraham Maimonides, xvii, 71, 73
Regev, Shaul, 163n2
Reines, Alvin J., 161n43, 162n56
Reuven, 113–114
Revelation, xv–xvi, 15, 21, 24, 26, 30–32, 41–42, 54–57, 60, 66, 75–77, 95, 125–127, 131–132, 154n18, 158n24, 162n56, 163n9, 165n26, 185n13
For Abraham Maimonides, 15, 54–55, 77, 95, 125–127, 131–132, 163n9
For Maimonides, xvi, 24, 26, 30–32, 41–42, 60, 66, 77, 162n56
For Saadya, 76, 131
For Halevi, 55–57
Rosenberg, Shalom, 165n23
Rosenblatt, Samuel, 135n14
The High Ways to Perfection of Abraham Maimonides, 135n14, 137n1
Roth, Rabbi David, 172n3
Russ-Fishbane, Elisha, xiv, 3, 11, 17, 135n14, 137n1, 142n33, 146n60

Saadya Gaon, xi, xiii–xv, xvii–xviii, 3, 6–7, 23, 31, 33, 36, 39, 42, 71–72, 76, 89, 94–95, 100–111, 115, 121–122, 126, 130–131, 137n2, 137n6, 138n8–9, 149n19, 155n2, 156n8, 158n29, 159n31, 160n37, 164n10, 167n10, 174n7, 174n7–8, 175n14, 175n3, 176n3–5, 176–177n1–3, 178n6–7, 179n10
Book of Doctrines and Beliefs, 6–7, 36, 76, 138n8, 155n2, 159n31, 165n26

Commentary to Exodus, xviii, 72, 89, 101–102, 104–109, 130, 159n31, 160n37, 164n10, 177n2, 177–178n6, 179n10
Daniel, with the Translation and Interpretation of Rabenu Se'adyah Gaon, 138n7
Kitāb al-amānāt wa'l-i'tiqādāt, 108, 177n3
Sefer Yetsirah, commentary to, 76, 137n2, 138n8, 149n19, 159n31, 165n26
Tafsīr, xviii, 56, 100–101, 105, 107, 155n5, 159n31, 176n1, 177n3, 179n10
Sabbath, the, 14–15, 52, 128–129
Sands, Kristin Zahra, 12
Sarna, Nahum, 166n2
Scientific knowledge, xii, xiv, xvi, 10, 14, 17, 19, 38, 52–53, 57, 66, 127, 129, 130
As "divine science" for Maimonides, 51–52, 114
Knowledge of logic, mathematics, physics, and metaphysics for Maimonides, xvi, 47, 49, 53, 128, 130, 167n11
Schwartz, Dov, 133n2
Schwarz, Michael, 154n12, 157n18, 162n55
Schwarz, Yossi, 182n22
Sells, Michael, 139n10
Sensory knowledge, xiii, xv–xvi, 3, 6–7, 18, 20, 25, 29, 39, 43, 46, 49, 65, 126–127, 148n14, 161n43, 168n12
And perception of divine light (Abraham Maimonides), xiii, xv–xvi, 3, 6–7, 25, 49, 126–127, 148n14
Sensory perception, 18, 20, 29, 39, 65, 161n43, 168n12
Septimus, Bernard, 60–61, 152n15, 156n8, 157n17, 158–159n28–29, 159n31, 160n37, 164n20
Shaubi, Eli, 15–16, 44–46, 137n1, 138n6, 139n12
Shekhinah, 26, 30, 32, 36, 76–77, 80, 138n8, 151n11, 152n12
Shemini 'Atseret, 103
Shim'on, 113–114
Shinan, Avigdor, 97, 174n8
Sifre Devarim, 171n3
Sklare, David, 177n3
Solitude, xvi, 9, 12, 15, 23, 36, 43, 50–53, 127, 143n36, 168n13
External, 43, 51
Internal, xvi, 36, 43, 50–51, 53
Soul, parts of, 8, 10–11, 15
Spain, xi–xii
Speculative intellect, 5, 10, 17, 19, 22, 46, 48
Spinoza, Benedictus de, 17
Ethics, 17
Spiritual ascent, xiv, 10, 17–18, 49, 52, 140n23, 144n45
Goal is glimpse of the divine essence, for Abraham Maimonides, xv, 8, 85, 132
Spiritual practices, xv, 13–15, 21–22, 24–25, 36, 126
Spiritual purification, xiv, xvi, 11, 50, 53
Stern, Josef, 112, 158n24, 180n6, 181n14, 183n27
Stroumsa, Sarah, xii
Study, xiv, xvi, 8, 13, 18, 53, 128, 130, 162n56
Sufi pietism, xiii, 35, 50, 53
Sufi tradition, xiii–xiv, xvi, 12–15, 17, 19–21, 25, 34–36, 38, 50, 53, 56–58, 60, 126–128, 134n12, 135n15, 139n10, 140n23, 156n11, 164n14
Illuminationists, xiv, 12, 14, 20
In Egypt, xiii, 11–12, 21, 35, 127, 134n12, 139n10
Influence on Maimonides and Abraham Maimonides, xiii–xiv, xvi, 12–15, 17, 19, 25, 34–36, 38, 50, 53, 126–128
Meditation, 15
Mushāhada (witness), 19, 56–58
Mysticism, xiv
Terminology, 60, 127
Suhrawardī, 12

Targum Onqelos, 96, 102–103
Targum Pseudo-Jonathan, 96, 102–103
Targumim (Aramaic translations of the Torah), 96, 103
Taste (*dhawq*), 18–20, 145n58, 146n60
In Ghazali, 18–20
Temple, 36, 151n11–12, 171n1

Created at the time of the created word rather than before the existence of the world, according to Maimonides, 166n29
Treiger, Alexander, 18–19, 141n27

van Ess, Josef, 175n3

Vision, xv–xvii, 3, 10–12, 17–18, 20–22, 24–25, 27–29, 34, 38–39, 41–42, 48–49, 53–55, 57–61, 63, 78–85, 126–127, 132, 138n8, 152n22, 157n18, 157n20, 158n29, 161n43, 162n53, 166n2, 167–168n11, 168n12
Intellectual, 11, 18, 49
Internal, 11, 17, 22, 25, 48
Physical, xvii, 20, 39, 42
Prophetic, xvi, 10, 24–25, 27–29, 38, 42, 54–55, 57–61, 63, 78–79, 127, 138n8, 152n22, 157n18
Vision of the Glory, xv, 3, 34, 39, 126, 161n43
Vision of the Nobles, 3, 78–85, 126
Contents of the vision, for Abraham Maimonides, 78–79
Maimonides' criticism of the Nobles' physical and anthropomorphic vision of God, in contrast to Moses' perfect intellectual apprehension of God, 80
The nobles not properly prepared but spared punishment for trying to see God, according to Maimonides; nobles spiritually prepared for the vision according to Abraham Maimonides, 80–81
Visual, external event and intellectual apprehension, for Abraham Maimonides, 79
Voice at Mount Sinai, the, xvi, 24, 27, 61–70, 75, 77, 127, 161n46, 163n2, 165n24
All at Sinai heard a real created voice and attained some form of prophecy, according to Abraham Maimonides, 127
Experiential-affective nature of the event, according to Abraham Maimonides, 127
Level of prophecy achieved by the people at Sinai, for Abraham Maimonides, 67, 70–73
Metaphorical for Maimonides, to represent knowledge of God attained by the intellect and knowledge communicated through prophecy to Moses, 75
Moses alone hears and apprehends the Ten Words, according to Maimonides, 77
Not auditory but represents the Active Intellect or information from it, for Maimonides, 65
Sensory, experiential aspect, but an unintelligible sound, according to Abraham he-Ḥasid, xvi–xvii, 69–70, 75
Sub-prophetic auditory and visual elements heard by the people, for Maimonides in early texts, 60–63, 73
The great voice heard by the people but not contents of speech, for Maimonides, 62
Traditional rabbinic interpretations, 63, 67–68
Used to impress upon the people the prophecy received by Moses, for Maimonides, 63
Voice heard and experienced by the people, and Ten Commandments heard by the people, according to Abraham Maimonides, 67, 73–75, 77
Voice heard by people authenticates Moses' prophecy, according to Abraham he-Ḥasid, 69

Wiesenberg, E.Y., 70, 166n4, 185n8
Witness (*mushāhada*), see *Mushāhada*
And communal assembly, 55, 156n6
For Ghazali, 18–19
Prophetic, *see* Prophecy
Worship, 8–9, 51–52, 132, 168n13, 186n4
And glimpsing God's exalted essence, for Abraham Maimonides, 8–9, 132
And intellectual apprehension, for Maimonides, 9

Yannai, 102, 175n10

Zayd, 180n4

Zev Harvey, Warren, 92, 137n2, 138n6, 158n22, 179n13, 181n11, 183n32
"Judah Halevi's Interpretation of the Tetragrammaton," 92

www.ingramcontent.com/pod-product-compliance
Ingram Content Group UK Ltd.
Pitfield, Milton Keynes, MK11 3LW, UK
UKHW020738250226
468390UK00008B/163

9 781644 695371